Rivers, Fish, and the People

RIVERS, FISH, AND THE PEOPLE

TRADITION, SCIENCE, AND HISTORICAL ECOLOGY OF FISHERIES IN THE AMERICAN WEST

edited by
Pei-Lin Yu

THE UNIVERSITY OF UTAH PRESS
Salt Lake City

The Defiance House Man colophon is a registered trademark
of the University of Utah Press. It is based on a four-foot-tall
Ancient Puebloan pictograph (late PIII) near Glen Canyon, Utah.

19 18 17 16 15 1 2 3 4 5

CIP data on file with the Library of Congress.

ISBN 978-1-60781-399-6 (paper)
ISBN 978-1-60781-400-9 (e-book)

Cover art by Pei-Lin Yu (stylized salmon) and Emilie Zelazo (white sturgeon).

Printed and bound by Sheridan Books, Inc., Ann Arbor, Michigan.

Contents

Figures

Tables

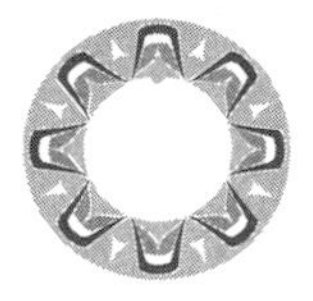

Introduction

PEI-LIN YU

In the American West, human beings have been a part of river ecosystems since the Pleistocene epoch. Their lifestyles have spanned a broad range of organizational diversity: The archaeological evidence indicates that the earliest Native use of rivers involved ephemeral occupations by small mobile groups, but over thousands of years some Native peoples "mapped onto" riverine habitats by maximizing aquatic resources. Innovative tactics to reduce resource risk and maximize benefit transformed technology, mobility, architecture, settlement and social structure, and spiritual life. The diversity of Native lifeways broadened, from generalized, mixed-use subsistence to river-focused occupations marked by strong seasonal variability and sophisticated techniques of resource capture, processing, storage, and consumption. Thus there is no one traditional lifeway associated with western American river ecosystems but, rather, many.

Most scholarly investigations of traditional human–river relationships have focused on subsistence—specifically fishing as an adaptive strategy. Fish have been assessed in cost/benefit terms that weigh the constraints and opportunities faced by people living in certain habitat conditions (Plew 1996). These analyses are usually based on detailed osteological analysis and/or the quantification of fish remains in archaeological assemblages to estimate dietary contributions and seasonality of site use (Plew 1996).

But in making these inferences archaeologists must consider the effects of varied techniques of fish processing, differential preservation of remains, and other taphonomic and site formation processes. To address gaps in archaeological knowledge, ethnographic information can help to flesh out detail in fishing practices or shed light on traditional tool manufacture. This information is situated in the bigger picture of "how and why" people fish, the relationship between fishing and other food resources, and economic and social implications of fishing. In some cases, intensive fishing supported the development of complex, fishing-focused cultures; in others, fishing was only one leg of diverse foraging strategies that incorporated terrestrial and aquatic resources.

Questions about the tempo and mode of the cultural change that led to all this variability have been tackled mostly in the academic sector. However, since the 1960s, a growing body of archaeology, ethnography, and traditional ecological knowledge (i.e., specific indigenous knowledge about environments) has been collected during legally mandated compliance activities for publicly funded undertakings. These studies have generated thousands of pages of technical reports and, less often, book-length treatments (e.g., Moss and Cannon 2011; Plew 1996).

For the nongovernmental researcher these data are not always easy to access. In recent decades concerns about the looting of archaeological sites and disclosure of culturally sensitive knowledge have caused well-meaning agencies and other entities to restrict dissemination. In addition, publicly funded compliance work is increasingly subject to market forces, which can limit the use of ethnographic and culture-historical data to simple diagnostic tools for rapid assessment and mitigation treatments. Finally, the continued focus on Native fishing per se in western North America, with heavy emphasis on salmon, leaves gaps in our understanding of complementary (and in some cases significant) use of resident fish species and other aquatic resources. This in turn leaves gaps in our knowledge about Native practices for monitoring and management of a wide spectrum of river resources and habitats and the implications for social organization, stability, and change.

Fortunately, recent collaborations between researchers and Native peoples are giving rise to mutually agreed best practices for disseminating scientific information and traditional knowledge while safeguarding heritage value and relevancy. The contributions in this volume reveal new avenues opening for information-sharing, querying current assumptions about the adaptive capacity of Native relationships with river resources, and probing the limits of variability in human relationships with river environments. New data presented here include diversified aquatic food resources, implications for traditional land use and technology, and the improvement of techniques to investigate past relationships using the material record available to us. Understanding the range of Native people–river relationships and changes over time is directly relevant to the future of western American rivers.

Human Use and Adaptive Limits of River Ecosystems

Modern American rivers have been impacted by dams, recontouring, pollution, development, and overcommitment for irrigation. Rapid climate change is altering river flows, temperature, and chemistry, as well as entire basin ecosystems (Baron et al. 2009; Loehman and Anderson 2009). Along the once-mighty Colorado River, tree ring reconstructions indicate that the interval beginning in 2000 is one of the lowest in more than 1,200 years (U.S. Bureau of Reclamation 2013). Keystone migratory and resident species, especially in the inland West, have vanished or are in steep decline, disrupting entire ecological communities in a synergistic fashion (U.S. Geological Survey 2007). Across the West, river and wetland restoration is a priority for public land management agencies, Native American tribal governments, and local communities.

River ecosystems are made up of interdependent species and communities operating at multiple trophic levels (see Cramer and Witty 1998), so defining "target" states for restoration planning requires some flexibility. Restoration ecologists usually choose the time of contact between Native Americans and Euro-American immigrants as an appropriate reference point (see Gulf of Maine Historical Ecology Research 2011). This is not necessarily a problem, but it can lead to unwarranted assertions of a "pristine" or "natural" state (sensu the Wilderness Act of 1964, sec. 2[c]) utterly devoid of human influence.

Yet scientific and traditional knowledge provides irrefutable evidence that people have inhabited the Americas for at least 13,000 years and possibly millennia more; *therefore all post-Pleistocene American landscapes have been potentially influenced by human presence.* The concept of "naturalness" in ecosystem descriptions clearly needs to be revisited (Boyd 1999; Cole and Yung 2010). The time of European contact was not one day, or one year, but in many cases spanned centuries. And constantly changing climates and environments in prehistory mean that target conditions for any given areas may need to shift in space as well as time (Kondolf et al. 2006).

Historical ecology, a term coined by biologists to describe changes in phylogenetic relationships (see Mayden 1992), now includes the reconstruction of reference conditions for ecosystems. In order to describe system states at a given point in time, researchers try to unpeel intervening layers of historic impacts (e.g., Gulf of Maine Historical Ecology Research 2011; Lotze and Milewski 2004; Moss and Cannon 2011). But historical sciences are largely inductive, so that the inconsistent validity of empirical data reduces confidence in extrapolations. The ever-receding historical record simply may not leave enough evidence to address certain questions. Further, modern-day analogies for some ancient ecosystems may not exist (Swetnam et al. 1999:1192).

Scientific approaches can alleviate this problem by identifying historic variability and trends in healthy river ecosystems, using frames of reference to characterize a system's dynamic properties (e.g., stabilizing mechanisms and thresholds), and proposing causal relationships. Hypotheses can be tested and revised through field experiments, model simulations, and controlled observations of naturally occurring phenomena (Binford 2001; Swetnam et al. 1999:1192).

Multidisciplinarity and Frames of Reference

Where traditional knowledge and river ecosystems intersect, the scientific approach relies heavily on qualitative data such as ethnographic documentation. The chapters in this volume reevaluate historical and contemporary ethnography to "unpack" existing normative models and highlight the complex adaptive relationship between ecology and traditional knowledge systems. Historic relationships between Native societies and rivers are germane to the health and viability of river ecosystems today. Admittedly, the great variability, geographic scope, and time span of Native life and river environments cannot provide fine-grained data points for current conditions, for example, the population of a species that should be present for a given locality.

Instead, the antiquity and mutually influential nature of traditional human–river relationships can help guide management ethics and restoration planning through contributing to testable hypotheses about system stability thresholds of "no return." For example, we know from archaeology and traditional knowledge that prehistoric Native American use of certain river resources could be quite intensive. Some salmon species were harvested en masse, using sophisticated methods of capture, distribution, and processing (see Yu and Cook, this volume). This was apparently accomplished without irreversible damage to the viability of this economically important species. Even in the 20th century, salmon have shown remarkable resilience when harvested at industrial scales (Newell 1988; O'Bannon 1987; Price 1990). This suggests that if ecosystem characteristics that facilitate species resilience remain intact, some populations can tolerate relatively high rates of harvest.

The archaeological record alone cannot generate explanations about Native relationships with river ecosystems: archaeological data are indirect and often ambiguous static traces of past dynamic processes (Binford 2001). Strong warranting arguments for selecting and analyzing data about the precontact use of riverine resources call for a disciplinary mosaic of biology, archaeology, ethnography, and traditional sources of environmental knowledge. Traditional ecological knowledge can be acquired directly from traditional holders of knowledge and targeted to specific environmental questions (in contrast to ethnographic information, which is filtered through changing anthropological objectives and techniques).

The Chapters

The contributing chapters in this volume cover biogeographic regions ranging from the Sacramento River delta up through the Snake River Plain and the Columbia River plateau, east to the Pend Oreille, and northwest to the Fraser River in British Columbia (see Figure I.1). These river ecosystems were conditioned by constantly changing climate and environments, such that migratory fish were suitable as a primary food source under some—but not all—predictable conditions. The first chapter, by Grabowski, lays a foundation of behaviors, salient life history characteristics, and environmental factors for economically important anadromous and resident fish species, including Pacific lamprey. This information is presented in terms that are understandable and useful to nonbiologists.

In the West and particularly the Northwest, anadromous fish have been central to the opportunities and constraints experienced by Native peoples. Yet fish productivity and movements were subject to seasonal and interannual variance; the productivity of remote marine feeding grounds; and unpredictable natural events such as landslides, wildfires, and river course changes along key migratory routes or breeding habitats. Too,

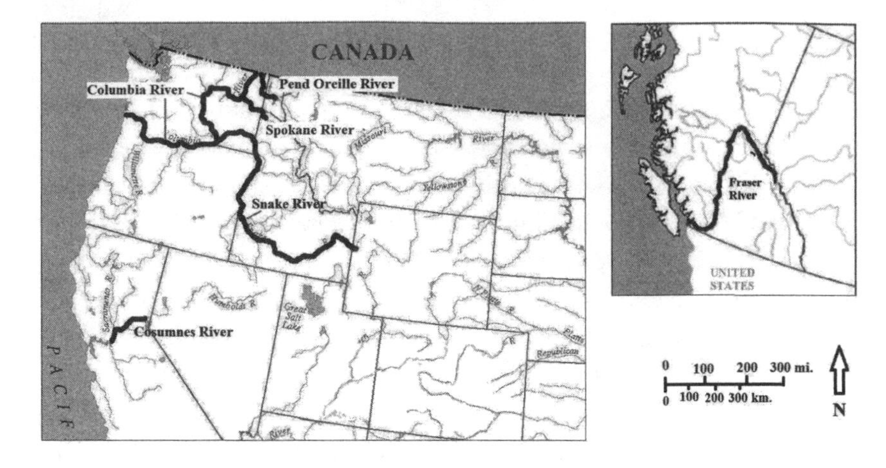

FIGURE I.1. North American rivers discussed in the volume.

demographic shifts or new technological developments could influence economically important species. Even in good years for high-value species such as salmon, random cultural phenomena (war, disease, spoilage of critical stores of food, etc.) could make alternative foods more desirable.

Historical contingencies leave archaeological signatures that are subject to equifinality (Moss and Cannon 2011). Normative assumptions about the role of migratory fish in Native life, such as the argument that changes in fish species indicate ethnic replacement, cultural evolutionary advances and retreats, and so on (sensu Chance and Chance 1985), cut off our ability to recognize and explore real variability. On the Snake River Plain, Plew and Guinn caution that equifinality may lead to unwarranted analogies between mobile foragers in desert river habitats and semi-sedentized peoples of densely populated, highly productive coastal rivers. They argue that if the predictability of salmon runs decreased below a certain ratio of cost to benefit, people could shift from anadromous fish to resident fish and terrestrial resources. This would condition for a wide-spectrum foraging strategy and higher mobility.

In addition, considerations *other* than procurement costs could have favored the use of nonanadromous fish. For example, children are vulnerable to hypervitaminosis D (a debilitating and potentially fatal condition), and salmon contains high amounts of vitamin D, especially in dried form (Lazenby and McCormack 1985). If Native parents were aware of this risk, they may have been motivated to include more terrestrial or nonsalmon aquatic foods in the diets of young children (Lazenby and McCormack 1985).

On the Spokane Arm of the Columbia River, Jones shows how foods described by optimal foraging proponents as "low ranked" could situationally acquire high resource value, leaving evidence for abundant shellfish middens and cooking facilities in areas that appear to favor anadromous fish. And in the Pend Oreille watershed, where anadromous species have been historically excluded by natural geographic barriers, Lyons provides fine-grained descriptions of economically important resident fish species, habitat, and behaviors that entailed diverse traditional strategies and tools for procurement. Lyons argues that resident species can be economically significant even if they are procured by individuals or small groups of people in dispersed contexts.

Inferences about past fish procurement and processing depend on direct evidence, usually in the form of actual fish remains in archaeological settings or traces (e.g., lipid, protein) on tools used for fish processing. Soil chemistry and dynamics are not always conducive to the preservation of fish remains, and trace analysis is not economically feasible at large scales. In the absence of direct evidence, diagnostic characteristics of fish-processing tools could lend insight into fishing activity, but these characteristics are not yet well understood. Thus the extent of the use of fishery resources is almost certainly underrepresented in most river sites of the American West. On the Upper Columbia River, Cook and I describe the relationship among the organization of labor, gender, stone tool production, and tool use in intensive salmon processing to delineate functional properties of fish-processing tools that can be applied in other fishing contexts.

Reactive or passive characterizations of Native relationships with the environment are implicit (if not explicit) in some sources, but we argue that traditional peoples were not simply "end users." Rather, they considered themselves trustees and sometimes managers of river resources (Moss and Cannon 2011) and behaved accordingly. It is likely that most river ecosystems encountered by early Euro-Americans were the result of millennia of Native activities that enhanced the productivity of important local resources. In some cases spiritual and technological practices formed a comprehensive system of guidelines to enhance key species productivity and overall habitat health. Early Euro-American observers (David

Thompson [1968], J. Teit [1930], and others) describe tactics that included keeping riverbanks scrupulously clean of offal and daily monitoring and redistribution of salmon catches by specially designated persons.

In central California, volume contributors Stevens and Zelazo provide ethnographic descriptions of fisheries habitat improvement by fire, resource rotation, and other techniques. This offers insights into active traditional resource management that complement information from other parts of the world, such as earthen fish enclosures in the flooded forests of Bolivia (Erickson 2000) and indigenous floating hatcheries in montane lakes of central Taiwan (personal observation, 2011). The manipulation of riverine wetland habitats can optimize conditions for fish breeding and maturation and encourage technologically important plant species used for nets, baskets, and line. Several fish and plant species present in Cosumnes archaeological assemblages are now extinct, suggesting that the cessation of traditional resource management practices combined with habitat disruption and other anthropogenic activities has impacted some river ecosystems irreversibly.

Traditional subsistence and resource management practices, and their modification over time, not only were important to Native diets and economies but also conditioned the organization of families, households, communities, and societies. In her synthesizing chapter, Prentiss evaluates the preceding chapters in the light of long-term cultural adjustments to changing climate, environment, demography, and other factors. Historic events are evaluated as processes of change in society and settlements: Did coastal peoples immigrate to the interior West, bringing with them semi-sedentary lifestyles and salmon-intensive economies? Or did intensification develop in situ as a response to local conditions? What factors might have kept people from moving farther east and south to the desert river systems of the Snake River Plain? Can the Columbia Plateau be considered intermediate between coastal and desert systems of river use?

Prentiss presents new evidence from the Middle Fraser Canyon of British Columbia that shows that the increasing density of human populations altered the balance between supply and demand for highly ranked foods such as salmon. This in turn affected community size and structure, economic and political hierarchies, and spiritual life. Increasing competition for desired fish species favored innovative practices to enhance productivity, capture, and storage capacity.

The research in these chapters points to intriguing new domains of variability of human–river–fish relationships. New data, and new light shed on old assumptions, will aid future researchers in forming new frames of reference for Native use of riverine ecosystems and implications for stability and change. The powerful combination of scientific knowledge and traditional expertise is opening up new tactics for learning: Native traditional knowledge safeguards and perpetuates detailed, place-based descriptive information and heritage values, whereas scientific research pursues trends, patterns, and causal relationships for the ways that people interacted with the natural world around them. Scientists and traditional stakeholders share a common goal of improving understanding of human–natural relationships to better inform future use and stewardship of river resources and ecosystems. We hope that the offerings in this volume move us closer to that goal.

Editor's Acknowledgments

The contributors to this book hope that the information presented here provides new scientific insights into Native–river relationships while giving all due respect to Native stewardship, ingenuity, perseverance, and heritage. This would not be possible without the active participation and contributions of Native scientific and traditional experts. The living memories of Elders and their sharing of memories complement and enrich scientific explorations of the material record of the past. The information provided directly by tribal experts in this volume is published with awareness of its sensitive nature, and the authors have obtained permissions from tribal governments as appropriate (also see the individual chapter acknowledgments). For me, as volume editor, it is a pleasure and privilege to see this work become available to new audiences—particularly students, tribal professionals, and tribal community members. I wish to express my deepest gratitude to the Confederated Tribes of the Colville Reservation, the Kalispel Tribe of Indians, the Spokane Tribe of Indians, the Plains Mewuk tribes, and the Bridge River (Xwisten) and Pavilion (Ts'kway'laxw) bands (both St'át'imc Nation) of the Middle Fraser River in British Columbia for sharing information that went into this volume, keeping traditional knowledge alive, and their continued advocacy in the stewardship of river ecosystems. Many thanks go to Lynne MacDonald of the U.S. Bureau of Reclamation, for her encouragement of this project in its earliest stages, and to the anonymous peer reviewers, whose comments made the volume stronger, clearer, and more coherent. Clint Hughes and his red cataraft have taken me on, over—and sometimes into—the rivers of Idaho, Utah, and Montana. I thank him for his love and support.

References Cited

Baron, J. S., L. Gunderson, C. D. Allen, E. Fleishman, D. McKenzie, L. A. Meyerson, J. Oropeza, and N. Stephenson

2009 Options for National Parks and Reserves for Adapting to Climate Change. *Environmental Management* 44:1033–1042.

Binford, L. R.

2001 *Constructing Frames of Reference: An Analytical Method for Archaeological Theory Building Using Ethnographic and Environmental Data Sets.* Berkeley: University of California Press.

Boyd, R.

1999 *Indians, Fire, and the Land in the Pacific Northwest.* Corvallis: Oregon State University Press.

Chance, D. H., and J. V. Chance

1985 *Kettle Falls: 1978.* Anthropological Reports no. 84. Moscow: Laboratory of Anthropology, University of Idaho.

Cole, D. N., and L. Yung

2010 *Beyond Naturalness.* Washington, DC: Island Press.

Cramer, S. P., and K. L. Witty

1998 *The Feasibility for Reintroducing Sockeye and Coho Salmon in the Grande Ronde Basin.* Technical report prepared for Bonneville Power Administration and the Nez Perce Tribal Executive Committee. On file at Bonneville Power Administration, Portland, OR.

Erickson, C.

2000 An Artificial Landscape-Scale Fishery in the Bolivian Amazon. *Nature* 408: 190–193.

Gulf of Maine Historical Ecology Research

2011 What Is Historical Ecology? Electronic document, http://www.gomher.org/what.php, accessed March 2, 2010.

Kondolf, G. M., A. J. Boulton, S. O'Daniel, G. C. Poole, F. J. Rahel, E. H. Stanley, E. Wohl, A. Bång, J. Carlstrom, C. Cristoni, H. Huber, S. Koljonen, P. Louhi, and K. Nakamura

2006 Process-Based Ecological River Restoration: Visualizing Three-Dimensional Connectivity and Dynamic Vectors to Recover Lost Linkages. *Ecology and Society* 11(2): article 5. Electronic document, http://www.ecologyandsociety.org/vol11/iss2/art5/, accessed March 30, 2010.

Lazenby, R. A., and P. McCormack

1985 Salmon and Malnutrition on the Northwest Coast. *Current Anthropology* 26(3):379–384.

Loehman, R., and G. Anderson

2009 *Understanding the Science of Climate Change—Talking Points: Impacts to Western Mountains and Forests.* Natural Resource Report NPS/NRPC/NRR—2009/090. Ft. Collins: Department of the Interior, National Park Service.

Lotze, H. K., and I. Milewski
2004 Two Centuries of Multiple Human Impacts and Successive Changes in a North Atlantic Food Web. *Ecological Applications* 14(5):1428–1447.
Mayden, R. L.
1992 *Systematics, Historical Ecology, and North American Freshwater Fishes*. Stanford, CA: Stanford University Press.
Moss, M. L., and A. Cannon
2011 Introduction. In *The Archaeology of North Pacific Fisheries*. M. Moss and A. Cannon, eds. Pp. 1–15. Fairbanks: University of Alaska Press.
Newell, D.
1988 The Rationality of Mechanization in the Pacific Salmon-Canning Industry before the Second World War. *Business History Review* 62(4):626–655.
O'Bannon, P. W.
1987 Waves of Change: Mechanization in the Pacific Coast Canned-Salmon Industry, 1864–1914. *Technology and Culture* 28(3):558–577.
Plew, M. G., ed.
1996 *Prehistoric Hunter-Gatherer Fishing Strategies*. Boise: Boise State University Press.
Price, R. E.
1990 *The Great Father in Alaska: The Case of the Tlingit and Haida Salmon Fishery*. Douglas, AK: First Street Press.
Swetnam, T. W., C. D. Allen, and J. L. Betancourt
1999 Applied Historical Ecology: Using the Past to Manage for the Future. *Historical Variability* 9(4):1189–1206.
Teit, J. A.
1930 *The Salishan Tribes of the Western Plateaus*. F. Boas, ed. Pp. 23–296. 45th Annual Report of the Bureau of American Ethnology. Washington, DC: U.S. Government Printing Office.
Thompson, David
1968 *David Thompson's Narrative*. J. B. Tyrrell, ed. New York: Greenwood Press.
U.S. Bureau of Reclamation
2013 Statement of Michael L. Connor, Commissioner, Bureau of Reclamation, U.S. Department of the Interior, before the Energy and Natural Resources Committee, Subcommittee on Water and Power, U.S. Senate on Colorado River Basin Water Supply and Demand Study, July 16, 2013. Electronic document, http://www.usbr.gov/newsroom/testimony/detail.cfm?RecordID=2421, accessed September 5, 2013.
U.S. Geological Survey
2007 Impacts of Climate Change on Water and Ecosystems in the Upper Colorado River Basin. Electronic document, http://www.crwcd.org/media/uploads/200708_climate_change_impacts_USGS.pdf, accessed September 5, 2013.

Structure of a Resource

Biology and Ecology of Pacific Salmon in the Columbia River Basin

STEPHEN J. GRABOWSKI

This chapter will describe the biology and ecology of Pacific salmon and steelhead, with emphasis on those species that occur in the Columbia River basin, in the context of the availability of fish resources for use by Native people. The usually abundant annual runs of Pacific salmon provided a seasonal, dependable, major food resource and trade item for Native Americans living in both coastal and interior areas of the Columbia River basin. The chapter will include general life history characteristics of several species of Pacific salmon found in the Columbia River basin, life cycle and population structures, historical basin-wide distribution, estimates of historical abundance, and some of the factors contributing to recent population decline from historic levels. Information regarding some other fish species of traditional importance to people of the basin, such as the Pacific lamprey and white sturgeon, and some native resident species will be presented as well.

This chapter will describe the variable nature of the fishery resources that were available to hunter-gatherers for thousands of years in their quest for a reliable food source and items for trade with other hunter-gatherer groups and how stochastic environmental or climatological events such as El Niño–Southern Oscillation may have altered the annual or cyclical abundance of those resources. Other chapters will discuss how these cyclical changes in abundance may have affected the behavior, migration, and even survival of Native people who inhabited the Columbia River basin.

This chapter will provide some information about the unique ecological function that returning adult Pacific salmon and lamprey had beyond simply providing a sustainable food supply and items for trade throughout the basin and beyond. Returning Pacific salmon contributed marine-derived nutrients to the nutrient budget of aquatic, riparian, and terrestrial ecosystems—especially those far removed from the ocean—that enhanced and sustained the productivity of these ecosystems. The chapter will discuss and explain the complex and variable life cycles and habitat requirements of Pacific salmon and the ways in which those characteristics contribute to the salmon's resilience in the face of short- and long-term natural disturbances.

The wide range of complex and variable Pacific salmon life histories contribute substantially to the maintenance and health of aquatic, riparian, and terrestrial ecosystems and have important cultural and social implications for Native Americans in the Columbia River basin even today. Many of the same Pacific salmon species and life history characteristics are manifest in other West Coast river systems that produced salmon and steelhead and were populated by Native people.

The Columbia River basin has an estimated 65 species of native resident, migratory, and anadromous fish (Stanford et al. 2005); this chapter will focus on several species of anadromous Pacific salmon and steelhead and to a lesser extent Pacific lamprey, sturgeon, and cutthroat and bull trout. These latter fish species were less abundant than the annual returning runs of salmon and steelhead but were also used opportunistically by Native people, as described in subsequent chapters of this volume.

Along with Pacific salmon, Pacific lamprey were both culturally and ecologically important components of the basin's aquatic ecosystem, used as a traditional source of food and medicine. This chapter will discuss some aspects and attributes of Pacific lamprey and their life history as well.

To provide some context for the discussion of Pacific salmon and steelhead and some other fishery resources in the Columbia River basin, a description to aid understanding of the vast and ecologically diverse Columbia River basin is germane. Other chapters in this volume will discuss the actual use of the available fishery resources by Native people in the basin. This chapter will form a foundation for those discussions by describing the anadromous fishery resource and how interannual variability in the number of returning adult salmon could affect the relationship between the hunter-gatherer "predators" and their aquatic prey.

Description of the Columbia River Basin

The vast Columbia River basin is ecologically, culturally, and economically diverse. It is the largest river system in the northwest United States and contains the fourth-largest river that flows to sea in North America (Stanford et al. 2005). The basin is about the size of France and drains an area of approximately 219,000 square miles in Washington, Oregon, Idaho, Montana, Wyoming, Nevada, and Utah and an additional 39,500 square miles within Canada, for a total of about 258,500 square miles (Figure 1.1).

Columbia Lake, at an elevation of 809 meters (2,650 feet) in Canada's Selkirk Mountains, is the river's Canadian source. After flowing about 1,200 miles through a varied landscape, the river enters the Pacific Ocean near Astoria, Oregon. The environmental and climatic conditions in the Columbia River basin span the range from arid in the upper and interior basin to wet and coastal in the lower basin. The range of annual temperatures in the basin can be extreme. Numerous tributaries contribute to the river's overall annual flow. The annual water supply to the river is due in large part to the accumulated snowpack in the various mountain ranges within the basin, including parts of the Northern Rockies and the Cascades.

The Snake River is the Columbia's largest tributary and represents about 40 percent of the Columbia River basin area. Its most distant origin is on the Yellowstone Plateau in Wyoming. The Snake River flows through a varied landscape for about 854 miles to its confluence with the main stem Columbia River. The basin exhibits great landscape diversity and complexity; it includes mountains, subalpine lakes, meadows, and streams, as well as lower-elevation arid lands (Stanford et al. 2005). It covers parts of 13 terrestrial and three freshwater ecoregions (the Columbia Glaciated ecoregion, the Columbia Unglaciated ecoregion, and the Upper Snake River ecoregion). Anadromous fish occurred throughout the basin but could not pass Shoshone Falls and therefore could not access the Upper Snake River ecoregion. Other U.S. Columbia River tributaries from upstream to downstream include the Okanogan, Entiat, Wenatchee, Yakima, Klickitat, Umatilla, John Day, Deschutes, Wind, Willamette, Lewis, Cowlitz, and a few others along the lower river.

Prior to modern development of the Columbia River (principally

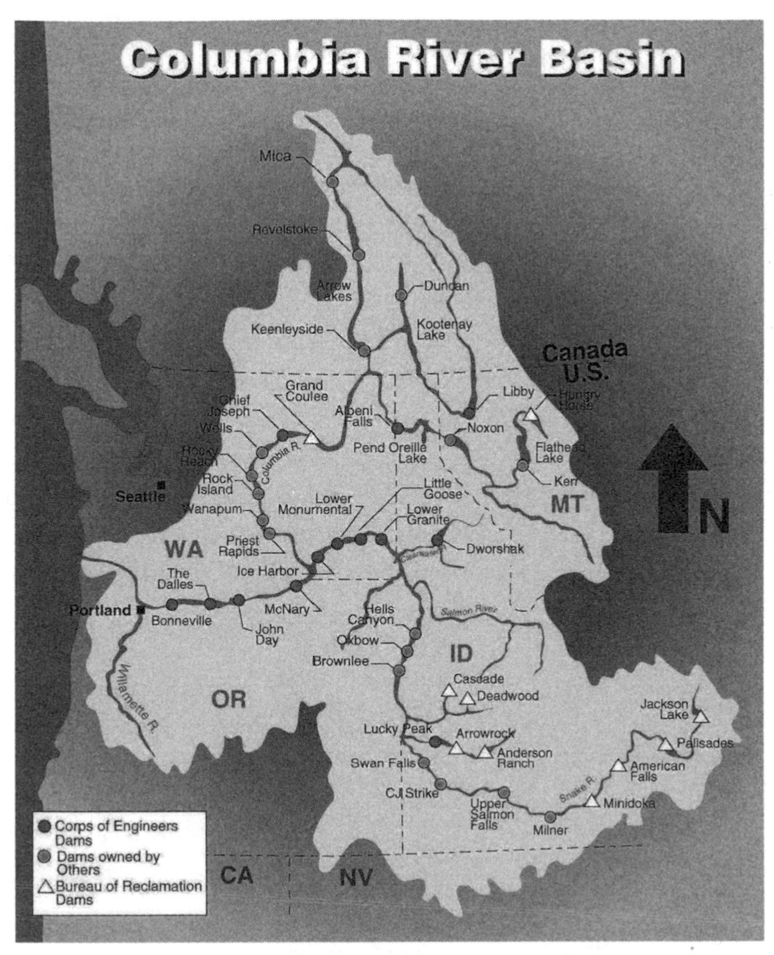

FIGURE 1.1. Generalized map of the Columbia River basin, its major river systems, and hydropower and water development projects (from http://www.nwr.noaa.gov/Salmon-Hydropower/Columbia-Snake-Basin/).

the construction of dams for power production and irrigation), flows were much higher in the spring and lower in winter, and water velocity was significantly greater. The operation of several dams for hydropower and irrigation has altered the river hydrology. The average annual flow for the Columbia River as measured at The Dalles, Oregon, is approximately 190,000 cubic feet per second. The annual discharge rate fluctuates with precipitation and runoff and ranges from 120,000 cubic feet per second in a low water year to 260,000 cubic feet per second in a high water year. The average annual discharge at The Dalles is about 134.1 million acre feet.

The Snake River prior to the 1960s was considered the most important Columbia River tributary for the production of anadromous fish; and the Salmon River and its tributaries contributed substantial production to the overall Snake River salmon production (U.S. Army Corps of Engineers 2002). Changes in riparian and river productivity due to hydrologic modification of the Snake River have occurred downstream from Shoshone Falls. The Upper Columbia River also produced substantial runs of salmon and steelhead, with lesser production occurring in smaller tributaries. About 40 percent of the historic habitat for Pacific salmon in the basin is now inaccessible because of the construction of impassable hydropower projects on the main stem Columbia River, the Snake River, and the North Fork of the Clearwater River in Idaho (National Research Council [NRC] 1996; National Science and Technology Council 2000). Numerous small dams on the Columbia and Snake River tributaries also blocked access to historic salmon and steelhead habitats (Mighetto and Ebel 1994).

Pacific Salmon in the Columbia River Basin

Several culturally, ecologically, and economically important species of anadromous salmonid fish occur in the Columbia River basin. The Columbia River has a high number and diversity of Pacific salmon species and stocks (Augerot 2005). More than 200 different runs or stocks of Pacific salmon spawned in the river system (Stanford et al. 2005). This salmonid stock diversity reflects adaptation to the vast range of local habitat conditions in the basin (Stanford et al. 2005).

Six *Oncorhynchus* species occur in the basin, with fewer species occurring farther south along the Pacific coast, such as in the Sacramento River. The species of interest in the Columbia Basin include Chinook salmon (*Oncorhynchus tshawytscha*), coho salmon (*O. kisutch*), sockeye salmon (*O. nerka*), chum salmon (*O. keta*), and pink salmon (*O. gorbuscha*); the steelhead (*O. mykiss*) is another important anadromous salmonid in the basin, but it exhibits some life history differences from salmon. In the Columbia River basin, Chinook, coho, and sockeye salmon were more widely distributed and abundant than chum or pink salmon (Wydoski and Whitney 2003); the latter two species are generally low in abundance and limited to the lower basin, with pink salmon having the most restricted distribution. Pacific salmon have three unique characteristics: They are anadromous, they home back to their natal streams to spawn, and they are semelparous (they spawn once and die) (NRC 1996; Quinn 2005).

Several species of freshwater or resident salmonid fish such as cutthroat trout and bull trout also occur in the basin; they also exhibit diverse life histories (defined as everything a fish does from birth until death [Behnke 2002]). The high diversity of Columbia Basin's Pacific salmon species and their varied adult run timing (Augerot 2005) had implications for traditional Native American subsistence and trade. The reduction or impairment of one species or returning run of adult salmon due to local environmental perturbation could be offset by abundant returns of runs in other locales. Ocean conditions partly dictate the survival of juvenile fish entering the ocean and, as will be discussed later, may affect several species or runs in a given year, but localized events such as landslides or fires in particular tributaries might only affect a particular fish stock.

The different annual distribution and abundance of anadromous salmonid species from the lowlands to the higher elevations of the interior resulted in a variable array of ecological and economic contributions of the fish to the basin. In addition, spawning fish provided marine-derived nutrients to the spawning tributaries that contributed substantially to primary and secondary production in aquatic, riparian, and terrestrial ecosystems, in turn contributing substantially to salmon production.

Some General Life History Characteristics of Pacific Salmon

The different anadromous salmonids in the Columbia Basin have complex and interesting life cycles, life history strategies, habitat requirements, and ecological interactions. Different life stages of individual species have substantially different habitat requirements. Anadromy, or the movement of juvenile fish from freshwater spawning and rearing habitats to oceanic feeding areas and back to freshwater streams as mature adults to spawn, provides Pacific salmon with enhanced opportunities for growth, primarily from the greater abundance of food available in the ocean, which promotes more rapid growth compared with a freshwater environment (NRC 1996). Anadromous salmonids generally acquire more than 90 percent of their adult weight from ocean feeding (Montgomery 2003). After leaving the ocean to return inland, adult salmon do not eat and must use their accumulated energy reserves for migration and reproduction.

Even before Euro-American settlement of the Columbia River basin and construction of dams and other obstacles to migration along the West Coast, anadromous fish encountered challenges during migration that were not necessarily encountered by resident salmonids. Migration challenges include local and regional events such as landslides, wildfires, and glacial activity that altered the structure and nature of drainages (also see chapter 2, this volume). These events could cause altered or blocked waterways, unfavorable water temperatures, or the accumulation of sediment. In addition, physiological stress from the transition from freshwater to seawater and back again and predation on several life stages (including humans for thousands of years) affected populations of anadromous salmonids.

Nevertheless, Pacific salmon are relatively robust and resilient against natural climatic and environmental disturbances, and over time their populations can rebound from natural short-term and longer-term environmental perturbations that affect habitats and population abundance (chapter 3 discusses the resiliency of this species to industrial-scale human harvest). Pacific salmon can recolonize a degraded habitat that has been improved through either the passage of time and natural ecological processes or active intervention and habitat improvement projects.

Although adult Pacific salmon are well known for their ability to home back to their natal streams to spawn and die, a small percentage of fish stray to other watersheds (Quinn 2005), which over the long term is a necessary and beneficial attribute that provides an opportunity for the population to colonize restored habitats or expand their range into nearby suitable habitats. The straying of natural-origin fish also provides gene flow among local populations, which is important in maintaining the population in the event of the destruction or degradation of a portion of their habitat. The straying of returning adult salmon does not create isolated populations that over time could result in speciation or subspeciation (Behnke 2002).

Population Structure

Populations are groups of fish found in a particular location at a given time (Meehan and Bjornn 1991). A "deme" is a local breeding population that is reproductively isolated from other breeding populations of the same species and which is generally uniquely adapted to local environmental conditions (Meehan and Bjornn 1991; NRC 1996). Biologists have grouped West Coast and Columbia River basin Pacific salmon populations into evolutionarily significant units (ESUs) and steelhead into distinct population segments (DPSs) under the Endangered Species Act (ESA [Waples 1991]). The basis of these groupings invokes the genetic relatedness of populations and of fish within populations; the geographic, geologic, and climatic setting where the fish occur; the run timing of adults; the behavior and ecology of juvenile fish and the timing of downstream migration; and other factors.

Today, eight Chinook salmon ESUs are designated in the Columbia River basin; five are listed as threatened or endangered under the ESA, as are some coho and sockeye salmon ESUs. The delineation of Pacific salmon ESUs, with their major population groups and populations, provides some framework for understanding the wide range of life history characteristics of these fish and the way this structured availability in time and space for Native communities. Table 1.1 shows the current ESA listing status of Columbia River salmon ESUs and steelhead DPSs.

Columbia River basin and some other West Coast salmon ESUs and steelhead DPSs have been listed under the Endangered Species Act, indicating the substantial decline in population levels from historic abundance in the 19th century and dramatic changes in anadromous fish population robustness and distribution since Euro-American settlement of the basin. Nehlsen et al. (1991) describe factors contributing to the decline of many Pacific salmon stocks and their current precarious condition. They note that different stocks are uniquely adapted to particular rivers and subareas, an unknown number of stocks have become extinct, and others may have been impacted by historic hatchery practices that did not recognize the importance of individual stocks of Pacific salmon to the well-being of the whole species.

Pacific Salmon Abundance

Large runs of Chinook salmon and sockeye salmon historically returned annually to the Columbia River, as did smaller runs of coho salmon and steelhead. Estimates vary for the historic abundance of Pacific salmon in the Columbia River basin. Chapman (1986, 1988) estimates the predevelopment abundance of all species of Pacific salmon and steelhead as 7.5–8.9 million fish, on the basis of peak-period commercial catch estimates and

TABLE 1.1. Endangered Species Act Status of Pacific Salmon and Steelhead in the Columbia River Basin.

Species	Evolutionarily Significant Unit/Distinct Population Segment	Endangered Species Act Listing
Chinook salmon	Upper Columbia River, spring run	Endangered
	Snake River, spring/summer run	Threatened
	Snake River, fall run	Threatened
	Lower Columbia River	Threatened
	Upper Willamette River	Threatened
	Middle Columbia River, spring run	Not warranted
	Upper Columbia River, summer/fall run	Not warranted
	Deschutes River, summer/fall run	Not warranted
Coho salmon	Lower Columbia River	Threatened
Sockeye salmon	Snake River	Endangered
	Okanogan River	Not warranted
	Lake Wenatchee	Not warranted
Chum salmon	Columbia River	Threatened
Steelhead	Upper Columbia River	Threatened
	Snake River basin	Threatened
	Lower Columbia River	Threatened
	Upper Willamette River	Threatened
	Middle Columbia River	Threatened
	Southwest Washington	Not warranted

probable optimum exploitation rates. Chapman (1986) reckons 2,253,000 to 2,623,000 sockeye salmon, 2,000,000 to 2,500,000 summer Chinook salmon, 1,250,000 fall Chinook salmon, 500,000 to 588,000 spring Chinook salmon, 560,000 to 618,000 coho salmon, 449,000 to 748,000 chum salmon, and 449,000 to 554,000 steelhead. The Northwest Power Planning Council (now the Northwest Power and Conservation Council) (1986) estimates an overall predevelopment run of ten to 16 million adult salmonids combined.

Chapman (1986) cautions that estimates of historic abundance prior to the 1850s may not accurately represent overall annual population abundance and fluctuations due to the numerous environmental perturbations (e.g., warm and cool spells, fires and landslides, etc.) that could have occurred over thousands of years. Localized events in tributaries and larger-scale events in the ocean could have had profound effects on overall population abundance.

Populations of Pacific salmon declined with the onset of widespread commercial fishing in the late 1800s, as well as other anthropogenic activities such as timber harvest, irrigated agriculture (with its water diversions), mining activities, livestock grazing, hydropower development, excessive harvest, and habitat degradation both in spawning tributaries and in the migratory corridor. Recently, federal agencies responsible for salmon and steelhead recovery in the Columbia River basin consolidated the numerous factors for the decline of West Coast Pacific salmon populations in the basin into four "*Hs*": habitat, harvest, hatcheries, and hydropower development (National Marine Fisheries Service 2000).

Besides the direct influence of human activity, ocean environmental conditions such as water temperature, coastal upwelling and ocean productivity, and the abundance and distribution of prey and predators also affect the survival of juvenile fish entering the ocean and ultimately the number of returning adults. Short-term manifestations of large-scale atmospheric–oceanic linkages such as El Niño–Southern Oscillation and La Niña events and longer-term phenomena such as the Pacific Decadal Oscillation have profound effects on ocean productivity and environmental conditions and therefore juvenile survival and the number of returning adult Pacific salmon. Survival to adulthood of a cohort of juvenile salmon entering the ocean is largely determined during the first four to six weeks after initial entry (Pearcy 1992).

The harvest of Pacific salmon ramped up with the establishment of salmon canning operations on the Lower Columbia River in the late 1800s. Of the three annual Chinook salmon runs, the summer run was most abundant and was targeted early on by commercial fishery. The total Chinook salmon catch peaked about 1883, the river coho salmon catch peaked in 1895, the sockeye salmon catch peaked in 1898, and the steelhead catch peaked in 1892. The chum salmon catch peaked much later, around the late 1920s, after the abundance of the more desirable salmon species had declined. Summer-run Chinook salmon were more abundant overall than they are currently. Summer-run Chinook salmon were relatively large fish, and some of those that ascended the Upper Columbia River were referred to as June hogs (Mighetto and Ebel 1994).

The Pacific Salmon Life Cycle

Simply stated, in the overall life cycle of anadromous West Coast Pacific salmonids, mature adults spawn in suitable gravel substrates in freshwater tributaries in the fall, followed by a variable period of incubation of the fertilized eggs over the winter, with hatching and emergence of the fry the following spring. A variable period of residence in freshwater (from months to years) by the young fish is followed by eventual migration downstream to the ocean and then a variable period of growth to adulthood in the ocean. Some species undertake substantial oceanic migrations, while other species remain closer to the coast. Finally, the fish migrate upstream back to their natal streams as mature adults to spawn and die and complete the cycle.

Migration to the ocean provides an opportunity for substantial and rapid growth to adulthood in the generally more highly productive ocean environment, compared with limited opportunities for growth in inland tributaries (Quinn 2005). Navigation in the ocean during this life history stage is thought to be mediated by magnetite in the head of the fish.

As noted above, homing back to natal streams is a unique characteristic of some anadromous fish species and is in part the result of olfactory imprinting of the smolts on the sequence of odors they encounter on their downstream migration (Mighetto and Ebel 1994; Quinn 2005) and recognition of the sequence in reverse order for adult upstream migration. The nares and nasal sacs provide the olfactory sense by which the fish recognize odors (Behnke 2002).

This general overall life history strategy varies among the Pacific salmon species. Some have rigid life spans and strategies, while others are more variable. For example, Chinook salmon can be long-lived and have a variable life span and time spent both in freshwater and in the ocean, and they have several different adult run timings in the same river (Healey 1991), whereas pink salmon have a rigidly fixed two-year life span (Heard 1991). The Chinook salmon in the Columbia River basin is a relatively long-lived species that exhibits spring, summer, and fall runs of returning adults.

Despite substantial intraspecies variability, there are some basic similarities in life histories. Pacific salmon are generally considered to be fall spawners, although "fall" can range from July to late fall and even into January or February in some chum salmon populations (Quinn 2005), while the unique winter-run Chinook salmon of the Sacramento River in California spawn during late spring and summer (Fisher 1994; Moyle 2002). The eggs have a relatively long incubation period over the winter in the gravel substrate, with eggs hatching and fry emerging from the gravel the following spring. Prior to fry emergence, the newly hatched "alevins" (the recently hatched fish prior to absorption of the yolk sac) remain in the gravel for several weeks absorbing their yolk sac. Upon absorption of the yolk sac, the fry emerge into the stream at a length of about one inch and begin feeding.

Pacific salmon are semelparous (spawn once and die), but steelhead and trout are iteroparous (do not necessarily die after spawning). Steelhead can return to the ocean to grow another year and then spawn a second or even a third time, although the incidence of repeat spawning among steelhead decreases the farther inland or upstream the fish originate. Steelhead are spring spawners, in contrast to the usual fall spawn timing of other Pacific salmon species.

The several Pacific salmon species in the Columbia River basin have different spawning and rearing habitat requirements. Once the adults have returned to their natal stream, mature females construct redds or nests in gravel, generally in an area at the downstream end of a riffle where there is adequate groundwater flow through the several pockets in the redd that contain the eggs. Redd location and construction are not random events; females are highly selective of particular attributes of substrate size, water quality, water temperature, dissolved oxygen, and flow. This ensures the incubation of the embryos and survival of the alevins before they emerge from the gravel as fry.

After redd construction and during spawning, as the female fish releases the eggs, the accompanying male releases milt to fertilize them. The fertilized eggs drift down into the egg pocket, and as the spawning process continues, gravel dislodged by the female from upstream is displaced downstream to cover and protect the recently deposited eggs. Larger fish can move larger-sized gravel and therefore dig a deeper pocket, resulting in eggs being deposited deeper in the substrate and therefore better protected from potential bed load movement that could occur during high streamflow events.

After a variable time spent rearing in freshwater (especially among Chinook, coho, and sockeye salmon), young fish undergo a physiological change, transforming into smolts, which generally out-migrate to the ocean during high river flows in spring. The physiological transformation from a "parr" (a juvenile fish rearing in the stream) to a "smolt" (a process referred to as smoltification) involves primarily the ability of the fish to osmoregulate to survive in the salty ocean environment. In freshwater environments, juvenile salmon bodies have a higher osmotic pressure than the medium in which they live, so fish take in water and must eliminate excess water to maintain osmotic balance. In the ocean, on the other hand, seawater has a greater osmotic pressure than the body of the fish, resulting in water being drawn from the fish. In this case, to maintain osmotic balance, the fish needs to drink water and excrete excess salt (Bond 1979). During smoltification, other changes occur such as alterations in enzyme activity and metabolism; externally the smolts become more slender and silvery in coloration, and their scales are more easily removed or dislodged.

Detailed Accounts of Several Pacific Salmon Species in the Columbia River Basin

Chinook Salmon

Chinook salmon occur in the Columbia River basin in some life history stage most of the year; either eggs are incubating in the gravel, juveniles are rearing or overwintering, or smolts or adults are migrating. Chinook salmon are widely distributed throughout the basin, from low elevations to high elevations. This species has three historic run timings in the Columbia River basin; for convenience and management purposes, these three runs are designated as spring, summer, and fall (Fish Passage Center 2012). Adult spring Chinook salmon pass the area of Bonneville Dam from March to May 31, summer Chinook salmon pass from June 1 to July 31, and fall Chinook salmon pass from August 1 to the end of the counting season in November. These dates are lagged progressively as the adult fish migrate upriver and pass successive dams or hydropower projects. In the Snake River, spring Chinook salmon pass Lower Granite Dam from March to June 17; summer Chinook salmon, from June 18 to August 17; and fall Chinook salmon, from August 18 to the end of counting in November. Historically this resulted in a continuum of adult salmon returns to some parts of the basin over a large portion of the year. In the Sacramento River there are four runs of Chinook salmon.

Chinook salmon throughout their range have what are referred to as "stream-type" and "ocean-type" life histories (NRC 1996). In the stream-type life history, such as that exhibited by Upper Columbia River spring Chinook salmon and the Snake River spring/summer Chinook salmon, juvenile fish remain in freshwater and rear for one year before migrating downstream to the estuary and open ocean as smolts, and the adults return to the river before they are mature and thus require additional time in the river or in headwater streams before spawning. Stream-type fish generally migrate farther inland and spawn and rear in higher-elevation tributaries. Their earlier upstream adult migration timing provides the additional time needed to reach these higher-elevation and inland spawning tributaries.

After eggs hatch and the fry emerge in the spring, the young fish reside in freshwater for about a year, overwinter, and then out-migrate to the ocean in their second year of life as one-year-old smolts or yearlings. Ocean-type fish such as Upper Columbia River summer/fall Chinook salmon and Snake River fall Chinook salmon adults return to the river later in the year and are either sexually mature or nearly so. They are therefore much closer to spawning and are considered ocean-maturing fish. These fish typically occupy and spawn in the main stems of the Columbia and Snake rivers and in some cases the lower reaches of major tributaries (Healey 1991). Once eggs of these fish hatch and the alevins emerge from the gravel the following spring, they relatively quickly begin a protracted downstream rearing migration as subyearling fish and generally make it to the estuary or ocean during their first year of life. Some juveniles may overwinter in the estuary, growing to a larger size, which reduces the threat of predation once they move into the ocean the following spring. Once in the ocean, they are more coastline oriented than stream-type Chinook salmon.

In the upper main Columbia River, stream-type spring Chinook salmon are genetically distinguishable from the ocean-type summer/fall Chinook salmon. In the Snake River, the spring/summer Chinook salmon are stream-type fish, while the fall Chinook salmon are ocean-type fish. Figure 1.2 shows the ten-year average daily count of Chinook salmon at Bonneville Dam, which illustrates both the season-long timing of the returning adults and the timing and separation of the spring, summer, and fall runs. Figure 1.3 shows the ten-year average daily count of Chinook salmon at Lower Granite Dam as well as the timing differentiation of the Snake River spring/summer Chinook salmon ESU and the fall Chinook salmon ESU.

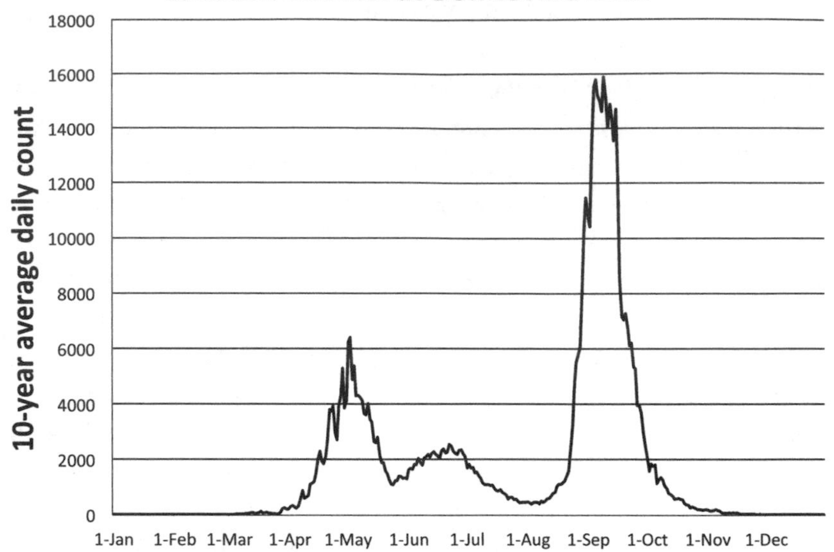

FIGURE 1.2. Ten-year average daily count of Chinook salmon at Bonneville Dam.

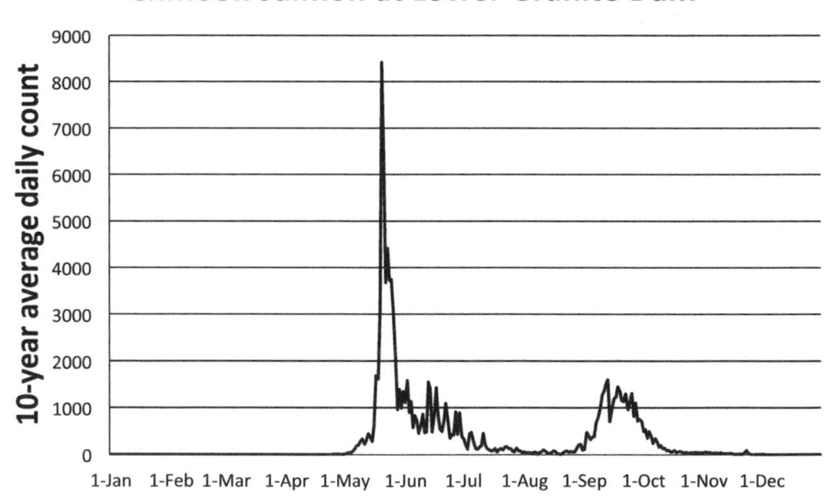

FIGURE 1.3. Ten-year average daily count of Chinook salmon at Lower Granite Dam.

Coho Salmon

Coho salmon are found from central California northward to Point Hope, Alaska, and in Asia (Sandercock 1991; Simpson and Wallace 1978). National Oceanic and Atmospheric Administration Fisheries has designated several West Coast ESUs for coho salmon (Weitkamp et al. 1994). Coho salmon were present and abundant historically in tributaries of the Columbia up to the Wenatchee River of the Upper Columbia and in the Grande Ronde River of the Snake River (Frissell 1993; Wahle and Pearson 1987, cited in Sandercock 1991). Coho salmon are not as abundant as Chinook salmon in the Columbia River basin and generally return to the Columbia River from early August to late November, with a few adults migrating earlier and later, with a peak migration about early September (Columbia River DART, http://www.cbr.washington.edu/cgi-bin/dart/makegraph/dart/makegraph/html-src/adultpass.config). Coho salmon are relatively resilient and can utilize a broader range of habitats than other anadromous salmon (Meehan and Bjornn 1991). They are found in small tributaries of large rivers as well as in some small urban streams, if water quality and other habitat requirements are suitable.

Coho salmon build redds for spawning similarly as described above for Chinook salmon, and the juveniles rear in freshwater habitats for about a year prior to downstream migration. They do not exhibit the highly variable life history noted above for Chinook salmon. Their abundance in the Columbia River basin has been much less than that of Chinook salmon. Some populations were extirpated, and some recent actions have been implemented to restore coho salmon to some of the areas they occupied historically (Nez Perce Tribe and FishPro 2004).

Sockeye Salmon

Sockeye salmon are found along the Pacific coast from the Columbia River up to the Yukon River in Alaska and westward to Japan (Wydoski and Whitney 2003). Sockeye salmon reported south of the Columbia River are thought to be strays and not established populations (Behnke 2002; Moyle 2002). In the Columbia River basin, there are currently two Upper Columbia River sockeye salmon populations, in Wenatchee River and Okanogan River (Lake Osoyoos); and one Snake River population, in Redfish Lake in Idaho in the Upper Salmon River basin near Stanley (Waples et al. 1991). Sockeye salmon occurred historically in areas throughout the basin where lakes were associated with river systems. They were historically more widely distributed in the Snake River basin in areas such as the tributaries to Payette Lake in the Payette River drainage (Simpson and Wallace 1978).

Some sockeye salmon populations spawn in tributaries to nursery lakes, while some populations spawn on the lakeshore. Snake River (Redfish Lake) sockeye salmon are lakeshore spawners, whereas Wenatchee River sockeye salmon are tributary spawners. Sockeye salmon are somewhat unique among Pacific salmon species in that soon after hatching and emerging from the gravel, the young fish begin a downstream (or in a few cases, an upstream) migration from the spawning grounds to lakes in which to rear for about a year before out-migrating as yearling fish. Those fish that spawn on lakeshores emerge directly into the lake to rear. Juvenile sockeye salmon in nursery lakes feed heavily on zooplankton, which is much more abundant in lakes than in streams (Foerster 1968). Commonly, sockeye salmon nursery lakes are oligotrophic, that is, of low productivity that is nonetheless generally sufficient to support the populations of salmon.

Chum Salmon

Chum salmon are found along the Pacific coast from the Sacramento River up to the Bering Sea (Wydoski and Whitney 2003). Chum salmon are now generally limited to streams of the Lower Columbia River up to about the Wind River above Bonneville Dam, although Wydoski and Whitney (2003) note that chum salmon have migrated long distances upstream in the Columbia River basin. Spawning occurs in the late fall in several tributaries and in some areas of the lower main stem Columbia River such as near Ives Island below Bonneville Dam. Chum salmon fry differ behaviorally from Chinook, coho, and sockeye salmon fry in that they migrate downstream to the estuary and ocean soon after they emerge from the gravel. They constitute a smaller component of the overall Pacific salmon abundance in the Columbia River. They were important to the traditional Alaskan diet and acquired the common name "dog salmon," since this species was sometimes used to provide food for dogs in some northern areas. Mature chum salmon spawners also develop exceptionally large canine teeth, which may have led to the name. The Columbia River ESU of chum salmon is listed under the ESA.

Pink Salmon

Like chum salmon, pink salmon are found along the Pacific coast from the Sacramento River up to the Bering Sea (Wydoski and Whitney 2003). They are a minor contributor to the salmonid fishery resources in the Columbia River basin, but in some northern areas they contribute substantially to the salmon harvest. Some pink salmon enter the Lower Columbia River, but few are counted at Bonneville Dam. Interestingly, a few adult pink salmon have been reported occasionally in the Lower Snake River in Idaho. Like chum salmon, pink salmon generally spawn lower in river systems, closer to the ocean, since fry of this species also migrate downstream to an estuary and the ocean relatively soon after emerging from the gravel. West Coast pink salmon are not listed under the ESA.

Steelhead

Steelhead were historically widely distributed in the Columbia River basin. They occupied most of the area and habitat accessible to anadromous salmonids. They were able to negotiate higher stream gradients and velocities and occupied habitats farther upstream than those of Chinook and coho salmon. Steelhead exhibit some life history characteristics similar to salmon, that is, spawning and rearing in freshwater tributaries, migrating downstream to the ocean with relatively large excursions in the open ocean over a period of from one to several years, and finally returning to the Columbia River basin and migrating upstream to spawn in their natal streams. Steelhead are differentiated from other species of Pacific salmon in that they are iteroparous: they do not necessarily die after spawning and may migrate back downriver to the ocean, resume feeding and growth, and migrate upstream another time or two to spawn again. Another difference is that steelhead spawn in the spring.

Steelhead in the Columbia River basin have both summer-run and winter-run populations. Generally, in the more coastal populations the adult fish migrate into the Columbia River and its lower river tributaries in the fall–winter and early spring period to spawn. Summer-run fish, on the other hand, are generally destined for the many upstream tributaries above the Columbia River Gorge and begin migrating into the Columbia River starting about May. These fish generally migrate to the interior of the basin and spawn at higher elevations. Summer steelhead require additional time to migrate to natal streams. Depending on their destination and distance to natal streams, adult summer steelhead may overwinter in the main Columbia or Snake rivers and resume migration to their natal streams the following spring after water temperatures have warmed.

To complicate matters somewhat, summer steelhead migrating to inland habitats in the Columbia River basin have two runs, the "A-run" and "B-run." A-run fish are differentiated by passage timing and size at Bonneville Dam. A-run fish return before August 25 and are less than 77.5 centimeters (30.5 inches) in length, while B-run fish are larger and return after August 25. Most of the interior summer steelhead that populate the Upper Columbia River and Snake River tributaries are A-run fish, while some of the fish that return to the Lower Salmon River, Middle Salmon River, and Clearwater River are B-run fish. In the Snake River basin, the larger size of those fish passing Lower Granite Dam in the late summer and fall rather than actual passage date distinguishes the B-run fish from the A-run fish. The B-run fish spend an additional year rearing in the ocean and attain the larger size.

Steelhead spawn in the spring, and the eggs hatch later in the spring–early summer. Eggs hatch in about 50 days at an incubation temperature of 10 degrees Celsius (50 degrees Fahrenheit). Juvenile steelhead generally occupy riffle areas and consume a variety of invertebrates. Where both steelhead and coho salmon occur in the same streams, there is some separation of the species due to the steelhead's preference for riffle areas and the juvenile coho salmon's preference for a pool-type habitat (Bjornn and Reiser 1991). Juvenile steelhead spend a variable amount of time rearing in freshwater, anywhere from one to seven years, before out-migrating to the ocean (Busby et al. 1996).

Current Status of Salmon and Steelhead in the Columbia River Basin

The current status of salmon and steelhead reflects the dramatic change in Columbia Basin fishery from pre-Euro-American days. The recent ten-year averages of Pacific salmon returning to the Columbia River as counted at Bonneville Dam are shown in Table 1.2, along with historic estimates of abundance from Chapman (1986). In some runs 80 percent or more of adult salmon and steelhead returns to the river are hatchery-origin fish,

TABLE 1.2. Ten-Year (2002–2011) Average Counts of Pacific Salmon at Bonneville Dam and Estimates of Historic Abundance ($7.5–8.9 \times 10^6$).

Species or Run	10-Year Average at Bonneville Dam[a]	Historic Estimate[b]
All Chinook salmon	645,570	
Spring Chinook salmon	152,015	500,000–588,000
Summer Chinook salmon	92,437	2,000,000–2,500,000
Fall Chinook salmon	401,116	1,250,000
Coho salmon	123,066	560,000–618,000
Sockeye salmon	130,981	2,253,000–2,623,000
Chum salmon	107	449,000–748,000
Pink salmon	84	
Steelhead	386,083	449,000–554,000
Wild steelhead	116,554	

[a] Fish Passage Center 2012.
[b] From Chapman 1986.

while historic estimates are based on wild or natural-origin fish. Hatcheries have been established for a variety of reasons, such as mitigation for hydropower development and the consequent loss of historical habitat for anadromous Pacific salmonids. Hatchery production of anadromous salmonids may have detrimental effects on natural-origin fish.

Pacific Lamprey

Pacific lamprey (*Entosphenus tridentatus*) occurred historically throughout the Columbia River basin and coast-wide. Lamprey are a more primitive fish species than Pacific salmonids and should not be confused with eels, even though Pacific lamprey are sometimes referred to as "eel." As seen in Jones (this volume), they could represent a significant source of traditional Native food. Substantial numbers of adult Pacific lamprey were harvested by Native Americans near Asotin, Washington, as well as at some other sites. These fish are also important ecologically in providing an additional source of marine-derived nutrients to enhance aquatic, riparian, and terrestrial production in inland tributaries; buffer predation on young salmon; and provide a source of food to young salmon. Also, upstream-migrating adult Pacific lamprey helped to offset predation by sea lions on adult Pacific salmon migrants in the Lower Columbia River.

Historically, Pacific lamprey were found as far upstream as Kettle Falls in the Columbia River and Spokane Falls in the Spokane River (Wydoski and Whitney 2003). Grand Coulee Dam and Chief Joseph Dam blocked the upstream migration of Pacific lamprey. Simpson and Wallace (1978) report that in Idaho, Pacific lamprey once migrated to all waters where salmon and steelhead occurred, which included the main stem Snake River upstream to Shoshone Falls and the several large and small tributaries. That upstream migration is now blocked by Hells Canyon Dam.

Pacific lamprey share numerous traits with Pacific salmon. Pacific lamprey are anadromous, with adults spawning in freshwater redds or nests of fertilized eggs. Pacific lamprey spawn in the spring, after which they die. After the young hatch in a few weeks the larval ammocoetes reside in suitable freshwater habitats usually downstream from spawning locations, generally in sandy-silty areas, filter feeding on desmids and diatoms for a period of up to seven years (Simpson and Wallace 1978). The ammocoetes then transform physiologically and behaviorally into "transformers" or macropthalmia in preparation for a downstream migration to the ocean, where they parasitize a range of host organisms by attaching to the hosts with their oral disc. They grow in the ocean for several years, and in response to environmental or physiological cues they return to freshwater as adults to spawn.

Pacific lamprey are less well studied than Pacific salmon, and many aspects of their life history are not well known, especially during their ocean residency. They have been found in deep water far offshore (Wydoski and Whitney 2003). Although they return to freshwater to spawn and die, little is known about their homing instincts. It is thought that lamprey may not necessarily return to natal streams to spawn but instead are stimulated to ascend streams in response to chemical cues such as bile acids or pheromones released by ammocoetes rearing and filter feeding in the sediments of tributary streams.

Recently, populations of Pacific lamprey in the Columbia River basin have plummeted compared with estimated historic abundance, and many efforts are in progress to restore degraded lamprey habitats and improve passage conditions at Columbia River basin hydropower and irrigation projects (Jackson and Moser 2012). In addition, some restoration projects in the basin are translocating adult Pacific lamprey to suitable habitats upstream of barriers to migration (Ward et al. 2012).

White and Green Sturgeon

White sturgeon (*Acipenser transmontanus*) and green sturgeon (*A. medirostris*) both occur in the Columbia River basin and were another potential source of traditional Native food. White sturgeon are found in marine waters and freshwaters along the Pacific coast from Monterey, California, to Cook Inlet, Alaska, while green sturgeon are found along the Pacific coast from Ensenada, Mexico, to southeastern Alaska (Wydoski and Whitney 2003). White sturgeon are large and slow-to-mature fish that were historically widely distributed throughout the Columbia River basin, in the Snake River up to Shoshone Falls (Stanford et al. 2005), and in the Lower Salmon and Clearwater rivers.

The construction of hydropower facilities on the Columbia and Snake rivers isolated populations of sturgeon that had migrated throughout the river system to the estuary and ocean. These populations are no longer migratory. Lower Columbia River populations of white sturgeon still have access to the ocean, while those populations farther upstream have a more limited migration and are mostly landlocked due to the presence of impassible hydropower projects. Large white sturgeon cannot ascend fish ladders. These fish generally remain in particular reservoirs for their entire lives. Green sturgeon have a much more limited distribution in the Columbia River but do occur in the Lower Columbia River, where they spend some time rearing.

Resident Fish

Numerous species of resident fish are found throughout the Columbia River basin (Behnke 1992, 2002; Simpson and Wallace 1978; Wydoski and Whitney 2003), and populations of resident fish provided an alternative food source for Native people in the Northwest (see Lyons, this volume). Below is a description of some of the more prominent and widespread species.

Bull Trout

Bull trout (*Salvelinus confluentus*) historically occurred from northern California up the coast to about 60° north latitude in Alaska and in the Pacific Northwest and far inland (Wydoski and Whitney 2003). They occurred in numerous far inland waters of the Pacific Northwest including many of the tributaries to the Columbia River, which provided specific habitat requirements such as cold water, stable stream channels, clean spawning and rearing gravel, and complex cover (http://ecos.fws.gov/speciesProfile/profile/speciesProfile.action?spcode=E065). Bull trout are not found on offshore islands in British Columbia (Behnke 2002; Wydoski and Whitney 2003). As far south as California, the Wintun tribe of Native Americans referred to a fish in the McCloud River in California now recognized to be bull trout as *wye-dar-deekit* (Behnke 2002), which indicates the tribe's use of the species. Lyons (this volume) provides a detailed description of Native use of bull trout in the Pend Oreille Basin.

Bull trout require relatively cold and clean water. They can tolerate water temperatures up to about 10 degrees Celsius (50 degrees Fahrenheit). Lower water temperatures are preferable. This requirement for cold clean water limits their distribution. Bull trout are generally slow growing, especially those that remain resident in small headwater tributaries. Bull trout exhibit several life history strategies to adapt to a variety of resource types. In addition to the resident fish, there are fluvial bull trout, which migrate from the small headwater tributaries to larger rivers to grow and mature; adfluvial bull trout, which migrate from headwater tributaries through larger rivers to lakes (or reservoirs) to grow and mature; and anadromous bull trout, which migrate into coastal environments. After these migratory fish mature, they migrate back upstream to their natal streams to spawn. The fidelity of adult fish to spawning sites is thought to be high.

Bull trout spawn in the fall as water temperatures drop, starting at about 9 degrees Celsius (48 degrees Fahrenheit). The female fish constructs a redd in which to deposit the eggs, which require a long incubation time in the stream substrate (up to about 200 days). After hatching and emerging from the gravel substrate, the young fish rear in tributaries and forage on larval and adult aquatic insects and crustaceans. Young fish rearing in lakes feed opportunistically on mysid shrimp (*Mysis relicta*) when they are available. As bull trout grow, they shift their diet to fish. The adult fish that migrate to rivers or lakes to grow and mature can be relatively large when they return to spawn in small headwater tributaries and are vulnerable to predators and human harvest.

In recent times, populations of bull trout throughout their range have declined due to habitat degradation resulting from livestock grazing, timber harvest, mining activities and mineral extraction, water withdrawal for irrigated agriculture, road construction, and so on. Numerous populations of bull trout in the Columbia River basin have been listed as threatened under the Endangered Species Act.

Cutthroat Trout

Cutthroat trout (*Oncorhynchus clarki*) are a widely distributed species along the West Coast and inland. The original distribution was greater than that of any other salmonid species in North America except for lake trout (Behnke 1992). Several of the 14 subspecies of cutthroat trout occurred historically in the Columbia River basin (Behnke 1992). These include the coastal, westslope, Yellowstone, and Snake River fine-spotted cutthroat trout. Lahontan cutthroat trout have been introduced into the Columbia Basin. Westslope cutthroat trout were the most widespread of the subspecies and included populations in the Upper Columbia River basin, in the John Day River basin in Oregon, and along the east slope of the Cascades (Behnke 1992). Some of the populations occurred upstream from natural barriers to migration. Yellowstone and Snake River fine-spotted cutthroat were sympatric (overlapped in habitat) above Shoshone Falls. It is difficult to assess the historic abundance of these fish. Their numbers were probably low compared with the annual returning runs of adult anadromous salmonids.

Like bull trout, cutthroats exhibit several life history strategies. Some are resident fish that remain in smaller headwater streams for their entire lives; others migrate to rivers (fluvial) or lakes (adfluvial) to grow and mature and then return to natal streams to spawn. Some coastal populations are anadromous and migrate to the ocean to grow. These migratory fish have access to the food resources in the large rivers and lakes, which are generally more abundant than that which is available in their natal streams.

Cutthroat trout, like other salmonid fish, return to natal streams to spawn; they spawn in spring or early summer and require gravel in which to construct redds, along with adequate water flow and temperature. Cutthroat trout interact with other trout species and in some cases hybridize with rainbow trout. Food habits differ among the subspecies, but in general they are opportunistic feeders (Wydoski and Whitney 2003). Westslope cutthroat trout typically feed on *Daphnia* spp. and other invertebrates, while other subspecies prey on fish and therefore grow larger.

Rainbow/Redband Trout

The nonanadromous form of *O. mykiss* were historically fairly widely distributed throughout the Columbia River basin, except above several impassable barriers, such as Shoshone Falls on the Snake River in southeastern Idaho, Spokane Falls on the Spokane River, Kootenay Falls in western Montana, and Albeni Falls on the Pend Oreille–Clark Fork drainage in western Idaho (Behnke 2002). Behnke (1992) recognizes three main evolutionary groups of *O. mykiss*, the redband trout of the Sacramento–San Joaquin basin, the redband trout of the Columbia and Fraser basins, and the coastal rainbow trout. He (2002) considers *O. mykiss* west of the Cascades to be *O. m. irideus* (the rainbow trout) and those east of the Cascades to be *O. m. gairdneri* (the redband trout). Behnke (1992) notes that anadromous steelhead populations are found in both the coastal and redband trout groups. He classifies the redband steelhead as those fish that ascend the Columbia River to east of the Cascade Range.

Other representatives of *O. mykiss* occur in other basins throughout the West. Their history and evolutionary relationship are complicated, and in recent times the integrity of native stocks has been influenced by the introduction of hatchery-produced fish into areas occupied by other subspecies. In part due to the much larger area of the Columbia Basin east of the Cascades, the *gairdneri* subspecies was more abundant in the Columbia Basin than the *irideus* subspecies west of the Cascades, as were the anadromous forms. The evolutionary relationships among the several groups of *O. mykiss* are beyond the scope of this chapter (for details, see Behnke 1992).

As discussed above for anadromous *O. mykiss*, the nonanadromous *O. mykiss* are spring spawners and iteroparous. Since they remain in smaller tributaries where food resources are more limited, they do not attain the much larger size of anadromous *O. mykiss*. However, some populations are migratory and move downstream to larger rivers and lakes to rear. The fish rearing in lakes during some part of their life cycle can attain a relatively large size, due to their consumption of forage fish (Quinn 2005). The smaller stream-resident *O. mykiss* seek smaller gravels with somewhat slower flows for spawning than their larger steelhead conspecifics. Since movement of the gravel during the construction of a redd is dependent on the size of the female fish, larger females can move larger-sized gravels than smaller females.

Nonanadromous *O. mykiss* (redband trout) were likely known to Native people and available to them for food. It is not known how abundant these fish were historically, but they are not likely to have been as numerous as the concentrations of annually returning adult steelhead; however, in some locations they would have been available during most of the year.

Summary

Anadromous and resident fish contributed substantially to the life and culture of West Coast Native people, with Pacific salmon and lamprey providing a relatively dependable and important source of fish for food, trade, and medicine. The available information indicates that the historical abundance of Pacific salmon in the Columbia River was much greater than present-day abundance, and the several species of Pacific salmon were differentially distributed throughout the Columbia River basin. Some estimates indicate that up to 40 percent of the historic salmon habitat has been rendered inaccessible to anadromous salmonids by large and small dams and other barriers to migration (NRC 1996). Chinook, coho, and sockeye salmon were the more abundant and widely distributed anadromous salmonids in the basin. Chum and pink salmon were far less abundant and generally occurred in the lower river. Chinook salmon were and are the most widespread and abundant anadromous salmonid in the Columbia River basin, reaching farther inland and occurring at higher elevations than coho salmon, which with few exceptions are now restricted to the Lower Columbia River and its tributaries.

Chinook salmon occupy low-elevation tributaries as well as high-elevation habitats in the interior of the basin in Idaho, Washington, and Oregon. Many populations are currently enhanced by artificial propagation to increase abundance and provide commercial, recreational, and cultural harvest opportunities and in some cases to conserve populations at risk. Sockeye salmon make long-distance interior migrations to Redfish Lake in the Upper Salmon River drainage and to Lake Wenatchee in Washington and Lake Osoyoos in Canada, but they are more restricted in their basin-wide distribution by their requirement for a nursery lake to provide a rearing habitat for juvenile fish prior to downstream migration. Returning adult Pacific salmon and lamprey provided a substantial nutrient subsidy to interior aquatic, riparian, and terrestrial ecosystems, which enhanced productivity. There has been a substantial reduction in populations of Pacific lamprey in the Columbia River basin as well as coast-wide. This reduction in Pacific lamprey abundance is a serious concern to Native American communities and agencies tasked with the management of fisheries and river ecosystems.

References Cited

Augerot, X.

2005 *Atlas of Pacific Salmon*. Berkeley: University of California Press.

Behnke, R. J.

1992 *Native Trout of Western North America*. American Fisheries Society Monograph 6. Bethesda: American Fisheries Society Press.

2002 *Trout and Salmon of North America*. New York: Free Press.

Bjornn, T. C., and D. W. Reiser

1991 Habitat Requirements of Salmonids in Streams. *American Fisheries Society Special Publication* 19:83–138.

Bond, C. E.

1979 *Biology of Fishes*. Philadelphia: W. B. Saunders Co.

Busby, P. J., T. C. Wainwright, G. J. Bryant, L. J. Lierheimer, R. S. Waples, F. W. Waknitz, and I. V. Lagomarsino

1996 *Status Review of West Coast Steelhead from Washington, Idaho, Oregon, and California*. NOAA Technical Memorandum NMFS-NWFSC-27. Seattle: National Marine Fisheries Service, Northwest Fisheries Science Center and Southwest Region.

Chapman, D. W.

1986 Salmon and Steelhead Abundance in the Columbia River in the Nineteenth Century. *Transactions of the American Fisheries Society* 115:662–670.

1988 Critical Review of Variables Used to Define Effects of Fines in Redds of Large Salmonids. *Transactions of the American Fisheries Society* 117:1–21.

Fisher, F. W.

1994 Past and Present Status of Central Valley Chinook Salmon. *Conservation Biology* 8:870–873.

Fish Passage Center

2012 FPC Adult Metadata. Electronic document, http://www.fpc.org/documents/metadata/FPC_Adult_Metadata.Html.

Foerster, R. E.

1968 *The Sockeye Salmon* Oncorhynchus nerka. Bulletin 162. Ottawa: Fisheries Research Board of Canada.

Frissell, C. A.

1993 Topology of Extinction of Native Fishes in the Pacific Northwest and California. *Conservation Biology* 7(2):342–354.

Healey, M. C.
1991 Life History of Chinook Salmon (*Oncorhynchus tshawytscha*). In *Pacific Salmon Life Histories.* C. Groot and L. Margolis, eds. Pp. 311–393. Vancouver: University of British Columbia Press.
Heard, W. R.
1991 Life History of Pink Salmon (*Oncorhynchus gorbuscha*). In *Pacific Salmon Life Histories.* C. Groot and L. Margolis, eds. Pp. 121–230. Vancouver: University of British Columbia Press.
Jackson, A., and M. Moser
2012 Low-Elevation Dams Are Impediments to Adult Pacific Lamprey Spawning Migration in the Umatilla River, Oregon. *North American Journal of Fisheries Management* 32(3):548–556.
Meehan, W. R., and T. C. Bjornn
1991 Salmonid Distributions and Life Histories. *American Fisheries Society Special Publication* 19:47–82.
Mighetto, L., and W. J. Ebel
1994 *Saving the Salmon: A History of the U.S. Army Corps of Engineers Efforts to Protect Anadromous Fish on the Columbia and Snake Rivers.* Seattle: Historical Research Associates, Inc.
Montgomery, D. R.
2003 *King of Fish: The Thousand-Year Run of Salmon.* Boulder: Westview Press.
Moyle, P. B.
2002 *Inland Fishes of California.* Rev. and expanded edition. Berkeley: University of California Press.
National Marine Fisheries Service
2000 *Endangered Species Act Section 7 Biological Opinion on the Reinitiation of Consultation on Operation of the Federal Columbia River Power System, Including the Juvenile Fish Transportation Program, and 19 Bureau of Reclamation Projects in the Columbia Basin.* Seattle: National Marine Fisheries Service, Northwest Region.
National Research Council
1996 *Upstream—Salmon and Society in the Pacific Northwest.* Washington, DC: National Academy Press.
National Science and Technology Council
2000 *From the Edge: Science to Support Restoration of Pacific Salmon.* Washington, DC: National Science and Technology Council, Committee on Environment and Natural Resources.
Nehlsen, W., J. E. Williams, and J. A. Lichatowich
1991 Pacific Salmon at the Crossroads: Stocks at Risk from California, Oregon, Idaho, and Washington. *Fisheries* 16(2):4–21.
Nez Perce Tribe and FishPro
2004 *Coho Salmon Master Plan Clearwater River Basin.* Port Orchard, WA: HDR.

Northwest Power Planning Council
1986 Council staff compilation of information on salmon and steelhead losses in the Columbia River basin. On file at Northwest Power and Planning Council Office, Portland, OR.

Pearcy, W. G.
1992 *Ocean Ecology of North Pacific Salmonids*. Seattle: University of Washington Press.

Quinn, T. P.
2005 *The Behavior and Ecology of Pacific Salmon and Trout*. Seattle: University of Washington Press.

Sandercock, F. K.
1991 Life History of Coho Salmon (*Oncorhynchus kisutch*). In *Pacific Salmon Life Histories*. C. Groot and L. Margolis, eds. Pp. 397–445. Vancouver: University of British Columbia Press.

Simpson, J. C., and R. L. Wallace
1978 *Fishes of Idaho*. Moscow: University Press of Idaho.

Stanford, J. A., F. R. Hauer, S. V. Gregory, and E. B. Snyder
2005 The Columbia River. In *Rivers of North America*. A. C. Benke and C. E. Cushing, eds. Pp. 591–653. Boston: Elsevier/Academic Press.

U.S. Army Corps of Engineers
2002 *Lower Snake River Juvenile Salmon Migration Feasibility Report and Environmental Impact Statement (Final FR/EIS)*. Walla Walla: Walla Walla District Corps of Engineers.

Wahle, R. J., and R. E. Pearson
1987 *A Listing of Pacific Coast Spawning Streams and Hatcheries Producing Chinook and Coho Salmon (with Estimates on Numbers of Spawners and Data on Hatchery Releases)*. NOAA Technical Memorandum NMFS-F/NWC-122. Seattle: U.S. Department of Commerce, National Marine Fisheries Service, Northwest Fisheries Science Center.

Waples, R. S.
1991 *Definition of "Species" under the Endangered Species Act: Application to Pacific Salmon*. NOAA Technical Memorandum NMFS-F/NWC-194. Seattle: U.S. Department of Commerce, National Marine Fisheries Service, Northwest Fisheries Science Center.

Waples, R. S., O. W. Johnson, and R. P. Jones Jr.
1991 *Status Review for Snake River Sockeye Salmon*. NOAA Technical Memorandum NMFS-F/NWC-195. Seattle: U.S. Department of Commerce, National Marine Fisheries Service, Northwest Fisheries Science Center.

Ward, D. L., B. J. Clemens, D. Clugston, A. D. Jackson, M. L. Moser, C. Peery, and D. P. Statler
2012 Translocating Adult Pacific Lamprey within the Columbia River Basin: State of the Science. *Fisheries* 37(8):351–361.

Weitkamp, L. A., T. C. Wainwright, G. J. Bryant, G. B. Milner, D. J. Teel, R. G. Kope, and R. S. Waples

1994 *Status Review of Coho Salmon from Washington, Oregon, and California.* NOAA Technical Memorandum NMFS-NWFSC-24. Seattle: U.S. Department of Commerce, National Marine Fisheries Service, Northwest Fisheries Science Center.

Wydoski, R. S., and R. R. Whitney

2003 *Inland Fishes of Washington.* Seattle: University of Washington Press.

Assessing the Potential Impacts of Natural Events on the Holocene Productivity of Anadromous Fish Populations in Western Idaho

MARK G. PLEW AND STACEY GUINN

The historic use of anadromous fish on the Snake River Plain has been the source of considerable discussion and debate (Gould and Plew 1996; Pavesic and Meatte 1980; Plew 1983). Traditionally, archaeologists have argued that abundant fall Chinook runs provided the foundation for winter storage and a level of resource intensification that served as the basis for the "emergence of village life" (Pavesic and Meatte 1980:21). Other, more contemporary approaches have utilized optimal foraging models as a means of examining the harvest, processing, and storage costs associated with a bulk procurement strategy (Gould and Plew 1996) and have examined resource rankings and nutritional values of fish harvests (Plew 1983). In a recent article Plew (2009) reviews the zooarchaeological evidence of diet breadth and prey choice shifts during the Archaic period (7000–150 BP). Notably, data suggest limited use of fish until approximately 1,500 years ago. The increased use of fish, particularly during the Late Archaic, is argued to result from the emergence of modern, more arid environmental conditions that saw increasing numbers of artiodactyls aggregating in riverine settings. This chapter, however, assesses the potential of natural and cultural agencies to affect the productivity of the fishery by degradation or enhancement. It examines the potential of landslides, paleoseismic events, and range fires as events that could have altered/influenced conditions affecting the availability and productivity of the anadromous fishery in western Idaho. These impacts are argued to include cultural influences associated with the indigenous population and Euro-Americans. Environmental alterations beginning in the early historic period are argued to be in part the basis for the pattern of bulk procurement described by ethnographers and historians. This chapter discusses in greater detail the potential short-term/longer-term impacts of alteration of the Snake River corridor as a foundation for thinking about the extent, constancy, and timing of the use of the anadromous fishery. As the use of salmon has been seen as the basis for a pattern of increasing intensification and ultimately the emergence of village life on the Plain (Pavesic and Meatte 1980), assessment of the potential impacts of natural events disrupting the availability and/or productivity of salmon resources, both short and longer term, provides a means of evaluating the evolutionary trajectory of cultural developments in the region.

The Geographic Area and Historic Distribution of Anadromous Fish in Western Idaho

The study area encompasses most of western Idaho from the Oregon border to Shoshone Falls in the Snake River Canyon near Twin Falls, Idaho. To the north it extends south from the Salmon River country where deep canyons are cut through the Idaho Batholith. South of the city of Boise, the area extends to the Nevada border, encompassing the Owyhee, Bruneau, and Jarbidge river systems. This area, which has sometimes been referred to as the Middle Snake River in Idaho, lies largely within what is more strictly defined as the western Snake River Plain, a relatively open plain cut by the Snake River and the canyons within the Owyhee Province (Figure 2.1).

Prior to dam construction and other water control systems, anadromous fish migrated into river drainages throughout southern Idaho. Salmon migrated as far east as Shoshone Falls; into the Bruneau, Jarbidge, and Owyhee rivers; and to Salmon Falls Creek and northern Nevada (Evermann 1896, 1897; La Rivers and Trelease 1952) south of the Snake. North of the Snake River salmon spawned in the Boise, Payette, and Weiser rivers. Salmon runs occurred three times a year. An early spring (March–April) run consisted largely of steelhead trout (*Oncorhynchus mykiss*), with late spring (May–June) runs of Chinook salmon (*Oncorhynchus tshawytscha*). A fall run between September and November consisted largely of Chinook salmon.

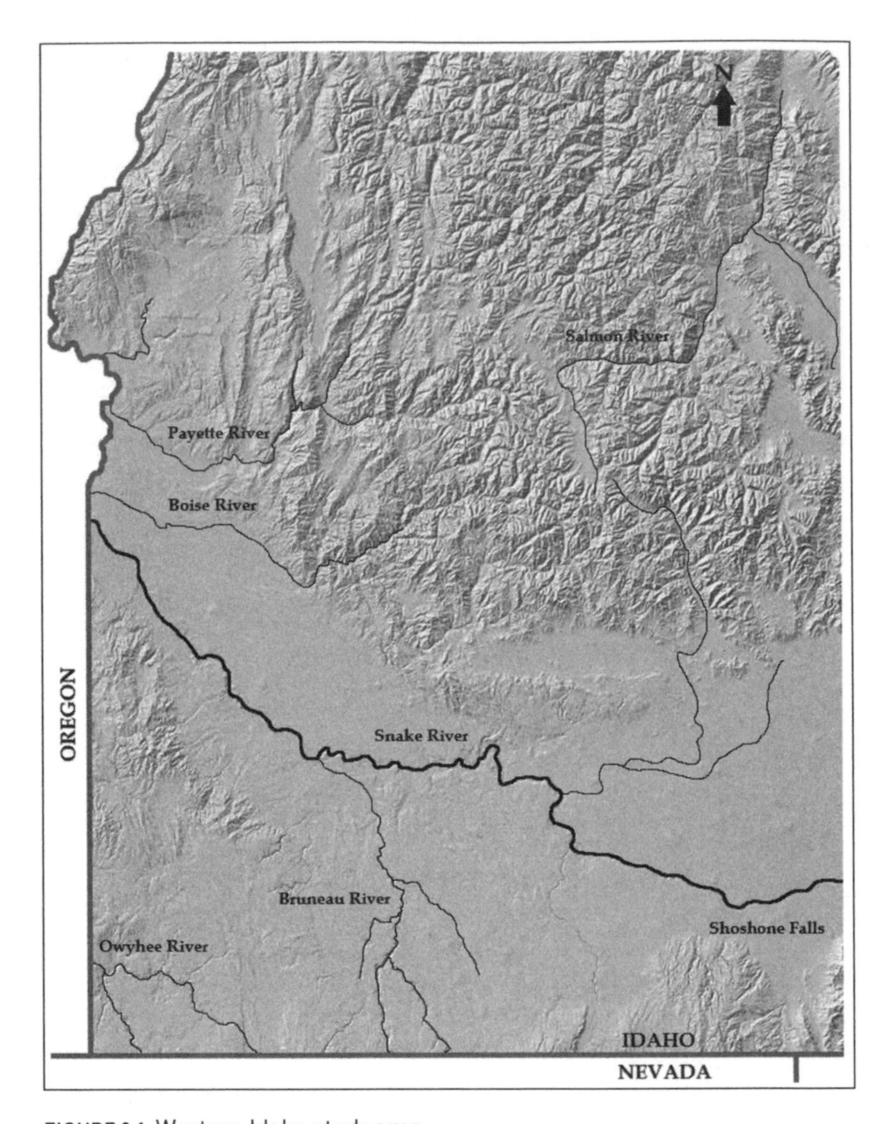

FIGURE 2.1. Western Idaho study area.

The Ethnographic Setting

The historic inhabitants of southern Idaho include the Northern Shoshone and Northern Paiute, the primary difference between them being linguistic (Murphy and Murphy 1986:284). Economic lifeways and sociopolitical organization were similar for the Shoshone—including the Boise, Bruneau, and Weiser subgroups—and the Northern Paiute, and both occupied southwestern Idaho at the time of historic contact (Murphy and Murphy 1960, 1986; Steward 1938; Walker 1978). The Northern Paiute comprised the Payette, Weiser, and Bannock subgroups, with the latter defining a group of mounted hunters who moved eastward to the Fort Hall area during the eighteenth century (Liljeblad 1957:81). The primary ethnographic sources for the Middle Snake River area are Murphy and Murphy (1960) and Steward (1938, 1943).

Murphy and Murphy (1960) provide a relatively detailed, if at times cautionary, view of the sociopolitical organization and economy of Middle Snake River groups. Following Steward (1938, 1943), they (1960:321) suggest that the Snake River Shoshone resemble the Western Shoshone of Nevada in social, political, and economic characteristics more than other Idaho groups, noting few horses, no bison hunting activities, and virtually no warfare. Further, there were no band chiefs, and winter villages lacked headmen. Generally, the sociocultural pattern was a rather loose organization in which individuals occasionally were chosen to coordinate specific tasks, such as being "fishing directors" (Steward 1938:168–169). In the predominant-settlement pattern, small aggregates of nuclear families—family clusters—camped together and performed subsistence-related activities together, but the composition of a cluster was highly fluid, in that allegiances shifted as families moved to pursue different resources (Steward 1970:129–130). A somewhat larger but substantially less common unit consisted of multicluster aggregates marking "temporary allegiances for a few corporate activities, such as hunting, or other associations where local resources could support unusual numbers of people" (Steward 1970:130). Although such corporate organizations are known, they certainly were the exception. When looking at the Shoshone of Nevada and those living along the Snake River, Steward is quite clear that "the household was very nearly a self-sufficient economic unit and as such an independent social and political unit" (1938:239). In general the pattern is similar to that described for the Owyhee area by Steward and Wheeler-Voegelin (1974).

The settlement pattern of the Middle Snake River in southwestern Idaho was highly dispersed, with small winter residences (Murphy and Murphy 1960:322). The splitting of residence groups into smaller winter camps of two or three lodges is important, in that the same people did not camp together at the same sites each winter (Liljeblad 1957:36; Murphy and Murphy 1960:322). This corroborates Steward's observation that the "true political unit was the village, a small and probably unstable group"

(1938:169). In this context the term *village* as it is now used in specific relation to ranked societies implies some greater sociopolitical complexity than was, in fact, the case among Snake River groups (see also Liljeblad 1957:35–36). The ambiguity of this language has fostered a situation in which the traditional focus on winter settlements (Pavesic and Meatte 1980) may be inappropriate when attempting to discuss the level of complexity. This is especially evident in discussions of storage in archaeological conjectures about the winter pattern (e.g., Meatte 1990:66–67, 69, 71; Pavesic 1978; Pavesic and Meatte 1980:21–23).

The major subsistence pursuits of Middle Snake River groups were fishing and camas collecting. Areas such as Glenns Ferry were considered better fishing sites since waters were shallow enough for weirs to be used (Murphy and Murphy 1960:322); however, the use of weirs along the Snake was not widespread. Steward notes that "dams and weirs could be used in few places in the Snake River, which is too wide and deep" (1943:226). Above Hagerman, salmon were speared, while basketry traps, sometimes used in conjunction with weirs, were employed in small streams. Steward (1938:43) notes fishing for species other than steelhead or salmon, including the three-tooth lamprey (*Entosphenus tridentatus*), Columbia River sturgeon (*Acipenser transmontanus*), cutthroat trout (*Oncorhynchus clarki*), and Rocky Mountain whitefish (*Prosopius williamsoni*), as well as winter fishing (1938:168).

This normative view of Middle Snake River ethnographic groups presents a picture of a mixed-mode foraging strategy—one marked by a subsistence emphasis on anadromous fish and camas, with groups establishing residential bases along the river. From the perspective of some archaeologists, the defining characteristic of the Snake River Shoshone is an intensive pattern of anadromous fish use that, in combination with longer-term settlements along the river, revolves around fish storage for overwintering purposes (Pavesic and Meatte 1980:20–23, 75–79). In brief, this marks a classic collector mobility pattern. Binford notes that "sites of major fish weirs or camas procurement on the Columbia plateau might be examples of [collectors'] locations with high archaeological visibility as opposed to the low-visibility locations commonly generated by foragers" (1980:10). If this "normative" pattern of intensive fish use is manifest in the archaeological record, such an adaptation necessarily results in a specific array of sites.

The river also was used by groups exploiting the same resources but practicing different mobility strategies. Murphy and Murphy (1960:321) indicate that only a small population wintered in the area, noting that greater use of the area's resources was made by the more numerous Shoshone and Bannock who wintered elsewhere. Having winter residences on or near the Humboldt River in northern Nevada, the Battle Mountain or "White Knife" Shoshone are known to have migrated to the Snake to exploit summer fish runs (Harris 1940:39, 44; Steward 1938:162). Likewise, mounted groups from the Fort Hall area of southeastern Idaho moved to the Snake below Shoshone Falls to harvest or trade for salmon (Steward 1938:200–205). To a lesser degree, the Grouse Creek Shoshone were known to have migrated to the river to fish for salmon (Steward 1938:175). Thus, sites on or near the river were frequented not only by the often-emphasized collectors but also by foragers.

The pattern of groups practicing a high degree of residential mobility is implicit in Murphy and Murphy's (1960:321) descriptions. As opposed to the normative situation of the Snake River Shoshone outlined above, two different strategies are implied in outside groups using the area. First is the case of mounted groups of Fort Hall Shoshone and Bannock using the area (Murphy and Murphy 1960:320–321; Steward 1938:166, 200–205, 1943:268–270). While these groups traded for salmon at Camas Prairie (e.g., Liljeblad 1957:47), they also moved to the Snake to directly exploit fish runs. There is a strong difference between their fishing strategy and the one outlined above for the Snake River Shoshone. A site class noted among the Snake River groups, dried fish caches most likely were extremely rare among Fort Hall groups. Because of the greater transport capability of horses, moving dried fish hundreds of kilometers to winter residences did not present a logistical problem. This contrasts with the Snake River Shoshone, whose winter residences were tethered to stores of fish. Steward notes that during the winter, Snake River groups preferred to base themselves in "the vicinity of the river so as to be near cached salmon" (1938:165). However, salmon caches along the river likely are absent among the sites formed by the Fort Hall people, who procured and dried fish in the area but then transported them back to southeastern Idaho. Furthermore, only field camps, not full-fledged residential bases, would likely result from the mounted groups' exploitation of the area. With regard to the site types believed to be manifest in the pattern described for the Snake

River Shoshone, two important deletions must be considered. The Fort Hall people's use of the area would have resulted in the formation of fishing field camps, processing locations, and harvesting locations. It is highly unlikely that caches or long-term residential bases would result from their use of the area. An adaptation marked by a significantly higher degree of residential mobility would be manifest in the Grouse Creek (Steward 1938:175, 1943:268–270) or White Knife (Harris 1940:39, 44; Steward 1938: 162, 166) Shoshone use of the Snake River area. The land use pattern associated with these two groups is one of small, residential groups coming to exploit fish during the summer. Most important, their use of the area is not marked by storage for winter consumption. The Grouse Creek groups seem to have used salmon in the Middle Snake (Steward 1943:268–270), but travel distances made such efforts rare (Steward 1938:175). To a much greater degree, northern Nevadan groups—specifically, the White Knife Shoshone—would have come, fished for their daily subsistence, and left when other resources became available or the fish runs tapered off. Harvesting a surplus, extensive drying and storage, and the transport of dried fish are not indicated within this strategy.

As noted, camas was an important food source for the Snake River Shoshone (Liljeblad 1957:37–38; Murphy and Murphy 1960:320, 322; Steward 1938:167–168). While the focus of ethnographic discussions has rested upon anadromous fish use, it does appear that camas was equally, if not more, important to Middle Snake groups (Plew 1990; Statham 1982:88–92). In fact, some Snake River groups spent the winter "at Camas Prairie near their caches of (camas) roots but returned to the river in spring for fishing" (Steward 1938:167). This, then, was a situation in which the Snake River Shoshone stored processed camas in order to winter in the prairie but came down to the river to catch fish during the spring run. It is unlikely that storage caches, intensively used locations, or field camps would have been produced by these groups when using the river.

The Archaeological Record and Fisheries Productivity

Beginning in the late 1970s the use of water separation techniques and ⅛-inch hardware mesh in dry screening has seen the recovery of fish remains from some 19 sites along the Middle Snake River (Plew 1981, 2008, 2009). Most sites contain evidence of the remains of Salmonidae, though nonsalmonid fish remains commonly occur or co-occur in sites. In addition, fishing gear consisting of weights has been found at site 10-AA-188 and at the Knox and Crutchfield sites (Murphey and Crutchfield 1985; Plew et al. 2002), as well as, in the case of Schellbach Cave, a cache of fish and bone harpoon points, fishhooks, and wooden spear foreshafts (Pavesic et al. 1987). The remnants of fish weirs have been described at three sites (see Pitkin 2010:52). The largest assemblages are from the Bliss site (19-GG-1) and Three Island Crossing (10-EL-294), where 19,000+ fish remains were recovered (Gould and Plew 1996, 2001; Plew and Gould 2001).

Based on these data it appears that fishing activity occurred as early as 11,000 years ago at the Hetrick site near Weiser, Idaho, and became increasingly common in the Late Archaic (2000–150 BP). While a total of three individual fish are documented for the Early and Middle Archaic periods on the Middle Snake River, 31 percent of Late Archaic sites contain salmonid (ubiquity = 13) and/or nonsalmonid (ubiquity = 14) remains. Notably, the ubiquity of nonsalmonids is greater than that of salmonids. Most interesting is that salmonids rank second only to cervids in relative abundance (Plew 2009). Previous studies have noted the relative absence of salmonids from earlier periods (Gould and Plew 1996; Plew 2008; Plew and Plager 1999) and their remarkably greater presence in the Late Archaic. Though sampling, differential preservation, and uneven discovery of taxa may partially account for this, it appears that the use of fish became increasingly common into the Late Archaic period. Calculation of the minimum number of individuals (MNIs) indicates few individual fish represented in the majority of assemblages. In some instances, as with Bernard Creek Rockshelter (Randolph and Dahlstrom 1977), approximately 60 percent of the remains are nonsalmonid.

The discoveries at Three Island Crossing address two competing hypotheses characterizing the extent and nature of fish procurement in southwestern Idaho and the Middle Snake River area in general. The first, as noted earlier, argues for a winter storage strategy based upon the bulk procurement of fall Chinook salmon and is vested in the presumption that an abundance of salmon resources provided the single largest protein source for aboriginal peoples and the basis for the emergence of sedentary village life (Pavesic and Meatte 1980). A second hypothesis argues for year-round fishing by many groups employing variable strategies in the short-term procurement of a variety of species. The latter hypothesis argues that only a few groups engaged in large-scale fall harvests for winter storage as the resource was not cost-effective or optimal (Gould and Plew 1996; Plew 1990).

The primary sources for the storage model are historic, ethnohistoric, and ethnographic works, particularly those by Steward (1938), Murphy and Murphy (1960), and Liljeblad (1957). Without belaboring criticisms of 19th- and early 20th-century ethnography, it is important to note the anecdotal nature of these accounts. While the accounts of ethnohistories tend to be seasonally and event specific, ethnographic accounts detail the "memory culture" of peoples who never resided on the Snake River Plain and who did not practice the aboriginal lifeway. The accounts provide sweeping generalizations about subsistence, as is exemplified by Steward's 1938 account of Great Basin subsistence that contains but two pages pertaining to the Middle Snake River area. Such accounts fail to document the variability of aboriginal lifeways at different points in time and as they evolved over time. Strategies most certainly changed in the recent period—a point made by Kelly in his observation that "all too often, ethnographic data are used as whole cloth analogies of the past without considering the context of those data" (1996:213).

The storage model of fish procurement adheres to the uncritical assumption predicated upon historic bias that aboriginal peoples utilized abundant resources because such resources were abundant and remained constant over time. This assumption, which is at odds with much hunter-gatherer research, is not archaeologically demonstrated. Further, the model fails to account for the ways in which these assumptions must be related to biological and ecological factors affecting fish, particularly salmonids.

Schalk (1977) has demonstrated that fluctuations in water temperature in southern mid-latitudes often result in short winter spawning seasons with greater competition from nonanadromous fish, which periodically reduced harvests. He has further demonstrated that the distance from the mouth of the river to the point of return determines the duration of the run, a demonstration that means fewer fish on the Snake River than on the Columbia. With regard to distance of migrations, Plew (1983) has noted the relevance of significant nutritional losses (78–96 percent fat and 31–61 percent protein losses by sex) for spawning runs covering distances as great as those to the Middle Snake River. At issue in all instances are the numbers of fish migrating annually. Chatters (1995) and Chatters et al. (1995; see also Neitzel et al. 1991) model middle Holocene stream conditions to estimate the effects of warmer temperatures on the salmon fishery of the Columbia River between 8000 and 6000 BP. Their findings suggest a 30–60 percent loss of adults returning after 100 years of warmer conditions. Less significant fisheries such as the Snake River might have seen even greater losses. The archaeological evidence suggests that salmon were not only relatively less available but smaller, with a mean weight of returning adults of only 6.2 kilograms.

An appropriate assumption is that tactical responses were driven by the contingencies of resource encounters, a consideration consistent with optimal foraging models. As such, there is some likelihood that different groups employed variable strategies in utilizing Middle Snake River resources. The latter is exemplified by what Plew (1990) has described as the "camas model," in which camas and other tubers were more optimal in terms of co-occurring harvest/processing times, nutritional values, portability, and storage.

Insights regarding the potential of aboriginal harvests have been traditionally based upon historic accounts of fish taken in the late 19th and early 20th centuries (Plew 1983; Walker 1993). Among common examples are the harvests at the historic Liberty Millet's Fishery near Salmon Falls in 1894 (Fulton 1968). Using techniques with some ethnographic parallel, two men employed a small boat and seine to harvest Chinook salmon between October 2 and November 1. This largest of the salmon runs was harvested by Native people engaged in procurement for winter storage. Though harvesting time and work schedule were not controlled, there are certain notable characteristics—specifically the temporal compression of the run—with days producing more than 200 kilograms occurring within a two-week period between October 14 and October 29. It appears that latitudinal position, distance from stream mouth, and discharge characteristics are reflected by the short period of availability and appear to have influenced the fishery in Hells Canyon (Butler and Chatters 1986; Chatters 1995; Chatters et al. 1991; Reid and Chatters 1997), where fluctuations in the availability of salmonids are noted at a number of sites.

Relevant to the consideration of the optimality of this resource are previously identified biological and ecological variables. Notable in this regard is that the harvest and handling time for salmon would have occurred over an extended period. Plew (1983) has estimated that it would require 1,270 kilograms (2,700 pounds) of fish to meet the nutritional requirements for the domestic unit from mid-December to mid-March—the winter period. It appears based on the historic Liberty Millet's Fishery harvest that an adequate amount of fish could be taken. Yet the extended period of harvest and processing time may have reduced the cost-benefit returns of the strategy, particularly since there is a lack of constancy in individual runs on an annual basis and over periods of years. Since processing time is linked to procurement, an extended harvest period only extends the processing time (though the winter season may well shorten this). Historic and ethnographic data from the Northwest where smoking fish was common suggest that processing occurred over a period of six to eight weeks. Whereas drying, the technique known on the Middle Snake River, may require less time, the investment must be calculated in assessing the overall return rates and thereby the overall ranking of resources (see Plew 2009). Of further importance is O'Leary's (1985, 1996) observation that salmon rarely stores for more than a month (due to decay, insect infestation, and canid activity)—in southern Idaho this "handling" equation might well have taken groups into the winter period. Increasing the harvest of nutritionally deficient fish (presuming they are available) only extends the handling time and provides little return.

Since groups would have remained near the river for an extended period of time, investing heavily in facilities and technology of the sort associated with bulk procurement, it seems odd that foragers would have opted for a strategy that likely placed them at greater risk through competition with resident and transient populations for local resources, especially since the fisheries are concentrated in specific locales along the Snake River (Pitkin 2010; Steward 1938). Here, as with other sites on the Middle Snake River, collections of fish remains span many occupational episodes. Of interest in this regard is Chatters's (1995) observation that the faunal assemblages from Hells Canyon and the greater Plateau contain little evidence of fish remains, despite ethnographic evidence for extensive exploitation. Beyond the presence of fish remains, the sites in question lack evidence of fishing gear (with the notable exception of Schellbach Cave) and processing areas, that is, cleaning areas, as well as drying and storage facilities. Indeed, the only evidence of storage is at Three Island Crossing, where two storage pits suggest the type of short-term storage described by Zeanah

(1980). Given the investment of time related to extended harvesting and processing schedules, we might expect evidence of residential structures. Yet, of the 24 residential structures described by Green (1993), few have produced fish remains. Only Three Island Crossing contains a single small structure in association with a large assemblage of fish remains.

While normative views embrace arguments relating to sampling and preservation as a rationale for explaining the lack of evidence for fishing activity, these remain inadequate explanations of the existing data. While processing and discard behaviors and gear produced from willow and cordage not surviving in the record may have affected the formation of the archaeological record, there are many items including weights, net sinkers, and spears that should be found in some contexts.

As noted, faunal assemblages along the Middle Snake River suggest a greater reliance on deer and rabbits than on fish, particularly salmon (Gould and Plew 1996; Plew 2009). The ubiquity of these species is most likely linked to their greater optimality. Analyses suggest an isomorphic relationship between harvested prey and variation in exploitive technology (Gould and Plew 1996). As noted, a high degree of redundancy exists in the number of functional tool classes; at no site are there clearly definable "specialized tools" (see Yu and Cook, this volume, for a relevant discussion of data relating to this issue). Notably, the absence of "specialized" gear is in contrast to the more task-specific gear described by Lyons (this volume). Differential functional elements are nearly the exclusive source of intersite variability. It appears that the same gear was used for harvest of both fish and terrestrial animals. In turn, the form of production reflects expedient manufacture of generalized items on an encounter basis, so as to suggest a pattern of direct feeding of the sort commonly associated with foragers, not the specialized or tactical tool kits of the type described by Steward (1938), a pattern recently reported by Reid and Chatters (1997) at Kirkwood Bar.

As noted above, fishing, presumably some preparation, and storage occurred at Three Island Crossing. But the assemblage of 19,000+ fish remains is substantially misleading. Calculation of MNIs, however, suggests relatively fewer individuals. Gould and Plew (1996) calculate on the basis of identifiable parts no more than 300 fish. Even if the correct number is twice that estimate, it does not appear to support the assumption of heavy dependence upon salmon. The Three Island assemblage, as we have estimated the probable quantity of fish, constitutes approximately two-thirds of the required poundage to meet nutritional requirements. However, a minimum of three occupations or uses have been radiometrically dated. With this in mind, the Three Island assemblage suggests a relatively minor use of salmon relative to the abundance of deer.

Those subscribing to the argument of "abundance" (Pavesic and Meatte 1980), and thereby the relative importance of salmon, may well argue that the recovery of few salmon remains is the result of aboriginal techniques of preparation, the friability of remains, and sampling bias. While preparation techniques may account for some obliteration of the record, the argument for lack of preservation in archaeological sites is not warranted (see Casteel 1976:88–92). Though sampling is a constant issue in archaeological excavation, the recovery techniques at sites including Three Island Crossing, Bliss (Plew 1981), and Clover Creek (Plew and Gould 1990) are comparable. Yet, in examining these assemblages, one finds little evidence of extensive fishing. The greater evidence at Clover Creek and Bliss is of the relative importance of ungulates and rabbits, which is true of other sites in the region. If the MNI estimates approximate the actual numbers, then the total of all assemblages may reflect no more than 500 individuals from fewer than 20 sites spanning 11,000 years.

Two additional matters are addressed by the Three Island data. The first regards the nutritional values of the harvests represented by the assemblage. Plew (1983, 1990) has estimated the probable needs of the domestic unit for the period from mid-December to mid-March to be, at minimum, 1,270 kilograms (2,800 pounds). Hence, we may not expect to find extensive evidence of storage or the same kinds of fishing gear at all localities, since they may be curated from one location to another or cached during off season, as may be the case with Schellbach Cave (Pavesic et al. 1987; Schellbach 1967). The isomorphic pattern of faunal remains and tools reflects gear selectivity and preservation. The MNIs for deer at Three Island Crossing provide evidence of what are probably fewer than 30 individuals. Yet the nutritional value of these resources is undoubtedly of greater importance than that of the fish. Simms's (1987) Great Basin analyses suggest that deer, along with bighorn sheep, were the most highly ranked resources in the region. Average edible weight (34 kilograms) and kilocalories per kilogram (1,258) affect ranking as it relates to pursuit and processing time. The return rate for average-sized deer (42,900 kilocalories/individual) ranged between 17,900 and 31,450 kilocalories/hour (Simms 1987), significantly greater than the value of the fish harvests at Three Island Crossing.

This finding suggests that the location represents the type of residential base more commonly associated with foragers than one typical of the collector strategy described by Steward (1938). The data from Three Island Crossing support the view (Gould 1990; Gould and Plew 1996) that extensive foraging activities were the primary strategy of peoples along the Middle Snake during Late Archaic times. While these groups used salmon, they used it variously and appear not to have been as dependent upon it as suggested by historic and ethnographic accounts.

Potential Impacts of Natural Events on Settlement Variability

A review of the ethnographic literature pertaining to the Snake River Plain suggests that somewhat varied settlement-subsistence strategies are associated with the different cultural groups utilizing the Plain. Gould (1990: 24–26) argues in this regard that these uses include fall–winter residential bases, field camps, extraction locations, and caches. He further argues that collapsing these site types into fewer spatial foci would be the most effective strategy for reducing transportation costs and forming the labor groups necessary for the large-scale procurement of salmon. Noting again the biological and ecological constraints on salmon availability/productivity, consideration of all factors influencing site location—both short and longer term—becomes critical in assessing the productivity of the western fisheries. To date, researchers have not examined the potential impacts of natural events on the productivity of the fisheries and locations that would be associated with the extraction and processing of fish. Assessment requires a description of anadromous fish ecology and the nature of naturally occurring events that would potentially affect resource availability and its relationship to variance in ethnographic settlement strategies.

Anadromous Fish Ecology

Davis (2007) provides an overview of fluvial conditions negatively impacting anadromous populations. These relate to the requirements of freshwater habitats and include the presence of channel substrates conducive to the construction of redds; moderate discharge rates; the stability of spawning gravels during floods; the absence of fine sediments inhibiting the hyporheic zone, resulting in egg suffocation; the connectivity of in-stream habitats; channel morphology avoiding overcrowding during low flows; the constancy of water temperature; inadequate discharge during periods of drought; and open gravels for the support of young fish and deeper pools for adult containment (also see Grabowski, this volume; Gregory and Bisson 1997; Hicks et al. 1991; Liss et al. 2006; Schalk 1997; Stanford et al. 2006). Naturally occurring or exogenous events as Davis (2007) describes them would include floods, fire-induced erosion, increased aridity, and above-average precipitation—the latter altering the physical configuration of the canyon and its floral and faunal communities—resulting in increased sediment load in the Snake and its tributaries. In this regard, Euro-American alteration of the Snake River corridor during and beyond the Oregon Trail period may well have contributed to the degradation of the landscape by the cutting of trees and shrubs and agricultural activities. Butler and Chatters (1986) hypothesize that salmon productivity in the Upper Columbia Basin varied significantly during the past 13,000 years as changing environmental conditions negatively impacted or improved fluvial conditions.

Geology of the Snake River Corridor: Implications for Holocene Settlement and Resource Use

Sediments in this region suggest a succession of alluvial and aeolian events (Bentley 1981) following the Bonneville flood. During this time the canyons, banks, and associated lowlands along the Snake River would have experienced a long developmental history (Bentley 1983; Malde and Powers 1972). Such a period would have consisted of torrential spring flooding, mudslides, debris flows, and alluvial fan development. Talus accumulating at the base of canyon rims would have been highly unstable and "given way," often affecting streamflow and sediment load discharge. Swanson and Muto (1975) report these periods of increased rockfall and increased bed load as coincident with the late Pleistocene/early Holocene (11,000–8000 BP) and as occurring again during the Medithermal period (4000 BP–the present). Bentley (1983) suggests that the region would not have been preferred by aboriginal peoples until after the warm/dry period of the Altithermal (8000–4000 BP) and after stabilization and aridity occurred in the canyons approximately 3000–2000 BP. A review of the depositional data from sites between Walter's Ferry and Hagerman indicates a pattern of successive accumulations of sediments to depths of one–two meters that lie above Pleistocene-age Bonneville gravels. While these deposits vary in depth and the precise nature of their depositional histories remains unknown, they appear to have accumulated during the late Holocene, a pattern characteristic of 10-EL-216. Regardless of the circumstances governing the rates of accumulation, they are critical in understanding why most sites along the Snake River are of Late Archaic age. If terrace formation and the stabilization of habitats did not occur until the late Holocene, that may provide a partial explanation for the discovery of so few Early and Middle Archaic–age occupations along the Snake River. Malde and Powers (1972) and Bentley (1983) describe the development of terraces on the Snake River during the Holocene as successions of surficial deposits transported through hydrologic seasonal draining and flooding. These surficial deposits are composed of both redeposited alluvium and loess. Bentley (1981, 1983) suggests that a minimum of six overbank floods occurred during the last several thousand years. Flood cycles would have impacted local fisheries. The rather late emergence of modern and relatively stable habitats where residential, procurement, and processing locations could occur, coupled with increasing aridity, may be the reason that salmon fishing is best documented in the late Holocene (2000–150 BP).

Paleoseismic Events and Their Impacts upon Anadromous Resources in the Salmon River Basin

In a recent article Davis (2007) argues convincingly that such stochastic variables as landslides and the neotectonic behaviors of local bedrock structures played an important role in shaping the natural history of the Salmon River basin—a phenomenon exemplified by the early 20th-century Hells Gate landslide on the Fraser River in British Columbia (Evenden 2000). Though noting the value of large-scale regional syntheses of the sort that have characterized interpretations of Plateau prehistory, he (2007; Davis and Muehlenbachs 2001) argues that we should apply geoarchaeological approaches focused at the scale of alluvial basins and subbasins as the basis for better understanding how regional conditions may be influenced by naturally occurring events. Traditionally, resource intensification focused on salmon productivity has been seen as the primary basis for the emergence of semisedentary villages and the so-called Winter Village Pattern on the southeastern Plateau (Ames and Marshall

1980). Coupled with the exploitation of root crops, the bulk procurement of salmon for delayed winter consumption is considered a hallmark of the pattern (Schalk and Cleveland 1983). While the Winter Village Pattern is considered a semisedentary foraging strategy (Lohse and Sammons-Lohse 1986), Prentiss and Chatters (2003:39–44) argue for a shift to a collector mode of logistical organization after 4200–3500 BP associated with cooler-wetter neoglacial conditions. Recent archaeological and geoarchaeological investigations along the Lower Salmon River indicate that evidence for bulk procurement in the Winter Village Pattern occurs only after 2000 BP and is thought to be associated with large-scale changes in the fluvial behavior of the Lower Salmon River (Davis 2007:235)—specifically, fluvial changes associated with neotectonic displacement along a local fault line. Davis (2007:235) hypothesizes that the fluvial changes increased the canyon's salmon fishery. In contrast to Butler and Schalk (1986), who attribute salmon productivity during the past 13,000 years to a combination of ecological requirements of salmon and effects of general environmental conditions, he (2007:252–256) argues that the increased productivity of the past 2,000 years correlates with geological events that have conditioned for an improvement in the fishery.

The Borah Peak Earthquake—Hydrologic Effects

In 1983 the Borah Peak earthquake increased the natural groundwater discharge and base flow of major rivers over an area of 18,000 square kilometers in south-central Idaho (Wood et al. 1985). The event saw the cessation of output from some springs and increased discharge in others. Though no data exist to assess the impact upon local fisheries within the region, it seems logical to assume that increased discharges might have impacted aquatic resources, if only for short intervals. Considering the impact of the Borah Peak event, we would argue that paleoseismic events may well have affected fisheries in areas of extensive discharge. In the area of Thousand Springs where the aquifer empties into the Snake River, it seems relatively certain that discharge levels would be affected by a major seismic event. Increased discharges would alter the local environment—almost certainly affecting the fishery, which in this reach of the Snake is well known historically. In addition, landslides often accompany earthquakes as delayed events. As we consider the potential impacts of paleoseismic events on fisheries, we must also consider that increased spring flows may well have resulted in aboriginal inhabitants shifting to terrestrial resources that are more common in areas with increased spring flows.

Fire-Induced Erosion on the South Fork of the Payette River

In a recent article Pierce et al. (2004) radiocarbon date fire-related sediment deposits in tributaries of the South Fork of the Payette River in Idaho as a basis for reconstructing Holocene fire history in xeric pine forests as it relates to millennial-scale climate change. The study is based upon data indicating that post-fire debris flow events and sediment-charged floods are produced by two mechanisms (Meyer et al. 2001). In the first, severe fires/burns reduce infiltration, and smooth soil surfaces increase surface runoff (Moody and Martin 2001), accompanied by heavy discharges of sediments through slope wash, rilling, and gullying (Meyer et al. 2001). The second relates to post-fire root loss promoting shallow landslides, usually during winter storms (Pierce et al. 2004). "Large"- and "small"-scale events are defined as debris flow units by the percentage of abundant coarse angular charcoal. Notably, small events dominate the overall record, save between 1000 and 750 BP. Peak recurrence at the South Fork of the Payette study site indicates frequent low- to mixed-severity fires producing limited sedimentation during the past 7,400 years. Larger versus small-scale fires are thought to correlate with drier versus cooler-wetter climates—with the latter inhibiting severe burns and increasing the understory grass growth that fuels low-severity fires (Pierce et al. 2004:89).

Though existing archaeological data do not corroborate the fire-related events occurring on the South Fork of the Payette, the area is known to have been utilized during the period (Plew et al. 1984). The implications of the Pierce et al. (2004) study for the anadromous fishery are, however, significant. Though Davis (2007) argues that fluvial shifts correlated with neotectonic fault line displacements increased the productivity of the Lower Salmon River fishery after 2000 BP, the South Fork study suggests the possibility of long-term periodic degradations of the fishery as associated with fire-induced erosional patterns. On the North Fork of the John Day River (Howell 2006) and in the Boise National Forest (Burton 2005) the effects of medium- to high-intensity burns are demonstrated to have impacted the salmonid fishery. In the case of the John Day, three tributaries having abundant salmonids immediately suffered the loss of entire runs following a 2003 burn. However, in both cases the fishery reestablished itself. In Boise National Forest, conditions improved dramatically over a period of five–ten years—with post-fire floods rejuvenating streams with fine sediment, gravel, cobbles, and woody debris, thus increasing nutrients and resulting in higher fish productivities (Burton 2005). Correlating fire-induced erosional episodes may provide a clearer understanding of the periodic use of some areas.

The Bliss Landslide: An Example of Localized Degradation

At Bliss, located some 90 miles east of Boise on the north side of the canyon rim of the Snake River, sediments consist of lacustrine and stream deposits, with thin-bedded clays and silts, sands and silts, fine gravels, and a thin basalt flow constituting deposits 200–400 feet in thickness (Gillerman 2001:3). Lying above the Tertiary Banbury Basalts are several hundred feet of Pliocene sediments of the so-called Glenns Ferry Formation (Malde 1982; Malde and Powers 1972). Though these deposits are relatively uniform between Bliss and Hagerman (upstream), they are complicated by pillow lavas of the so-called McKinney Basalt, which dammed the ancestral Snake River, creating McKinney Lake (Gillerman 2001:3). Deposited within the lake were bedded lacustrine clays named the Yahoo Clay by Malde (1982). In general, the interbedded clays and silts of the Glenns Ferry Formation have commonly slumped, creating landslide deposits. The basalts and sands of the Glenns Ferry Formation are sufficiently permeable as to transport considerable ground- and surface water into the deposits.

In 1993 a major landslide occurred on the north side of the canyon just below the city of Bliss. The landslide covered part of the existing roadway to the Bliss bridge and impacted more than 250 acres. More important, the slide reconfigured the channel of the Snake River (Gillerman 2001:1) and introduced considerable debris and sediment load into the river. Below the bridge the river has cut deeply into the Bliss archaeological site, a series of four Late Archaic (2000–150 BP) components that have produced evidence of salmon exploitation (Plew 1981). Gillerman (2001) reports that the local people indicate that an additional landslide feature visible on the south side of the river formed in the 1930s. Though we lack data pertaining to the rates of occurrence of landslides in the area, the capacity of the Glenns Ferry Formation to host numerous landslide events is well known. The local and perhaps extended downstream degradation (whether short or longer term) would certainly have impacted the use of the local fisheries as it pertained to productivity and the location of procurement and processing areas.

Yet the landscape alterations associated with landslides need to be considered in the context of area access—not just the presence/absence of anadromous fish. Resulting from a Ventura effect, in which crosswinds blow diagonally across the canyon, the Bliss site deposits are buried under some 1.2 meters of sterile sand deposited over the original site surface in fewer than 20 years after its original recordation (Bentley 1981). This type of rapid landscape alteration would certainly have been important in determining the location of fishing sites.

Conclusion

The primary purpose of this discussion has been to review natural events that could have influenced the short- and long-term productivity of the anadromous fishery in southwestern Idaho. The argument presented here is that natural events/disasters have periodically resulted in a disruption of the productivity of the fishery. Such paleoevironmental events include the geological evolution/devolution of Snake River system landscapes over several thousands of years, paleoseismic activity, fire-induced erosion (both natural and cultural), flooding, and localized landslides. These events, which commonly result in channel reconfiguration and increased sediment loads, are known to have a negative impact on the ecology of anadromous species (Burton 2005; Davis 2007; Grabowski, this volume; Gregory and Bisson 1997; Hicks et al. 1991; Howell 2006; Liss et al. 2006; Schalk 1977; Stanford et al. 2006). We further assume impacts associated with human use of the environment both prehistorically and beginning with the Oregon Trail period. Indeed, incidental or purposeful burning by indigenous peoples (Lewis 1985; Sauer 1950; Stewart 1951) may well have served to increase sediment discharge in some areas along the Snake River. Pitkin (2010) has recently examined the distribution of known fishing sites on the Snake River, demonstrating a general association of prehistoric fishing sites with islands, falls, and riffles. These features, given the impacts described here, are subject to rapid alteration. Further, periods of cooler-moister and warmer-drier conditions would have influenced, respectively, runoff and sediment loads—some resulting from fires during arid periods.

Yet the use of the salmonid fishery over thousands of years may have been configured by the geological evolution of the corridor. Malde (1965), Swanson and Muto (1975), and Bentley (1983) have argued that conditions within the Snake River canyon remained relatively dynamic for an extended period of time, with modern terraces stabilizing only 2,000–3,000 years ago. The conditions described by Swanson and Muto (1975) and Bentley (1983) would have significantly impacted the productivity of the fishery as it relates to water temperatures, runoff, silting, and food levels (Plew 2009:32; Willson and Plew 2007)—not to mention the location of residential bases and procurement and processing areas. While it is assumed that most natural events have largely degraded the environment, some events may have enhanced local conditions, as may be the case with increased spring discharges associated with seismic activity. This in turn, however, may have seen local groups utilizing terrestrial resources at greater distances from riverine settings.

A review of the archaeological literature from along the Snake River indicates little early/middle Holocene use of fish but a noticeable increase in the presence of fish in late Holocene contexts, which contrasts with the archaeological convention that salmon usage has a long history in western Idaho. Though Plew (2009) suggests that the increased use of fish may be associated with people utilizing artiodactyl populations that aggregated near water as a result of the increasing aridity of the late Holocene, Willson and Plew (2007) have proposed that it may reflect a lesser use of the corridor during the early and middle Holocene as relates to the formation of modern terraces and habitats. At issue are short- versus long-term impacts associated with natural events. These events suggest that over the course of the Holocene the alteration of the landscape may have periodically altered the availability or relative productivity of salmonids. A good analogue is the high-frequency wildfires that occurred in the Boise National Forest between 1986 and 2003. During this time post-fire debris flows reduced fish numbers and fish habitats (Burton 2005).

Given that prehistoric human populations were small and highly diffuse, these natural events, although short in duration, may have disrupted transhumant patterns, influencing shifts in prey choice and diet breadth—varied by the habits of different groups known to use the Snake River area. As resources including salmon were not uniformly distributed annually along the Snake River or equally exploitable using ethnographically documented techniques of salmon capture, it is important to note that the great fisheries of western Idaho are located in the Hagerman Valley area—an area notably subject to landslide events. Importantly, prey choice decisions, typically based on cost-benefit returns (Gould and Plew 1996; Plew 2009), may instead at the level of an individual site reflect decisions altered by natural events negatively impacting local habitats. The decreased availability of salmon may have increased competition/conflict among local groups, as Cannon (1992) has noted in the case of the Interior Plateau of British Columbia. Following Davis (2007), we argue that a more geoarchaeologically oriented approach placing greater attention on smaller spatial scales may provide a more detailed understanding of resource use in general and salmon usage in particular.

If we assume that tactical responses were driven by the contingencies of resource encounters, and that different groups then necessarily employed variable strategies in utilizing Middle Snake River resources as is known ethnographically, the potential impacts of such periodic and random natural perturbations need to be considered, as they potentially affected the rate or tempo and mode of cultural developments in the region. This has larger evolutionary implications for the rate and level of intensification based on salmon and thus arguments for the role of anadromous fish use in the emergence of villages in the Snake River Plain (Pavesic and Meatte 1980): the impacts of natural events disrupting the availability and/or productivity of salmon resources would have dramatically influenced their dependability as an intensifiable resource for foragers in this region.

References Cited

Ames, K. M., and A. G. Marshall

1980 Villages, Demography and Subsistence Intensification on the Southern Columbia Plateau. *North American Archaeologist* 2:25–52.

Bentley, Elton B.

1981 Geomorphic History and Soils Analysis of Archaeological Sites 10-GG-1 and 10-TF-352. In *Archaeological Test Excavations at Four Prehistoric Sites in the Western Snake River Canyon near Bliss, Idaho*. M. G. Plew. Pp. 198–233. Project Reports no. 5. Boise: Idaho Archaeological Consultants.

1983 Geomorphology and Human Land Use. Unpublished MS on file at the Bureau of Land Management, Boise.

Burton, Timothy A.

2005 Fish and Stream Habitat Risks from Uncharacteristic Wildfire: Observations from 17 Years of Fire-Related Disturbances on the Boise National Forest, Idaho. *Forest Ecology and Management* 211:140–149.

Butler, V. L., and R. F. Schalk

1986 Holocene Salmonid Resources of the Upper Columbia. In *The Wells Reservoir Archaeological Project, vol. I: Summary of Findings*. J. C. Chatters, ed. Pp. 232–252. Central Washington Archaeological Survey Archaeological Report, 86-6. Ellensburg: Central Washington University.

Cannon, Aubrey

1992 Conflict and Salmon on the Interior Plateau of British Columbia. In *A Complex Culture of the British Columbia Plateau*. B. Hayden, ed. Pp. 506–524. Vancouver: University of British Columbia Press.

Casteel, Richard

1976 *Fish Remains in Archaeology*. New York: Academic Press.

Chatters, James C.

1995 Population Growth, Climatic Cooling and the Development of Collector Strategies on the Southern Plateau, Western North America. *Journal of World Prehistory* 9(3):341–400.

Chatters, James C., V. L. Butler, M. J. Scott, D. Anderson, and D. A. Neitzel

1995 A Paleoscience Approach to Estimating the Effects of Climatic Warming on Salmonid Fisheries of the Columbia River Basin. *Canadian Special Publication in Fisheries and Aquatic Sciences* 121:489–496.

Chatters, James C., D. A. Neitzel, M. J. Scott, and S. Shankle

1991 Potential Effects of Global Climate Change on Pacific Northwest Spring Chinook Salmon (*Oncorhynchus tshawytscha*): An Exploratory Case Study. *Northwest Environmental Journal* 7:71–92.

Davis, Loren G.

2007 Paleoseismicity, Ecological Change, and Prehistoric Exploitation of Anadromous Fishes in the Salmon River Basin, Western Idaho, USA. *North American Archaeologist* 28(3):233–263.

Davis, Loren G., and Karlis Muehlenbachs

2001 A Late Pleistocene to Early Holocene Record of Precipitation Reflected in *Margaritifera falcata* Shell $\delta^{18}O$ from Three Archaeological Sites in the Lower Salmon River Canyon, Idaho. *Journal of Archaeological Science* 28:291–303.

Evenden, Matthew

2000 *Remaking Hells Gate: Salmon, Science, and the Fraser River, 1938–1948*. British Columbia Studies no. 127.

Evermann, Barton W.

1896 A Preliminary Report upon Salmon Investigations in Idaho in 1894. In *Bul-*

letin of the U.S. Fish Commission for 1895, vol. 15. Pp. 253–284. Washington, DC: Government Printing Office.

Fulton, Leonard A.

1968 *Spawning Areas and Abundance of Chinook Salmon (*Oncorhynchus tshawytscha*) in the Columbia River Basin Past and Present.* Special Scientific Report no. 571. Washington, DC: U.S. Fish and Wildlife Service.

Gillerman, Virginia S.

2001 *Geologic Report on the 1993 Bliss Landslide, Gooding County, Idaho.* Staff Report 01-1. Moscow: Idaho Geological Survey.

Gould, Russell T.

1990 Prehistoric Hunter-Gatherer Mobility and Anadromous Fish Use along the Middle Snake River, Southwest Idaho. Unpublished B.A. honor's project, Boise State University, Boise.

Gould, Russell T., and Mark G. Plew

1996 Prehistoric Salmon Fishing in the Northern Great Basin: Ecological Dynamics, Trade-Offs, and Foraging Strategies. In *Prehistoric Hunter-Gatherer Fishing Strategies.* M. G. Plew, ed. Pp. 64–83. Boise: Boise State University.

2001 Archaeological Excavations at Three Island Crossing, Boise State University. Unpublished MS on file at Boise State University, Boise.

Green, Thomas J.

1993 Aboriginal Residential Structures in Southern Idaho. *Journal of California Great Basin Anthropology* 15(1):58–72.

Gregory, S. V., and P. A. Bisson

1997 Degradation and Loss of Anadromous Salmonid Habitat in the Pacific Northwest. In *Pacific Salmon and Their Ecosystems.* D. J. Stouder, P. A. Bisson, and R. J. Naiman, eds. Pp. 277–314. New York: Chapman and Hall.

Harris, Jack

1940 The White Knife Shoshoni. In *Acculturation in Seven American Idaho Tribes.* R. Linton, ed. Pp. 39–118. New York: D. Appleton-Century.

Hicks, B. J., J. D. Hall, P. A. Bisson, and J. R. Sedell

1991 Responses of Salmonids to Habitat Change. In *Influences of Forest and Rangeland Management in Salmonid Fishes and Their Habitats.* W. R. Meehan, ed. Pp. 486–518. American Fisheries Society Special Publication 19. Bethesda.

Howell, Philip J.

2006 Effects of Wildfire and Subsequent Hydrologic Events on Fish Distribution and Abundance in Tributaries of North Fork John Day River. *North American Journal of Fisheries Management* 26:983–994.

Kelly, Robert L.

1996 Foraging and Fishing. In *Prehistoric Hunter-Gatherer Fishing Strategies.* M. G. Plew, ed. Pp. 208–214. Boise: Boise State University.

La Rivers, Ira, and T. J. Trelease

1952 An Annotated Checklist of the Fishes of Nevada. *California Fish and Game* 38(3):226–240.

Lewis, Henry R.
1985 Why Indians Burned: Specific and General Reasons. In *Proceedings, Symposium and Workshop on Wilderness Fire, November 15–18, 1983*. James E. Lotan, ed. Pp. 75–80. USDA Forest Service General Technical Report INT-182. U.S Forest Service, Ogden.

Liljeblad, Sven
1957 Indian Peoples of Idaho. Unpublished MS on file at the Idaho Museum of Natural History, Pocatello.

Liss, W.J., J.A. Stanford, J.A. Lichatowich, R.N. Williams, C.C. Coutant, P.R. Mundy, and R.R. Whitney
2006 Developing a New Conceptual Foundation for Salmon Conservation. In *Return to the River: Restoring Salmon to the Columbia River*. R.N. Williams, ed. Pp. 51–98. New York: Elsevier.

Lohse, E.S., and D. Sammons-Lohse
1986 Sedentism on the Columbia Plateau: A Matter of Degree Related to the Easy and Efficient Procurement of Resources. *Northwest Anthropological Research Notes* 20(2):115–136.

Malde, Harold E.
1965 Snake River Plain. In *The Quaternary of the United States*. H.E. Wright Jr. and D.G. Frey, eds. Pp. 255–263. Princeton: Princeton University Press.
1982 The Yahoo Clay, a Lacustrine Unit Impounded by the McKinney Basalt in the Snake River Canyon near Bliss, Idaho. In *Cenozoic Geology of Idaho*. Bill Bonnichsen and R.M. Breckenridge, eds. Pp. 617–628. Idaho Bureau of Mines and Geology Bulletin 26. Moscow.

Malde, Harold E., and H.A. Powers
1972 Upper Cenozoic Stratigraphy of the Western Snake River Plain, Idaho. *Geological Society of America Bulletin* 73:1197–1220.

Meyer, G.A., J.L. Pierce, S.H. Woods, and A.J.T. Jull
2001 Fires, Storms and Erosional Events in the Idaho Batholith. *Hydrologic Processes* 15:3025–3028.

Moody, J.A., and D.A. Martin
2001 Comparison of Soil Infiltration Rates in Burned and Unburned Mountainous Watersheds. *Hydrologic Processes* 15:2981–2993.

Murphey, Kelly, and M.J. Crutchfield
1985 *Archaeological Test Excavations at the Crutchfield Site: Hagerman Valley, Idaho*. University of Idaho Anthropological Reports no. 86. Moscow.

Murphy, Robert F., and Yolanda Murphy
1960 Shoshone-Bannock Subsistence and Society. *Anthropological Records* 16: 293–338.
1986 Northern Shoshone and Bannock. In *Handbook of North American Indians, vol. 11: Great Basin*. W.L. D'Azevedo, ed. Pp. 284–307. Washington, DC: Smithsonian Institution.

Neitzel, D. A., M. J. Scott, S. A. Shankle, and J. C. Chatters
1991 The Effect of Climate Change on Stream Environments: The Salmonid Resources of the Columbia Basin. *Northwest Environmental Journal* 7:271–293.

O'Leary, Beth S.
1985 Salmon and Storage: Southern Tutchone Use of an "Abundant" Resource. Unpublished Ph.D. dissertation, Department of Anthropology, University of New Mexico, Albuquerque.
1996 The Structure of a Salmon Resource: The Southern Tutchone Fishery in the Southwest Yukon, Canada. In *Prehistoric Hunter-Gatherer Fishing Strategies*. M. G. Plew, ed. Pp. 6–24. Boise: Boise State University.

Pavesic, Max G., and Daniel S. Meatte
1980 *Archaeological Test Excavations at the National Fish Hatchery Locality, Hagerman Valley, Idaho*. Archaeological Reports no. 8. Boise: Boise State University.

Pavesic, Max G., W. I. Follett, and William P. Statham
1987 Anadromous Fish Remains from Schellbach Cave No. 1, Southwestern Idaho. *Idaho Archaeologist* 10(2):23–26.

Pierce, Jennifer L., Grant A. Meyer, and A. J. Timothy Jull
2004 Fire-Induced Erosion and Millennial Scale Climate Change in Northern Ponderosa Pine Forests. *Nature* 432:87–90.

Pitkin, Travis J.
2010 Islands in the Stream: Searching for Structure in the Aboriginal Fishery along the Snake River. Unpublished M.S. thesis, Interdisciplinary Studies, Boise State University.

Plew, Mark G.
1981 *Archaeological Test Excavations at Four Prehistoric Sites in the Western Snake River Canyon near Bliss, Idaho*. Project Reports no. 5. Boise: Idaho Archaeological Consultants.
1983 Implications of Nutritional Potentials of Anadromous Fish Resources on the Western Snake River Plain. *Journal of California and Great Basin Anthropology* 5(1–2):58–65.
1990 Modeling Alternative Subsistence Strategies for the Middle Snake River. *North American Archaeologist* 11(1):1–15.
2008 *Archaeology of the Snake River Plain*. Boise: Boise State University.
2009 Archaic Hunter-Gatherer Diet Breadth and Prey Choice on the Snake River Plain. *Journal of Northwest Anthropology* 43(1):27–56.

Plew, Mark G., and Russell T. Gould
1990 Archaeological Test Excavations at the Clover Creek Site. *Idaho Archaeologist* 13(1):1–15.
2001 A Summary Report on the 1991 and 1992 Archaeological Excavations at the Bliss Site (10-GG-1), Middle Snake River Idaho. *Idaho Archaeologist* 24(1):3–13.

Plew, Mark G., Pamela Huter, and Richard Benedict
2002 *Archaeological Test Excavations at 10-EL-1577 near King Hill Idaho*. Boise: Boise State University.
Plew, Mark G., and Sharon Plager
1999 Fish Remains from Three Sites in Southwestern Idaho. *Idaho Archaeologist* 22(3):27–32.
Prentiss, W. C., and J. C. Chatters
2003 Cultural Diversification and Decimation in the Prehistoric Record. *Current Anthropology* 44(1):33–58.
Randolph, Joseph E., and Max Dahlstrom
1977 *Archaeological Test Excavations at Bernard Creek Rockshelter*. University of Idaho Anthropological Research Manuscripts Series no. 42. Moscow.
Reid, Kenneth C., and James C. Chatters
1997 *Kirkwood Bar: Passports in Time Excavations at 10-IH-699 in the Hells Canyon National Recreation Area, Wallowa-Whitman National Forest*. Rain Shadow Research Project no. 28. Pullman: Rainshadow Research.
Sauer, Carl O.
1950 Grassland, Climax, Fire and Man. *Journal of Range Management* 3(1):16–21.
Schalk, Randall F.
1977 The Structure of an Anadromous Fish Resource. In *For Theory Building in Archaeology*. L. R. Binford, ed. Pp. 207–249. New York: Academic Press.
Schalk, Randall F., and G. C. Cleveland
1983 A Chronological Perspective on Hunter-Gatherer Land Use Strategies in the Columbia Plateau. In *Cultural Resource Investigations for the Lyons Ferry Fish Hatchery Project, near Lyons Ferry, Washington*. R. F. Schalk, ed. Pp. 11–56. Laboratory of Archaeology and History, Project Report no. 8. Pullman: Washington State University.
Schellbach, Louis
1967 The Excavation of Cave No. 1, Southwestern Idaho. *Tebiwa* 10(2):63–72.
Simms, Steven R.
1987 *Behavioral Ecology and Hunter-Gatherer Foraging: An Example from the Great Basin*. British Archaeological Reports International Series no. 381. Oxford: British Archaeological Reports.
Stanford, J. A., C. A. Frissell, and C. C. Coutant
2006 The Status of Habitats. In *Return to the River: Restoring Salmon to the Columbia River*. R. N. Williams, ed. Pp. 99–172. New York: Elsevier Academic Press.
Steward, Julian H.
1938 *Basin–Plateau Aboriginal Sociopolitical Groups*. Bureau of American Ethnology Bulletin no. 120. Washington, DC: Smithsonian Institution.
1943 Culture Element Distributions: CCIII, Northern Gosuite Shoshoni. *University of California Anthropological Records* 8(3):263–392.

1970 The Foundation of Basin–Plateau Shoshonean Society. In *Languages and Cultures of Western North America: Essays in Honor of Sven S. Liljeblad*. E. H. Swanson Jr., ed. Pp. 113–151. Pocatello: Idaho State University Press.

Steward, Julian H., and Ermine Wheeler-Voegelin

1974 *The Northern Paiute Indians*. New York: Garland Publishing.

Stewart, Omer C.

1951 Burning and Natural Vegetation in the United States. *Geographical Review* 41(2):317–320.

Swanson, Earl H., Jr., and Guy Muto

1975 Recent Environmental Changes in the Northern Great Basin. *Tebiwa* 12(1): 31–38.

Walker, D. E., Jr.

1978 *Indians of Idaho*. Moscow: University of Idaho Press.

1993 Lemhi Shoshone–Bannock Reliance on Anadromous and Other Fish Resources. *Northwest Anthropological Research Notes* 27(2):215–250.

Willson, Christopher A., and Mark G. Plew

2007 *Archaeological Excavations at the King Hill Creek Site (10-OE-110): A Late Archaic Occupation near King Hill, Idaho*. Monographs in Archaeology no. 4. Boise: Boise State University.

Wood, Spencer H., Caroline Wurts, Ted Lane, Nick Ballenger, Mary Shaleen, and Dolers Totorica

1985 The Borah Peak (Idaho) Earthquake of October 28, 1983—Hydrologic Effects. *Earthquake Spectra* 2(1):127–149.

Zeanah, David W.

1980 Food Storage Strategies in the Great Basin. Paper presented at the 21st Great Basin Anthropological Conference, Park City, UT.

Scale and Organization in Traditional Salmon Fishing

Insights from Ancient Technology of the Upper Columbia River

PEI-LIN YU AND JACKIE M. COOK

Three generations ago the Upper Columbia River salmon fishery was eradicated by the construction of the Grand Coulee Dam and flooding of Lake Franklin D. Roosevelt. Fortunately, the vivid memories and oral traditions of Elders from the Spokane Tribe of Indians and the constituent tribes of the Confederated Tribes of the Colville Reservation (the Wenatchee, the Moses-Columbia, the Nez Perce, the Okanagans, the Lakes, the Sanpoils, the Nespelems, the Methow, the Palus, the Colville, the Entiat, and the Chelan) endure. Their detailed narratives describe important characteristics of traditional fishing (Pouley 2008:6). Numerous scientists and resource managers have been working to save salmon from extinction (Knudsen et al. 2000; Lackey et al. 2006; Levin and Schiewe 2001; National Research Council 1996; Stouder et al. 1997). Integral to that effort is the realization that traditional Native American use of fish is key to understanding the factors influencing the deep history of the salmon fishery (Butler and O'Connor 2004; Cone 1995; Lichatowich 1999). This is part of a global trend in which descendant communities, scientists, heritage managers, and policy makers are working together to incorporate indigenous knowledge about resource management into policy and procedures (U.N. Educational, Scientific and Cultural Organization 2002).

Archaeological investigations can complement the fine-grained knowledge of tribal Elders by examining the material record left behind

FIGURE 3.1. Illustration of typical fishing platform at Kettle Falls, ca. 1990. Illus. by P. Yu.

by ancient fishermen and -women. For thousands of years salmon helped support a remarkable mosaic of traditional cultural systems across the Pacific Northwest. Groups near the coast positioned themselves semipermanently near abundant, relatively stable aquatic and estuarine resources, but foragers who lived on the semiarid riverine plateaus needed to schedule mobility to maximize terrestrial and aquatic resources that varied by season and year. These Plateau groups coped with random, often remote, events that affected the timing and abundance of anadromous species such as salmon, lamprey, and steelhead. Successfully exploiting these animals required long-range planning, excellent communication, and rapid deployment of a labor force that was numerous, highly skilled, and well equipped. These dynamic processes manifest in the archaeological record as sites, features, ecofacts, and artifacts at locations such as the Fivemile area of The Dalles (Butler and O'Connor 2004) and others (Livingston 1985; Minor et al. 1999). The archaeological record shows that, with minor exceptions, salmon fishing along the Columbia and other rivers such as the Snake increased in intensity over a 10,000-year span, particularly in the last 1,500 years (Meengs and Lackey 2005; Plew and Guinn, this volume; Schalk

1986). Figure 3.1 is adapted from historical photos of traditional platform fishing on the Upper Columbia River.

The analysis of tools and features allows us to quantify and characterize the material components of a once-living system and investigate keystone relationships and properties of human ecology that are still relevant today. For more than 70 years, scientific excavations conducted at archaeological sites and locations of traditional significance that have been inundated and eroded by Lake Roosevelt have resulted in the collection of millions of artifacts from Kettle Falls and other key fishing locations. These artifacts, now curated by the Confederated Tribes of the Colville Reservation and the Spokane Tribe of Indians on behalf of the federal government, are valuable material expressions of traditional lifeways. Their heritage value and scientific importance increase every day.

Archaeological studies on the Upper Columbia River to date have focused on sites rather than collections, emphasizing settlement and subsistence, cultural continuity, and cultural evolution (Chance 1967, 1970, 1986; Chance and Chance 1977, 1985; Chance et al. 1977; Collier et al. 1942; Galm 1994; Larrabee and Kardas 1966; McKay and Renk 2002; Pouley 2008; Rice 1969; Ross 1969). However, information about the unique technology of the salmon fishery (tools and the functional requirements that influence their characteristics and uses) comes primarily from ethnographic information. This is not surprising given that most fishing gear (nets, harpoons, weirs, and baskets) is made of perishable wood, fiber, and/or bone, which have a lower likelihood of long-term preservation.

Organic preservation is better at sites on the Lower Columbia and Fraser rivers, which contain a robust record of fish bones and other structures such as otoliths (Belcher 2009; Butler and O'Connor 2004; Cressman et al. 1960; Graesch 2007). However, the Upper Columbia River depositional environment is characterized by acidic soil, erosion, wave action, currents, and dynamic stream and terrace morphology. These processes have a major influence on the presence and distribution of organic materials (Cannon 1996:27; Chance et al. 1977:126; Graesch 2007:590) and have probably resulted in underrepresentation of faunal and other organic material in the vicinity of Lake Roosevelt. Archaeologists should therefore exercise caution in making direct inferences based on the presence or absence of organics; for example, salmonid remains on the Snake River have been used to argue for very high dependence upon salmon without sufficient warranting arguments (Plew and Guinn, this volume), but on the other extreme, the scarcity of archaeological salmonid remains in northern California has been used to argue that the ethnographic record overstates the importance of salmon (Gobaleta et al. 2004) or that populations frequently abandoned and recolonized the Upper Columbia River (Chance and Chance 1985). Clearly, the complex depositional environments associated with salmon fishing sites preclude simple archaeological inferences from organic remains. We would add that such inferences do not take place in a vacuum; they have real social, political, and legal consequences for Native American communities today (Pouley 2008).

In the absence of organic evidence, archaeologists focus on durable stone tools associated with fish processing (which we define as all tasks from butchering and drying to packaging for storage). Stone tools were most often used for butchering (removal of fish heads and guts and filleting). However, fish-butchering tools vary in form and were likely multifunctional; therefore diagnostic criteria for tool use contexts remain elusive (S. Chen, personal communication, 2011; Gould and Plew 1996; Graesch 2007; Plew and Guinn, this volume). We propose that variability in these artifacts can be dimensionalized, and ultimately predicted in a testable manner, when examined within a frame of reference comprising the factors that influence the organization and technology of the fish-processing tool kit.

This chapter has two main goals. First, we will discuss conditioning effects of salmon life history upon ethnographically described fish-butchering technological systems. Second, we will create a model statement about the range of variation in the functional morphology of tools and assess the utility of the statement through analysis of a curated collection of archaeological tools from an ancient fishing locality. This will allow for the development of an independent but germane frame of reference about expected properties of fish-butchering tools.

Conditioning Effects of Salmon on Fishing and Fish Processing

In this discussion we focus on Columbia Plateau groups with ready access to large runs of salmon (for discussion of smaller-scale or more occasional salmon fishing, see Plew and Guinn, this volume; and Stevens and Zelazo, this volume). Groups that harvest and process migratory salmon intensively must take into account the characteristics of anadromous life history, habitat, and distribution that distinguish these animals from terrestrial or resident aquatic resources. These include

- large seasonal upriver migrations of thousands of individuals;
- uneven linear distribution, with concentrations at specific locations;
- decoupling from local environmental productivity (reproducing individuals rely on marine productivity and stop feeding once upstream migration has begun); and
- random interannual events driven by sea level changes, deglaciation, rockslides, streambed morphology, precipitation, global temperatures, migration routes, local runoff, sediment load, vegetative cover, and other factors (Butler and Chatters 1994; Cannon 1996; Davis 2007; Plew and Guinn, this volume; Schalk 1977).

These properties of salmonids required people to monitor and communicate, then aggregate at locations where the animals concentrated in space and time, organize the labor force, establish living and working spaces quickly, and build or refurbish infrastructure and tools. These hallmarks are well documented in ethnographic sources (Graesch 2007; Ray 1933; Teit 1930; Thompson 1968). With anadromous species the window of access is very narrow, and the likelihood of spoilage is high (Graesch 2007; Ray 1933; Teit 1930; Thompson 1968), so incentives to procure and process as many salmon as possible were probably extreme (Ames and Maschner 1999:115–116; Graesch 2007:581; Schalk 1977:226).

Although salmon could be cached temporarily in the river, generally butchering and drying were done as quickly as possible (Graesch 2007: 581). This required many hands. Binford's (2001:261) database, which uses known characteristics of foragers to project organizational characteristics in environments where they no longer reside, predicts very large primary foraging groups in regions with access to salmon. Task group sizes should covary with the bulk of resources processed per unit of time and the degree of dependence on stored resources (Binford 2001:261).

Salmon runs were far from predictable, and all other things being equal, longer migrational distances for fish stacked up the probabilities of exogenous impacts (Davis 2007; Gould and Plew 1996; Schalk 1977). Periodic, random collapses of local salmon fisheries—sometimes for decades—required logistical tactics to maximize fishing returns and minimize hunger. These included a sophisticated system of communication, rapid deployment of the labor force, regulation of access and distribution, rapid mass processing, and long-term storage (e.g., delayed return). If the run failed to materialize, people needed to redirect efforts quickly toward alternative bulk resources such as camas (Ray 1933; Thoms 1989).

Spiritual measures to minimize risk and uncertainty included an extensive array of prohibited activities and substances (Thompson 1968) and tight social controls at fishing locations to ensure that spiritual errors did not offend or frighten the migrating fish (Ray 1933:28, 70–71). If all went well and the fish run was strong, facilities and personnel for fish processing needed to be in place and ready for action. Preparation began weeks beforehand (travel, establishing camp, gathering of raw materials, constructing/refurbishing facilities, etc.), but from this point on we focus on activities associated with actual fish processing.

The Work of Butchering

It was the men's job to procure and deliver salmon to the women. The women "geared up" by constructing drying shelters and, on the Upper Columbia, preparing large "floors" of sunflower leaves, a plant connected spiritually to salmon (Ray 1933:28). Presumably they also prepped their fish-butchering tools during this time. Fishermen then used natural features and platforms and a wide variety of net forms, including J-shaped basket nets or dip nets (Graesch 2007; Ray 1933; Thompson 1968), or traps at major confluences (Ray 1933). The fishermen gaffed and clubbed the salmon and handed them to delivery men, who transported them to processing locations.

In North America, salmon butchery methods appear to have been standardized across cultural and geographic boundaries. On the Upper Fraser River of British Columbia, women cut open the fish along the backbone, removed the head, drained the blood, and removed the vertebral column and attached ribs (Graesch 2007:580–581). The head was split and set aside to dry separately, and then the body was laid open, and the remaining fillets, still connected by a section of ventral skin, were scored perpendicular to the length of the fish. Fillets were typically no more than one centimeter thick and were backed by the skin—backing was essential to the integrity of the fillet for drying and transport (Graesch 2007:580–581). The thickness of each row of scored flesh was determined by anticipated weather conditions (Graesch 2007:580–581). In central Alaska, Cup'ik women cut off the head just below the gills, split the belly, and removed the fish's internal organs (Frink et al. 2003:119). The fish were then split along both sides of the vertebrae, which were removed and either dried or discarded. Heads were also split. Filleting entailed leaving two flanks of meat attached at the tail, and the alternative method of stripping separated the fillets from the tail and cut them into strips (Frink et al. 2003:119). Scoring of the fillets, a step to facilitate drying, is not mentioned, perhaps due to the lower risk of spoilage in a cooler climate. Similar fish butchery techniques were observed among the Tutchone of the southwest Yukon (O'Leary 1992).

On the Upper Columbia River, women of the Lakes, Sanpoil, and Nespelem divided the task into two main phases. First, women removed the intestines immediately and placed the fish on drying racks for about one hour (Ray 1933:75). After several fish had accumulated, women cut off the heads and opened up the body:

> One flank was partially severed from the body by cutting along one side of the backbone, between the bones and the flesh. The fish was then turned over and a second cut was made from the ventral side extending almost to the backbone. Each flank, thus separated, was slashed transversely about every half inch. Long slender splints of cedar were used to hold the sides of the salmon apart. (Ray 1933:75)

Heads were also split and placed on drying racks. Salmon were hung from racks by piercing the tail and inserting a forked stick. Ten to 14 days were required to dry fillets, and twice as long was needed for heads and roe (Ray 1933:75). The drying rack shown in Figure 3.2 is adapted from historic photographs of Colville facilities.

It would be difficult for the modern fisherman or -woman to imagine the scale and scope of traditional Native salmon processing. The closest analogy is 19th-century salmon canneries prior to mechanization, in which hundreds of Asian and Native laborers worked around the clock for several weeks (Newell 1988:630; O'Bannon 1987:559–560; Price 1990:48). There are clear implications for the traditional processing labor force: women (Frink et al. 2003; Graesch 2007; Ray 1933; Rousseau 2004). In Alaska, Oswalt (1963:44) observed that even a small increase in salmon meant a significant jump in workload. On the Upper Columbia and in other

FIGURE 3.2. Illustration of typical Colville fish rack with drying salmon. Illus. by P. Yu.

camas-rich regions, women came into the spring salmon season having already expended significant energy on the camas harvest and processing it for storage (Ray 1933:27), entailing *two* closely linked workload surges in the spring. Romanoff (1992:235) estimates that each woman worked for about 12 hours continuously to process 60–100 fish, and Graesch (2007), citing Frink et al. (2003) and Schalk (1977:94), estimates between 67 and 100 salmon processed per woman per day. In western Alaska the average household took in about 150–300 salmon per annum (Frink et al. 2003), and in a maritime household the estimate is 54 woman-days of labor needed per year. When ritual/giveaway salmon are added to that estimate, the workload could double to 110 woman-days (Graesch 2007:581–582). A modern estimate of "continuous effort" probably does not include time for family-related interruptions, resting, eating and drinking, dealing with work-related injuries, refurbishing tools, and so forth. In our opinion, it is appropriate to add about 20 percent more time to a woman's annual salmon-processing budget, or 132 days—about one-third of her year.

We can now summarize ethnographically derived elements common to the organization of large-scale salmon-processing technology:

1. Processing was carried out by labor groups near key procurement locations.
2. Due to the messy nature of fish butchering and the need to monitor drying salmon (Marchand 1999; Ray 1933), the processing area was separate from, but near to, residential areas.
3. Skilled labor was organized by gender (men procuring and transporting; women butchering, drying, and packaging for storage).
4. High incentive to process salmon quickly during a strong run imposed physical and logistical demands on the processing labor force and their gear.

The physical traces of these organizational characteristics should be visible archaeologically (Cannon 1996:25). Salmon-processing tools, features, and by-products should be associated with residential areas but functionally and spatially separated. Activity levels varied with the strength and duration of a run, and incentives for intense processing effort could be high. Discarded tools should have accumulated in processing areas, covarying with the frequency and intensity of site use.

Fish-Butchering Tools: Characterizing Variability

Clearly, fish-butchering tools are *necessarily* linked with the mass processing of salmon (Graesch 2007:577)—but the relationship between function and morphology is not straightforward. In sub-Arctic North America, fish-butchering tools appear to be bimodal in form: hafted bifacial chert knives or handheld unifacial tools of tabular raw material. For example, slate fish-butchering knives are well documented on the Fraser River (Graesch 2007; Hayden 1997; Prentiss et al. 2007), but in northern California, Kroeber and Barrett (1960) collected hafted bifacially flaked

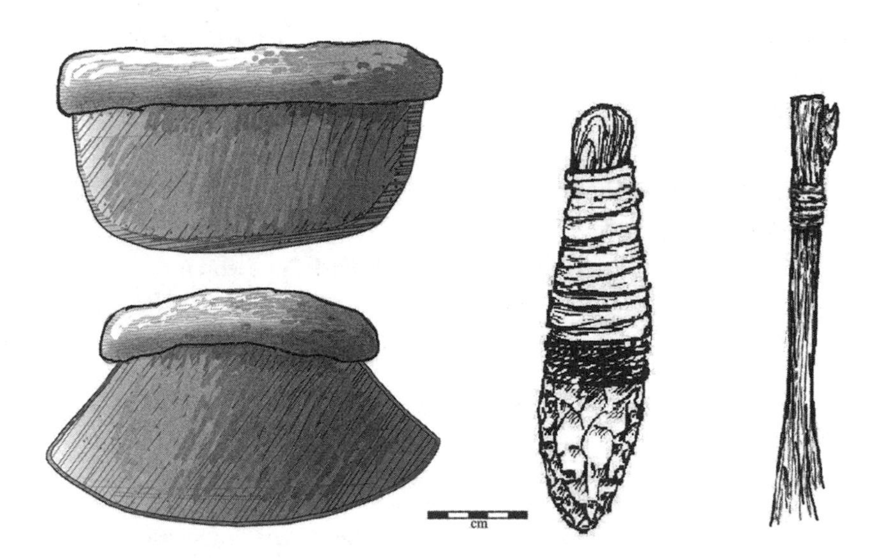

FIGURE 3.3. (*Right*) Slate fish-butchering knife forms (Graesch 2007:579) and (*left*) chert fish-butchering knife (drawing after Kroeber and Barrett 1960: 196, pl. 20).

knives. A typical knife is described as "a nicely chipped flint blade, hafted in a wooden handle, wrapped and pitched for firmness" (Kroeber and Barrett 1960:92). Rousseau (2004) proposes that prehistoric tools from the Canadian Plateau were bifacial and lanceolate, hafted with a blade on both the proximal and distal ends. He (2004:12) argues that these unusual tools (admittedly without an ethnographic basis) arose circa 3500–1200 BP as a result of increasing logisticality and functional specialization. At Fivemile Rapids in The Dalles, archaeological "blades" are described as made from thin conchoidal or lamellar flakes of chert with straight or convex edges occasionally on opposing sides (Cressman et al. 1960:48, 91). The case of Kettle Falls is more complex; on the Upper Columbia, Ray (1933:43) mentions hafted bifacial chert fish-butchering knives. Unifacial tabular knives are commonly reported as hide scrapers (Chance and Chance 1977:74; Mourning Dove 1990:103). However, Chance and Chance also state in the same sentence, "That at least some of the (tabular) knives were used for cutting fish is attested by numerous informants" (1977:74). Figure 3.3 shows morphological variation in ethnographic examples of fishing knives.

Multiple forms of fish-butchering tools may reflect distinctly different functional requirements. Cup'ik women have observed that more than one tool is required to butcher salmon (Frink et al. 2003): the first to pierce and chop and the second to make shallow slices. In British Columbia, Graesch reports,

> Because the beveled edges on slate knife blades are typically not sharp enough to penetrate the thick skin of most salmon...the initial dorsal incisions and removal of the head (which required cutting through the vertebral column) were likely accomplished with flakes, retouched flakes, or bifaces. (2007:582)

Slate knives may have been designed and used for a subset of salmon-butchery activities: the filleting and scoring of salmon flesh (Graesch 2007:582). Graesch (2007:582) also notes that slate cutting surfaces were finely ground and oiled to minimize sticking and blade edges were long to score the flesh without cutting the backing skin. Since similar qualities are desirable for processing hides, fish-butchering tools may have been multi-functional (as with the hide processing observation at Kettle Falls). Some of the slate Fraser River tools show both chipped and ground edges, which Graesch (2007:586) argues represent functionally different working edges.

We now have useful reference knowledge from ethnographic and traditional sources and can make linking arguments between technological requirements and tool morphology. Let us begin with the performance requirements for fish-butchering tools. Clearly, salmon processing required skill, concentration, and speed (Frink et al. 2003:117). These functional requirements conditioned for tools with superior piercing, slicing, and filleting capabilities as well as ease of manufacture and repair. The current literature on fish-butchering tools is dominated by slate examples (Burley 1980; Frink et al. 2003; Graesch 2007; Matson 1983), and Arctic ulus are often cited as the closest analogues to ancient North American tools. Slate offers several advantages: Along the Fraser River in British Columbia, outcroppings were close by, and toolmakers could acquire cobbles of good quality within a short walk's distance (Graesch 2007:585). Since foragers usually traveled to fishing grounds laden with equipment needed for camping, expedient tools from nearby sources minimized transported burdens (Graesch 2007:582).

Slates that were "soft and poorly cemented, breaking along bedding planes into thin plates or scales and terminating in joint-planes or irregular fractures" reduced the time required to make a tool (Graesch 2007:582); thin plates or sheets required no major thinning or cortical reduction. Frink et al. (2003:118) quote the preference of Cup'ik women of western Alaska for tools that are easy to use, speed processing, and require less resharpening. In a salmon-butchering experiment, the women compared replicas of traditional slate ulus with modern steel ulus with sharp pointed corners. Overall the women preferred steel ulus because the pointed corners could make the initial perforation, the blade was stronger, and the edge was more durable (Frink et al. 2003:120–121). However, they did determine that once the perforation was made with a piercing tool, the duller edge of the traditional slate ulu was better at filleting without cutting the essential "backing" skin (also see Morin 2004).

The use life of fish-processing tools may have been quite short, and the rate of discard, high. Frink et al. (2003) note that the Cup'ik women resharpened their slate knives after processing each salmon. Thus a woman processing circa 60 fish per day could exhaust one slate knife in a day! Knives made of more durable raw material such as chert or quartzite probably lasted for months or even multiple seasons. We expect that fish-butchering knives were also used for non-fish-related tasks, possibly hide scraping, while people resided at the fishing locality. Tools that were exhausted or broken beyond repair were likely discarded in higher numbers near fish-butchery locales (Graesch 2007:596); exhausted handheld unifacial tools made of tabular raw material should have reduced surface area–to–thickness ratios. Women may not have considered fish-butchering tools worthy of much curation or transport. Rather, we expect that most tools with utility value remaining after salmon processing were left on-site for recovery and refurbishing in future seasons.

We derive from these considerations some expectations for archaeological fish-butchering tools:

1. Varied morphologies that may be discernible at the level of an assemblage rather than between individual tools.
2. Formal characteristics that meet the functional requirements for both piercing/slicing *and* scoring/filleting.
3. Raw material that is easily accessed and worked (e.g., local, tabular fracture planes, etc.).
4. Large accumulations of exhausted or broken tools at processing localities, covarying with the intensity and frequency of site use.

5. Smaller numbers of tools with use life remaining also present at processing localities.

It is now possible to make a model statement regarding the expected characteristics of fish-butchering technology and tools:

> Bulk processers of salmon require tools with low transport and manufacture costs that are capable of performing both piercing and shallow slicing functions rapidly with minimal repair, refurbishment, or replacement. Multiple functionality may be reflected in the assemblage rather than in individual tools. To reduce resharpening, tools may have more than one slicing edge. Discarded and broken tools will accumulate in large quantities near key access locations, and tools may also be left on-site for later use.

Below, we evaluate an archaeological assemblage of tools from the Kettle Falls area (Figure 3.4) in terms of the model statement. Our objective is not to produce a classificatory system for salmon-butchering tools, or a range of expected variability in forms across space, or a systematic study of change in form over time. Rather, we will consider the utility of the model statement for describing the conditioning effect of larger organizational characteristics of fish processing upon specific traits in the morphology of tools, as well as implications for archaeological examples.

The Kettle Falls Collection

Human use of the Kettle Falls area extends back nearly 10,000 years (Pouley 2008). Due to erosion and other dynamic site-formational processes, artifacts recovered from Kettle Falls bracket a period of circa 9,000 years ago to Euro-American contact, with the majority dating to the Takumakst culture-historical period (ca. 2000–1700 BP; Chance and Chance 1982:63). The study sample of tabular tools from the known fishing site of Hays Island (45 FE-45; also known as the Ksunku site) and adjacent locations at Kettle Falls (Table 3.1) is curated at the Confederated Tribes of the Colville Archaeological Repository. More than 4,000 tabular tools have been recovered over decades of archaeological work, and many more are not yet recovered. We randomly sampled 253 tabular tools from six Kettle Falls–area sites (45 ST-119 and 45 FE-45 were excavated over several

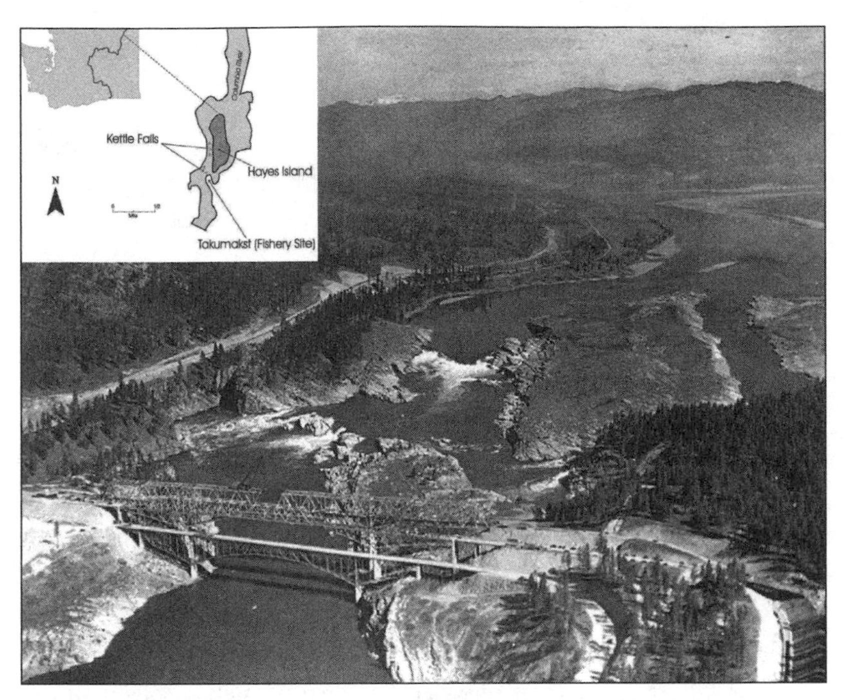

FIGURE 3.4. Kettle Falls and Hayes Island in northeastern Washington State (map from Pouley 2008:4, used by permission of the author) and aerial view of Kettle Falls prior to Grand Coulee Dam construction.

TABLE 3.1. Kettle Falls Area Sites Sampled.

Site	*N* Sampled
45 FE-43	9
45 FE-45 A	176
45 FE-45 B	21
45 ST-95	18
45 ST-116	6
45 ST-119	17
45 ST-201	6

years and assigned multiple catalog numbers, but each is treated here as a single collection). Due to the nonrepresentative nature of the collection, our analysis will describe and evaluate characteristics of sampled tools relative to the model statement rather than arrive at a statistically derived conclusion. The Takumakst or Fishery site (45 ST-94) was not sampled but is a highly significant fishing locality and should be prioritized for future analysis.

We analyzed artifacts if they were

1. tabular (roughly equal thickness along both axes formed by parallel fracture planes in the source material)
2. one centimeter or less in maximum thickness
3. not clearly a projectile point or other bifacial tool

Chance and Chance (1977, 1982) view the tabular, bifacially retouched tools from 45 ST-45 and other sites as a distinct artifact class. Excavators, and subsequently curators, have labeled the artifacts and assigned them a functional category. After reviewing the collection catalog we feel that the above characteristics match well with prior designations of "tabular knife" in all but an insignificant number, although we use the more generic term *tabular tools*. The weight, maximum length, maximum width, and thickness of artifacts were measured, as well as maximum thickness and thickness at one working edge. The number of chipped or "working" edges was noted. Each artifact was photographed with a metric scale with two map views.

Results

From the model statement we address individual expectations for the Kettle Falls sample.

Fish-Butchering Tools Had Low Transport and Manufacture Costs

The Kettle Falls tools are made of tabular quartzite from the Colville Formation, located right at 45 FE-45/Hayes Island and nearby at 45 ST-98/the Kwilkin site, or micaceous quartzite interleaved with micaceous schist (also called argillite), from the mouth of the Kettle River circa 2.5 miles distant (Chance and Chance 1977, 1982; R. DePuydt, personal communication, 2009; B. Martinez, personal communication, 2009). A few small slate tools were present in these sites but not sampled. As with Graesch's tools on the Fraser River, the Kettle Falls tabular tools were easy to manufacture and transport by virtue of a raw material source within a day's stroll from the main fishing locality. This raw material fractures into circa one-centimeter-thick pieces that require minor retouch to become functional tools.

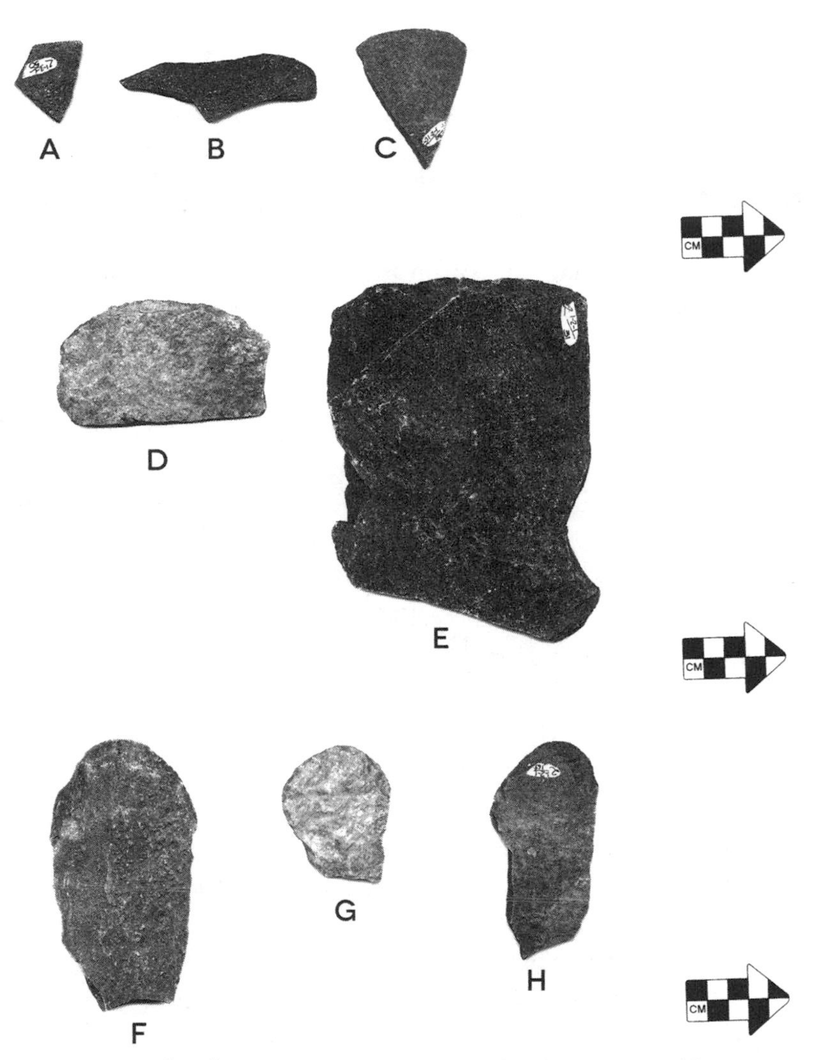

FIGURE 3.5. (a–h) Kettle Falls tabular tools showing a range of forms.

The Assemblage Should Reflect Multifunctionality in Which Tools Exhibit Piercing/Perforating Features as well as Shallow Curvate Ones

The sampled tools do show variability in form, with piercing functionality reflected in acutely angled (<90 degrees) sharp points (Figure 3.5a–c, g–h) and filleting functionality reflected in two- to three-millimeter-thick edges that are straight (Figure 3.5a, e), shallowly curved (3.5c–d), or tightly curved/ovate (Figure 3.5f–h). A subset of 171 tools was examined for morphological characteristics. Of these, 79 percent (135) exhibited both piercing and filleting characteristics (with a subset of tiny tools ca. 5–8 centimeters in maximum length that appear to be functionally different), and 21 percent (36) exhibited only filleting capability.

These categories agree somewhat with Chance and Chance's (1977, 1982) formal designations distinguishing the tabular tool assemblage as follows:

- Cornered or cutting knives, with angled edges between 90 and 180 degrees, most likely used to perforate or pierce;
- Pointed knives with angled edges more acute than 90 degrees, most likely used to make deeper perforations;
- Ovate or semilunar knives with tightly curved edges, most likely used for filleting; and
- Concave knives that they consider to be unfinished semilunar knives.

However, the Chance and Chance categories do not take into account the *combined* piercing and filleting capabilities of the Kettle Falls tools. In this sample, multifunctionality is observable both at the assemblage level and in individual tools.

Fish-Butchering Tools Should Have Multiple Working Edges to Minimize Resharpening Frequency

The Kettle Falls sample shows that the majority of tabular tools (56 percent) have one worked edge, excluding ovate examples (which make up 8 percent of the assemblage; see Figure 3.6). About 34 percent of the sampled tools have two or three straight edges. Our expectations were not supported by the sample, but a mitigating factor may be the durability of the Kettle Falls argillite and quartzite raw material.

Discarded and Broken Tools Will Accumulate in Large Quantities near Key Access Locations—Corollary: Still-Useful Tools May Have Been Left On-Site and Refurbished Upon Return

To date, the total number of tabular tools recovered in the Kettle Falls vicinity is 11,541 (see Figure 3.7, for example). Site 45 FE-45 (Hays Island) alone accounts for 6,005 tabular tools, and 45 ST-94 (Takumakst) accounts for 4,325. Most of these tools are densely packed in thin strata, with the highest numbers near the surface (Chance and Chance 1977), possibly as a result of reservoir-related deflation of sediments.

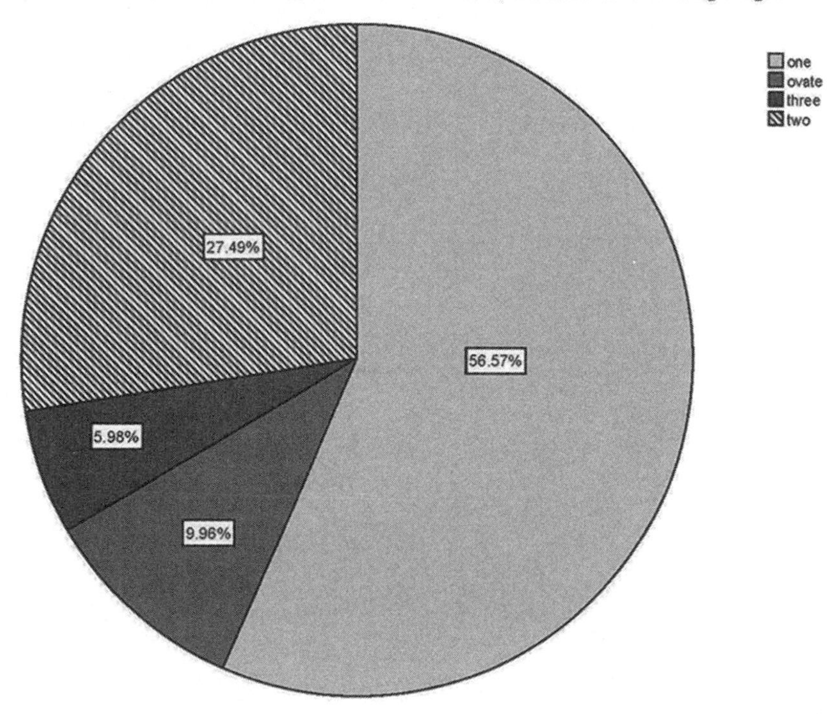

FIGURE 3.6. Number of working edges in the Kettle Falls sample of tabular tools (N = 253).

FIGURE 3.7. Tabular tool exposed on the surface at Hays Island, with water action visible (photo provided by Brent Martinez, 2004; used by permission).

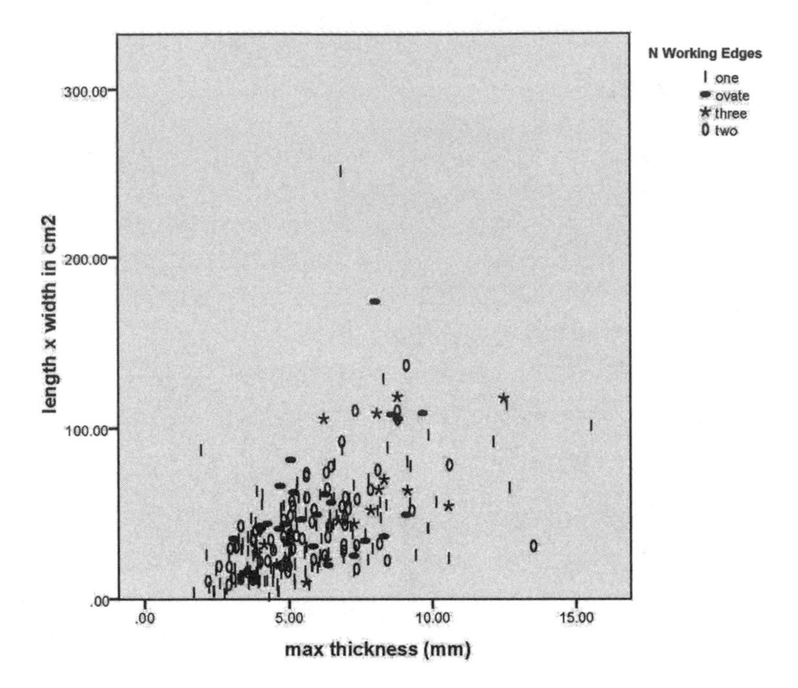

FIGURE 3.8. Ratio of surface area (approximated by maximum length × maximum width) to thickness by number of working edges.

The tabular tools at Kettle Falls should include some tools with use life remaining if women intended to refurbish them in later seasons. For a proxy of "exhaustedness" we used the ratio of surface area to thickness, with the expectation that exhausted tabular tools will be thicker relative to their surface area. Our analysis shows that, regardless of shape or number of working edges, the Kettle Falls sample is composed mostly of tools that retain some utility; their thickness relative to surface area is fairly consistent (Figure 3.8). Also, as can be seen in Figure 3.5, the piercing and slicing capabilities of the Kettle Falls tools are still present.

Discussion

Kettle Falls provides an interesting contrast to the Fivemile area of The Dalles, another renowned salmon fishery with major archaeological remains. The total number of artifacts that resemble fish-butchering tools there does not exceed 100 for all strata in Cressman's excavations, which were substantial. However, very large quantities of fish bone have been recovered from that locality (Butler and O'Connor 2004; Cressman et al. 1960). Several factors could contribute to the low numbers of fish-butchering tools at The Dalles: The destruction of large portions of the site for highway and other construction may have destroyed activity areas; and the original number of fish-butchering tools may have been smaller due to their manufacture from chert, a higher-quality raw material than quartzite that lends itself to longer use life and potentially curation and transport. If the Dalles raw material source was distant (not known), and thin flakes were a prerequisite for their manufacture, women may have made fewer fish-butchering knives and curated them rather than leaving them on-site. Thus we can expect that the workability and accessibility of raw material should directly influence the degree of accumulation of butchering tools at fish-processing locales.

The technology of fish butchering offers archaeologists and others interested in ancient fishing strategies for salmon (or other migratory aquatic species such as lamprey) a way to assess lithic assemblages for their association with fish-butchering activity. Characteristics of the Kettle Falls tabular tool sample supported our expectations that large-scale salmon processing produces assemblages of fish-butchering tools that are made of easily accessed and worked raw material. Our expectation of multifunctionality was partly supported; it appears that *individual* tools are highly likely to exhibit both piercing and filleting features (we feel that analysis at the assemblage level is more effective for archaeological collections, however). We expected tools to have more than one working edge to minimize resharpening time, but this does not appear to be the case at Kettle Falls. Our expectation that tools would accumulate in large numbers where processing was intensive and carried out over hundreds or thousands of seasons was supported, but it was surprising to see that every tool in the sample has plenty of use life remaining. These expedient but high-performing tools may have been a collective form of "site furniture" left by women intending to recover and use them season after season. Presumably the Kettle Falls assemblage gradually stopped being reused with the advent of alternatives such as metal knives.

To further evaluate the utility of our model statement, we recommend that the sample be increased to include tabular tools from Site 45 ST-95 (Takumakst). Edge-wear and residue analysis would also help refine the model statement. Our expectations for accumulations of tools would probably not apply to small-scale or occasional salmon fishing, but characteristics noted above may be useful in assessing whether tool morphology is consistent with fish butchering functionality.

In sum, the Kettle Falls archaeological record combines with ethnographically documented information to portray a large-scale, but flexible and adaptive, system of anadromous fish procurement and processing. This system of Columbia Plateau subsistence could mobilize very quickly in response to anticipated migrations and maximize energetic returns without (apparently) major effects on salmon populations. When the runs did not materialize, alternative resources were targeted, permitting fish populations to recover. The technology of salmon butchering is organized around these systemic requirements, allowing us to anticipate variability in the form and distribution of fish-butchering tools. We hope that our results will be useful to those who seek to increase the body of knowledge about prehistoric fishing, including researchers and descendant communities interested in inferring geographic and chronological scopes of ancient fishing and fish habitats. Humans and anadromous fish shared the landscape for thousands of years, and the archaeological record is a critical avenue toward understanding the evolution and nature of an intensive, sustainable ecological relationship.

Acknowledgments

Yu gives many thanks to the History and Archaeology Department, Confederated Tribes of the Colville Reservation, including Camille Pleasants, Brent Martinez, Brenda Covington, Guy Moura, and Donald Shannon. The Colville Tribal Repository is a paragon among archaeological repositories, and without Jackie Cook this project would not have been possible. Thanks also go to Ray DePuydt (National Park Service), Lynne MacDonald (Bureau of Reclamation), and Sacramento State University's College of Social Sciences and Interdisciplinary Studies. Ron Yoshiyama and three anonymous reviewers helped to improve this chapter and the volume as a whole.

References Cited

Ames, K. M., and H. D. G. Maschner

1999 *Peoples of the Northwest Coast: Their Archaeology and Prehistory*. London: Thames and Hudson.

Belcher, W. R.

2009 Understanding Ancient Fishing and Butchery Strategies of the Indus Valley Civilization. *SAA Archaeological Record* 9(5):10–14.

Binford, L. R.
2001 *Constructing Frames of Reference: An Analytical Method for Archaeological Theory Building Using Hunter-Gatherer and Environmental Data Sets.* Berkeley: University of California Press.
Burley, D.
1980 *Marpole: Anthropological Reconstructions of a Prehistoric Northwest Coast Culture Type.* Department of Archaeology Publication no. 8. Burnaby: Simon Fraser University.
Butler, V., and J. C. Chatters
1994 The Role of Bone Density in Structuring Prehistoric Salmon Bone Assemblages. *Journal of Archaeological Science* 21:413–424.
Butler, V., and J. O'Connor
2004 9,000 Years of Salmon Fishing on the Columbia River, North America. *Quaternary Research* 62:1–8.
Cannon, A.
1996 Scales of Variability in Northwest Salmon Fishing. In *Prehistoric Hunter-Gatherer Fishing Strategies.* M. G. Plew, ed. Pp. 25–37. Boise: Boise State University Press.
Chance, D. H.
1986 *People of the Falls.* Kettle Falls, WA: Kettle Falls Historical Center, Inc.
Chance, D. H., and J. V. Chance
1977 *Kettle Falls: 1976 Salvage Archaeology in Lake Roosevelt.* University of Idaho Anthropological Research Manuscripts Series, no. 39. Moscow: Laboratory of Anthropology, University of Idaho.
1982 *Kettle Falls: 1971 and 1974 Salvage Archaeology in Lake Roosevelt.* University of Idaho Anthropological Research Manuscript Series no. 69. Moscow: Laboratory of Anthropology, University of Idaho.
1985 *Kettle Falls: 1978.* Anthropological Reports no. 84. Moscow: Laboratory of Anthropology, University of Idaho.
Chance, D. H., J. V. Chance, and J. L. Fagan
1977 *Kettle Falls: 1972 Salvage Excavations in Lake Roosevelt.* University of Idaho Anthropological Research Manuscript Series no. 31. Moscow: Laboratory of Anthropology, University of Idaho.
Collier, D., A. E. Hudson, and A. Ford
1942 *Archaeology of the Upper Columbia Region.* Publications in Anthropology, vol. 9, no. 1. Seattle: University of Washington.
Cone, J.
1995 *A Common Fate: Endangered Salmon and the People of the Pacific Northwest.* Corvallis: Oregon State University Press.
Cressman, L. S., D. L. Cole, W. A. Davis, T. M. Newman, and D. J. Scheans
1960 *Cultural Sequences at The Dalles, Oregon: A Contribution to Pacific Northwest*

Prehistory. Transactions of the American Philosophical Society vol. 50, pt. 10. Philadelphia: American Philosophical Society.

Davis, L. G.

2007 Paleoseismicity, Ecological Change, and Prehistoric Exploitation of Anadromous Fishes in the Salmon River Basin, Western Idaho, USA. *North American Archaeologist* 28(3):233–263.

Frink, L., B. W. Hoffman, and R. D. Shaw

2003 Ulu Knife Use in Western Alaska: A Comparative Ethnoarchaeological Study. *Current Anthropology* 44(1):116–122.

Galm, J. R.

1994 Prehistoric Exchange Systems in the Interior Plateau of Northwestern North America. In *Prehistoric Exchange Systems in North America*. T. G. Baugh and J. E. Ericson, eds. Pp. 275–306. New York: Plenum Press.

Gobaleta, K. W., P. D. Schulz, T. A. Wackec, and N. Siefkind

2004 Archaeological Perspectives on Native American Fisheries of California, with Emphasis on Steelhead and Salmon. *Transactions of the American Fisheries Society* 133(4):801–833.

Gould, R. T., and M. G. Plew

1996 Prehistoric Salmon Fishing in the Northern Great Basin: Ecological Dynamics, Trade-Offs, and Foraging Strategies. In *Prehistoric Hunter-Gatherer Fishing Strategies*. M. G. Plew, ed. Pp. 64–83. Boise: Boise State University.

Graesch, A. P.

2007 Modeling Ground Slate Knife Production and Implications for the Study of Household Labor Contributions to Salmon Fishing on the Pacific Northwest Coast. *Journal of Anthropological Archaeology* 26:576–606.

Hayden, B.

1997 *The Pithouses of Keatley Creek*. New York: Harcourt Brace.

Kroeber, A. L., and S. A. Barrett

1960 *Fishing among the Indians of Northwestern California*. Anthropological Records vol. 21, no. 1. Berkeley: University of California Press.

Lackey, R. T., D. H. Lach, and S. L. Duncan, eds.

2006 *Salmon 2100: The Future of Wild Pacific Salmon*. Bethesda: American Fisheries Society.

Larrabee, E. M., and S. Kardas

1966 *Archaeological Survey of Grand Coulee Dam National Recreation Area, pt. 1: Lincoln County above Normal Pool*. Washington State University, Laboratory of Anthropology, Report of Investigations, no. 38. Pullman.

Levin, P. S., and M. H. Schiewe

2001 Preserving Salmon Biodiversity. *American Scientist* 89(3):220–227.

Lichatowich, J.

1999 *Salmon without Rivers: A History of the Pacific Salmon Crisis*. Washington, DC: Island Press.

Livingston, S.

1985 Summary of Faunal Data. In *Summary of Results, Chief Joseph Dam Cultural Resources Project, Washington.* S. K. Campbell, ed. Pp. 365–419. Seattle: Office of Public Archaeology, Institute of Environmental Studies, University of Washington.

Marchand, J.

1999 Oral History Interview. Unpublished MS on file at the History and Archaeology Department, Confederated Tribes of the Colville Reservation, Nespelem, WA.

Matson, R.

1983 Intensification and the Development of Cultural Complexity: The Northwest versus the Northeast Coast. In *The Evolution of Maritime Cultures on the Northeast and Northwest Coasts of America.* R. Nash, ed. Pp. 125–149. Department of Archaeology Publication no. 11. Burnaby: Simon Fraser University.

McKay, K. L., and N. F. Renk

2002 *Currents and Undercurrents: An Administrative History of Lake Roosevelt National Recreation Area.* National Park Service, U.S. Department of the Interior.

Meengs, C. C., and R. T. Lackey

2005 Estimating the Size of Historical Oregon Salmon Runs. *Reviews in Fisheries Science* 13(1):51–66.

Minor, R., K. A. Toepel, and R. L. Greenspan

1999 Bob's Point: Further Evidence of Pre- and Post-Mazama Occupation in The Dalles Area of the Middle Columbia River Valley. *Archaeology in Washington* 7:37–56.

Morin, J.

2004 Cutting Edges and Salmon Skin: Variation in Salmon Processing Technology on the Northwest Coast. *Canadian Journal of Archaeology* 28(2): 281–318.

Mourning Dove

1990 *Mourning Dove: A Salish Autobiography.* J. Miller, ed. Lincoln: University of Nebraska Press.

National Research Council

1996 *Upstream: Salmon and Society in the Pacific Northwest.* Washington, DC: National Academy Press.

Newell, D.

1988 The Rationality of Mechanization in the Pacific Salmon-Canning Industry before the Second World War. *Business History Review* 62(4):626–655.

O'Bannon, P. W.

1987 Waves of Change: Mechanization in the Pacific Coast Canned-Salmon Industry, 1864–1914. *Technology and Culture* 28(3):558–577.

O'Leary, B. L.

1992 *Salmon and Storage: Southern Tutchone Use of an "Abundant" Resource.* Occasional Papers in Archaeology. Whitehorse: Government of the Yukon.

Oswalt, W. H.

1963 *Mission of Change in Alaska.* San Marino, CA: Huntington Library.

Pouley, J. O.

2008 Analysis of the Kettle Falls Culture Chronology Temporal Gaps. *Archaeology in Washington* 14:3–20.

Prentiss, A. M., N. Lyons, L. E. Harris, M. R. P. Burns, and T. M. Godin

2007 The Emergence of Status Inequality in Intermediate Scale Societies: A Demographic and Socio-Economic History of the Keatley Creek Site, British Columbia. *Journal of Anthropological Archaeology* 26:299–327.

Price, R. E.

1990 *The Great Father in Alaska: The Case of the Tlingit and Haida Salmon Fishery.* Douglas, AK: First Street Press.

Ray, V. F.

1933 *The Sanpoil and Nespelem: Salishan Peoples of Northern Washington.* University of Washington Publications in Anthropology vol. 5. Seattle: University of Washington Press.

Rice, D. G.

1969 *Archaeological Reconnaissance, Southcentral Cascades, Washington.* Washington Archaeological Society, Occasional Paper no. 2. Seattle.

Romanoff, S.

1992 Frasier River Lilloet Salmon Fishing. In *A Complex Culture of the British Columbia Plateau:* Stl'átl'imx *Resource Use.* B. Hayden, ed. Pp. 222–265. Vancouver: University of British Columbia Press.

Ross, J. A.

1969 *The Spokan Indians.* Spokane: M. J. Ross Pub.

Rousseau, M. K.

2004 Old Cuts and Scrapes: Composite Chipped Stone Knives on the Canadian Plateau. *Canadian Journal of Archaeology* 28:1–31.

Schalk, R. F.

1977 The Structure of an Anadromous Fish Resource. In *For Theory Building in Archaeology.* L. R. Binford, ed. Pp. 207–259. New York: Academic Press.

1986 Estimating Salmon and Steelhead Usage in the Columbia Basin before 1850: An Anthropological Perspective. *Northwest Environmental Journal* 2(2): 1–29.

Stouder, D. J., P. A. Bisson, and R. J. Naiman

1997 Where Are We? Resources at the Brink. In *Pacific Salmon and Their Ecosystems: Status and Future Options.* D. J. Stouder, P. A. Bisson, and R. J. Naiman, eds. Pp. 385–387. New York: Chapman and Hall.

Teit, J. A.
1930 *The Salishan Tribes of the Western Plateaus.* F. Boas, ed. 45th Annual Report of the Bureau of American Ethnology. Washington, DC: U.S. Government Printing Office.
Thompson, David
1968 *David Thompson's Narrative.* J. B. Tyrrell, ed. New York: Greenwood Press.
Thoms, A. V.
1989 The Northern Roots of Hunter-Gatherer Intensification: Camas and the Pacific Northwest. Unpublished Ph.D. dissertation, Washington State University, Pullman.

Recognizing the Archaeological Signatures of Resident Fisheries

Considerations from the Pend Oreille Basin

KEVIN J. LYONS

Introduction to the Pend Oreille Fishery

The broadly distributed and varied life histories of Pacific salmonid fish native to the Columbia River basin (see Grabowski, this volume) provided a common experience for the Native peoples of the region and a broad picture whereby historic and contemporary ethnographers and archaeologists have long constructed interpretations about the region's past. Where these "first foods" existed in reliable numbers and could be accessed at predictable locations, Native peoples of the region devoted considerable energy to procure them. For regional experts interpreting the archaeological record, this necessary and faithful description of one of the region's defining resources is a comforting and useful orthodoxy. Yet, in places and/or times when this once-abundant resource was lacking, a nagging doubt persists that culminates in a singular question: Absent salmon, what happened in Native subsistence economies? This is not a trivial query; in this chapter it lends light to the incredible cultural variety in adaptive strategies exhibited by Native peoples of the region.

Plew and Guinn (this volume) provide ample historic examples of where and when geologic and climatic events impaired, disrupted, and in some cases eliminated migratory runs. Except for the last case, fish ecology has proved sufficiently robust enough to recoup periodic and even dramatic disruptions to accessing natal streams (e.g., the natural recolonization of Mount Saint Helens fisheries). Jones's (this volume) work in the Spokane watershed provides yet another cautionary tale against a salmon monoculture mind-set for interpreting the region's prehistory. And although the Kalispel bands were a "salmon people," this resource was not common to their homelands, thus making an examination of their family provisioning strategies within their home waters a worthy contribution to the broader question of "What, in the absence of salmon?"

The modern distribution of native fish in the Pend Oreille watershed (Figure 4.1) now listed on or eligible for the endangered species inventory belies their once-broad distribution and abundance. The degradation of their breeding habitats, fragmentation of populations into smaller far more vulnerable local communities, introgression of species, and outcompetition by invasive species have pushed westslope cutthroat trout (*Oncorhynchus clarki*) and bull trout (*Salvelinus confluentus*) to the brink of extinction in the Pend Oreille. The fortunes of mountain whitefish (*Prosopium williamsoni*), albeit at present not as desperate, are grim: there is a general downward trend in abundance resulting from the widespread distribution of a warm-water nonnative fish assemblage including northern pike (*Esox lucius*), a voracious keystone predator (see Connor 2010).

These native species, with the addition of less notable "game" fish to modern palates (Table 4.1), were the focus of both intensive (targeted) and pervasive (without preference) traditional harvest technologies that provided both in-season and winter-over family provisions. And conventional wisdom, as exemplified by the a priori assertion of Roll and Hackenberger that the "Barrier Falls sub-region" (1998:120) of the eastern Columbia Plateau had and has a de facto different prehistoric settlement and subsistence system than the salmon-rich watersheds to the south and west, can be called into question through a thorough review of the ichthyological, hydrological, and ethnographic data. Examination of social organization, scheduling of individual and group behaviors, and investment of a variety of directed and passive harvest technologies, coupled with no appreciable difference in human residency patterns between the neighboring watersheds, challenges the all-too-comfortable notion: *"As bison is to the Plains, so salmon is to the Plateau."*

Furthermore, I believe that it is not merely an abundance of a targeted species that can allow for hunter-gatherer intensification behaviors but also the spatial/temporal predictability of prey species that provides both dietary breadth and a quantity of calories that can (and in the case of the

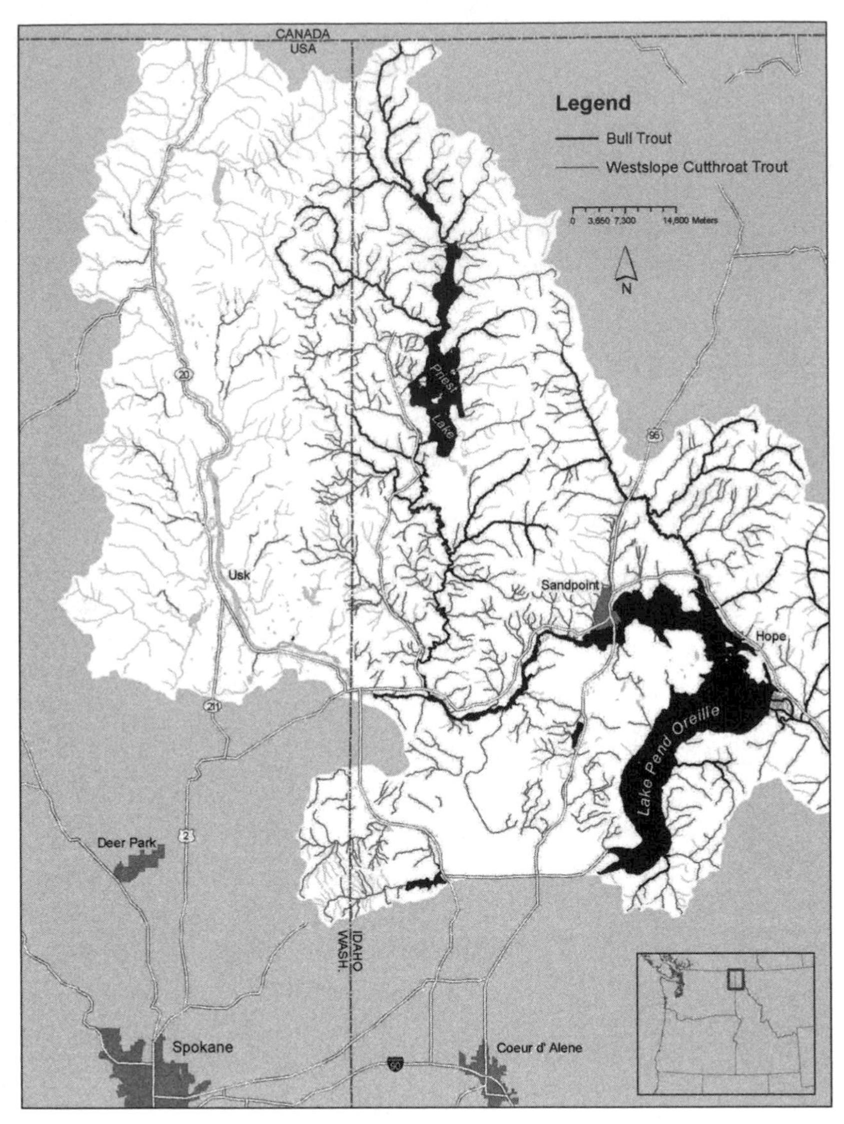

FIGURE 4.1. Contemporary distribution of bull trout and westslope cutthroat trout in the Pend Oreille watershed.

Kalispel bands, did) justify intensification on a broad spectrum of prey species. No less important to this discussion is the description of the associated material culture used in resident fisheries—which has hitherto been ignored. To aid in this discussion, I present below the essential ecological and ethnographic contextual data sets to construct a frame of reference sensu Binford (2001), whereby the spatial and technological associations

TABLE 4.1. Native "Game" Fish of the Pend Oreille Watershed.

Species	Common Name	Maximum Weight (kg)[a]	Spawning Window	Food Rank[b]	Optimal Harvest Setting
Catostomus castostomus	Longnose sucker	3.3	Early spring[c]	2	Shallow lateral margins of rivers
Catostomus macrocheilus	Largescale sucker	3[d]	April–June	2	Tributary gravel bars
Cottus spp.	Sculpin	?	April–May[c]	4	Rocky riffles in streams
Couesius plumbeus	Lake chub	?	May–June[e]	4	Gravel substrate of lakes and rivers
Lota lota	Burbot	34	January–April[d]	1	During spawn on sandy substrates
Mylocheilus caurinus	Peamouth	?	May–June[d]	4	Lateral margins of slow-moving waters
Oncorhynchus clarki lewisi	Westslope cutthroat	1.4	March–July	3	Tributaries to lakes and large rivers
Prosopium coulterii	Pygmy whitefish	?	?	4	Lakes
Prosopium williamsoni	Mountain whitefish	2.27	October–November	2	Tributaries to lakes and large rivers
Ptychocheilus oregonensis	Northern pike minnow	13	May–July[d]	1	Littoral margins of lakes and at tributaries
Rhicharsonius balteatus	Red side shiner	?	May–August[d]	4	Headwaters of streams and in lakes
Rhinichtys osculus	Speckled dace				
Rhinichtys falcatus	Leopard dace				
Salvelinus confluentus	Bull trout	9.07	August–November[f]	1	Low-gradient tributaries to lakes and large rivers

Source: After Scholz and McLellan 2009, unless otherwise noted.

[a] After http://www.fishbase.org, accessed April 23, 2010 (maximum normal weight, excludes world-record catches occurring in Lake Pend Oreille).

[b] As may be inferred by common lengths and relative abundance at time of maximum abundance.

[c] From http://www.rook.org, accessed April 24, 2010.

[d] From http://www.livinglandscapes.bc.ca, accessed April 24, 2010.

[e] Stasiak 2006.

[f] U.S. Fish and Wildlife Service 2002:11.

of the emerging Pend Oreille fishing tool kit(s) and site patterning can be more readily recognized and anticipated elsewhere in the Barrier Falls subregion.

Cold-Water Fish Ecology

In the following sections, the life histories of the three most abundant native fish species in the Pend Oreille watershed and their habitat requirements are described, with an emphasis on their potential to meet the needs of family provisioning. These data form the basis of a set of opportunities that would have been observable to human populations in the Barrier Falls subregion. In all three cases described, these species were predictable in their seasonal location and abundance, and for logistically organized hunter-gatherers they would have constituted a set of anticipatory resource patches in proximity to collateral resources that were either necessary or desirable for household survival and comfort. To aid in the formation of archaeological expectations of site placement and economic focus, the optimal harvest locations for each of these and other native fish within the system are provided in Table 4.1. This type of inference can be constructed from the temperature and substrate requirements of the targeted resource and source water body from which a species out-migrates.

Bull Trout

Bull trout (BT) is a cold-weather-adapted species, and as was the case for the woodland caribou, its viability in the warming post-Pleistocene environments of the western United States and Canada may have been subject to an inevitable decline with the reduction of its habitat. It has been estimated that BT historically occupied 60 percent of the Columbia Basin and have now been diminished to less than half of their former range (U.S. Fish and Wildlife Service [USFWS] 2002). The Pend Oreille watershed, located in the high and well-watered Selkirk and Bitterroot mountain ranges on the western flank of the Continental Divide, is among the handful of critical habitat units (USFWS 2002:3) actively being managed by federal, state, and tribal governments. With a growing sense of urgency, the hydroelectric industry has joined in a collaborative effort for species conservation and habitat restoration. Within the Pend Oreille's mountainous and numerous narrow valleys, the essential ecological attributes for BT viability and sustainability were once common. These included cover, complex in-stream structure, cool and abundant water, and connected breeding populations that allowed for both redundancy in the subpopulations and refugia from catastrophic events (Rieman and McIntyre 1993). A notoriously temperature-sensitive fish, BT is more commonly found in waters at or below 15 degrees Celsius (USFWS 2002:9). In short, BT are an exceptionally good indicator of water quality and if directly observable within the archaeological record, can function as an indicator species of a watershed's health and history.

Bull trout can behave as both migratory and nonmigratory fish (Rieman and McIntyre 1993). The former spend portions of their life in rivers and lakes and then ascend their natal streams to spawn. Nonmigratory stocks tend to be smaller than their migratory counterparts (Fraley and Shepard 1989; Goetz 1989). The spawning season, when fish's position within the system can be anticipated by people, is typically confined to a short two-week window triggered by an increased temperature in the rivers, pushing sexually mature individuals out of the main stem of the river and lakes into the cooler refuges of natal streams. Within the Lower Pend Oreille system this window typically occurred in August to September, when the highest ambient air temperatures coincided with the lowest water volume in the main stem. The sensitivity of this species to water temperature is most evident within their egg to fry stages (USFWS 2002:10).

Spawning areas are often associated with cold-water springs, groundwater infiltration, and the coldest streams in a given watershed (Pratt 1992; Rieman and McIntyre 1993; Rieman et al. 1997). Goetz (1989) suggested optimum water temperatures for rearing of about 7 to 8 degrees Celsius (44 to 46 degrees Fahrenheit) and optimum water temperatures for egg incubation of 2 to 4 degrees Celsius (35 to 39 degrees Fahrenheit).

As may well be suspected, such desirable conditions are driven as much by elevation as by proximity to the groundwater upwells that are patchily distributed throughout the watershed. Another factor affecting the relative abundance of bull trout is the presence of complex cover, important to this fish at all stages of its life history. Complex cover consists of large woody debris, boulders, pools, and undercut banks. BT also gravitate to low-gradient streams with clean gravel bars where their eggs can be immersed for an incubation period of 100 to 145 days (USFWS 2002:11). Within lake settings BT can grow to 9.07 kilograms (20 pounds) and live up to 12 years. Some ethnographic and historic accounts exceed these generalized biometrics, which shall be discussed below; it is sufficient to note here that BT was and is a large, seasonally and spatially predictable prey species. Its relative abundance and the necessary conditions for intensive harvest methods shall be discussed within the ethnographic materials below.

Westslope Cutthroat Trout

Westslope cutthroat trout (WCT) is native to the Columbia, Missouri, Saskatchewan, and Snake river drainages of the Pacific Northwest. It is far more prevalent in Montana and northern/central Idaho waters than elsewhere in its historic range, but a few scattered populations remain in Washington, Oregon, British Columbia, and Alberta. The modern distribution of this species is predominantly in isolated mountainous streams well removed from the habitat degradation that is now common downslope. Reproductive maturity occurs within four to five years, when individuals spawn in small tributary streams between March and July. This breeding schedule is also temperature-driven when the fish habitat has reached 10 degrees Celsius. As with bull trout, WCT can mature within their natal stream or migrate out to lakes and larger rivers, which creates three distinct potential life histories: resident, fluvial, or adfluvial. These differing life histories have ramifications for streams selected for subsistence fisheries, as they affect prey distribution relative to people's foraging patterns in the early season of the annual round and the potential size of harvestable fish that would warrant harvest.

Truly resident fish in the narrow sense consist of individuals that never leave their natal stream and are largely constrained by that stream's primary food productivity. Individuals that migrate to the main rivers to mature and return to their natal or an alternate stream to spawn are called fluvial, and those that migrate out to the watershed's lakes and return to spawn are labeled adfluvial. Essentially the body of water where an individual WCT resides determines its general size at maturity, as the surface area and volume of water set limits on food availability, as does general water temperature at the surface. Feeding upon insects, WCT inhabit the upper water column, in habitat and behavioral contrast to the BT's propensity to feed upon fish and insects deeper in the water column. As may be expected, the relative sizes of resident WCT are modest, at approximately 30 centimeters, whereas adfluvial and fluvial life histories can result in individual weights within the 0.9- to 1.4-kilogram range. Comparatively, WCT is a substantially smaller prey species than bull trout at their respective upper size ranges at maturity, yet their differing spawning schedules and spatial distributions within the watershed constitute contingent opportunities that hunter-gatherers would consider relative to the capacities of their technologies, the cost of their labor, and the expected rate of return for individual or communal efforts.

Mountain Whitefish

Mountain whitefish (MW) (see Holton 2003:95) gravitate toward streams but can be found in both riverine and lake habitats. This species is widespread throughout western Canadian provinces and the interior Pacific Northwest of the United States. The MW year-round range includes the Upper Colorado, Columbia, Fraser, Mackenzie, Missouri, Saskatchewan, and Snake river drainages. Their historic and modern ubiquity is coupled with an average size range within 25 to 40 centimeters, or above WCT and below BT in relative size. Maximal individual sizes of 2.27 kilograms were not uncommon. Within the Pend Oreille watershed's fish ecology, MW function as a forage species for the larger and more robust bull trout that occupy the same habitat—but whereas the former is an insectivore, the latter is more piscivorous. Having coevolved with trout in these waters MW are essentially noncompetitive, as they subsist upon macro-invertebrates and zooplankton in the lower water column. MW attain reproductive maturity within three years and congregate in large schools during the fall spawning season (late October to early November) in medium to large tributary streams with complex substrates of large and clean gravel bars, where eggs are deposited.

As will be demonstrated later, the MW stock associated with Priest Lake, Idaho, was of considerable importance to the Kalispel, particularly for its potential yield and spawning schedule. Priest Lake, located a scant 46.8 kilometers over the ridgeline from the principal winter villages of The Caves, Place of Many Bones, and Head of Lodge and only 50 kilometers upstream of the Priest River winter village site, was within the effective range of each of these communities, with a modest expenditure of effort in transportation. And as may be deduced from the life histories of this species and other fish in large lakes, it was a highly productive fishery. The lake was so productive that the Idaho State Game and Fish Commission allowed residents a harvest limit of 50 pounds of MW in fall 1939 (Sims 1999:6).[1]

Summary

The life histories, spawning schedules, sizes, and potential abundance of the fish described above suggest a number of implications for hunter-gatherer responses to these opportunities. The first is that locally none of these species' spawning schedules are coincidental with each other in either space or time, and thus they do not constitute mutually nullifying opportunities.[2] Further, the life histories of BT and WCT adfluvial/fluvial stocks (the larger of the potential resource options) narrow the range of possible tributaries that may have been deliberately visited by people for fishing. The mass spawning tendencies of MW also indicate that, although having a secondary food rank to BT, its spatial, temporal, and quantitative predictability may have made it a highly attractive prey accessible prior to the winter months when family provisioning for what was a long winter-over period was at the forefront of most providers' concerns.[3] Spatially discrete during their relative spawning seasons and tending toward tributary habitats with low gradients (BT) with ample cool, clean, and cobble-enriched substrates (BT and MW), these two species could at least be systematically predicted and intercepted with the appropriate harvest technologies and supporting labor that could maintain the harvest, process the catch, and transport it back home.

What will prove somewhat surprising in the ethnohistoric data analysis below is the scarce evidence for the cultural use of northern pike minnow and suckers and the absolute dearth of evidence of redband/rainbow trout use.[4] As may be deduced from Table 4.1, these underrepresented species in the ethnographic data set should be ranked relatively high in potential food value in their recorded maximum mass and inferred potential numbers; yet they only merited passing mention.[5] This indicates that a thoughtful process of cultural selection was at play. Ultimately some resources either lacked sufficient predictability in their encounter rates or conflicted with other opportunities (social and/or economic) to warrant specific harvesting strategies and thus were possibly bypassed. This assumes that the ethnographic record is sufficiently complete to account for this apparent discrepancy, an assumption that is fraught with its own hazards.

Hydrology

The Pend Oreille watershed is the second largest tributary to the Columbia River system and drains an area of 66,800 square kilometers (25,792 square miles). Its true headwater is located in Montana by way of the Clark Fork River and was historically called "the Clark Fork of the Columbia River." The Pend Oreille drainage is a very well-watered landscape with numerous cold-water upwellings essential for the various life stages of the native species listed above.

In terms of fish productivity (size and quantity) the preceding section briefly introduced the concept of primary food productivity; within the context of the Pend Oreille watershed's hydrology this highlights the importance of the area's lakes to resident fish ecology. Within these settings a relatively unrestrained food web developed that allowed for not only a high frequency of fish per hectare but also the production of significantly larger specimens on average. Adfluvial and fluvial life histories placed BT, MW, and WCT into an open range where macro-invertebrates and zooplankton, the foundation of the food web, were abundant in these broad and deep bodies of water. With well-fed and plentiful forage fish such as MW, suckers, and an assortment of native "minnows," keystone predators could attain significant sizes. Presently the world's-record BT is still held by N. L. Higgins, who caught a 32-pound specimen on October 27, 1949 (*Fisherman Review* 2010).

As significant as these lakes (Table 4.2) were for the size and quantity of native fish, the importance of the Pend Oreille River itself as a fish-rearing environment cannot be dismissed. In particular, the river would seasonally exceed its channel restraints and inundate the Calispell Valley floodplain to the west side of the river between river miles 69.6 and 61.7 within the Box Canyon reach.

This seasonal inundation (Figure 4.2) and localized increase in lentic habitat have all but been abated by the development of dikes (Northrop, Devine, and Tarbell, Inc. 1996), pumping stations, and hydroelectric projects above, below, and within the watershed. Chance recounts one historic observation of this seasonal inundation as follows:

TABLE 4.2. Summary of Local Lakes and Their Native Fish Inventory.

Lake	Depth (m)	Area (ha)	Elevation (ft amsl)	Native Fish Inventory[a,b]
Calispell[a]	1.52	768.91	2,034	?
Pend Oreille[a]	356.92	33,219.97	2,061	BT, WCT, MW, NPM, minnows
Upper Priest[c]	31.4	541	2,441	BT, WCT, MW, NPM, minnows
Lower Priest[a]	112	9,430		BT, WCT, MW, NPM, minnows
Sullivan[a]	100.58	56.56	2,562	Burbot(?)
Bead[b]	51.82	292.18	2,829	Peamouth, NPM, largescale sucker
Marshall[a]	28.04	76.89	2,730	WCT
Yokum[a]	18.29	19.02	2,953	WCT

Note: BT = bull trout; WCT = westslope cutthroat trout; MW = mountain whitefish; NPM = northern pike minnow; minnows = any variety of small forage species.

[a] See http://www.ecy.wa.gov/programs/eap/lakes/wq/docs/lksulpe1.html.

[b] See http://www.fs.usda.gov/recarea/colville/recreation/ohv/recarea/?recid=72032&actid=42.

[c] See http://geonames.usgs.gov/apex/f?p=136:3:0::NO:3:P3_FID,P3_TITLE:398012,Priest%20Lake.

> In May [1888] the spring flood began, and on June 28th it covered the entire Calispell Valley with a sheet of water measuring ten by twenty-five miles. This was the highest it had been in twenty years though early summer floods were the normal condition on the lower lands of the valley. (1993:19)

Prior to 1909, both historic and prehistoric populations adapted to this predictable (Figure 4.2) influx of waters into the system by vacating or avoiding significant residential development within areas that would be out of their direct access for as many as three to four months of the year. In 1909 the Idaho and Washington Northern Railroad constructed a grade on the west side of the valley, beginning a process whereby the river would be excluded from its floodplain—a process advanced by the formation of Pend Oreille County Diking Districts 1, 2, and 3. Diking District 2, the largest of these, is located about the Calispell Creek drainage and removes approximately 15 square miles of this portion of the valley from its annual flooding (Northrop, Devine, and Tarbell, Inc. 1996:8) and the associated seasonal fish habitat that it provided.

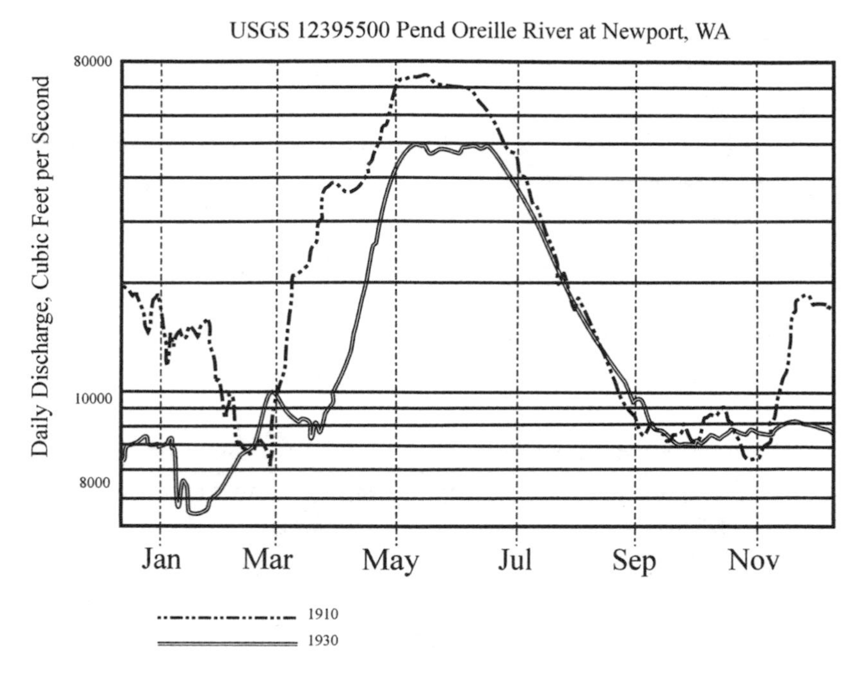

FIGURE 4.2. Pre-dam flows for the Oreille River. Hydrograph adapted from USGS data at Newport, Washington.

A Word on Ethnographic and Ethnohistoric Data Sets

To the uninitiated, the oral traditions of indigenous peoples often reside somewhere between polemic apocrypha and unassailable holy writ. Authors and readers of such data find themselves standing at one or the other end of this spectrum, ultimately as a result of biases unconsciously negotiated through the decades. It is arrogant to assert and naive to assume that the life experiences of one or even a handful of cultural mentors are sufficiently comprehensive to include all aspects of a society's behaviors, priorities, contingencies, or any of their variations, even among small-scale societies. Additionally, cultural mentors can get facts wrong—particularly when language and interpretation are a hindrance to understanding. Add to this the legion of "failed to ask" questions that can bedevil the conscience of any ethnographer, and it is amazing that a cogent understanding of many societies has ever resulted.

For these reasons this chapter begins with a description of the native fish resources that existed and the waters in which they were likely to be large and seasonally abundant. Such an objective grounding provides needful sideboards in the reading of ethnohistoric data. Despite ten years of reading the primary ethnographic materials gathered by Allan H. Smith (1936–1938), taught to him by One-Eye Tom, Blind Paul, Michael Bluff, and Robert Sherwood, the ethno-ichthyology of the Pend Oreille watershed is riddled with ambiguity. The fishery is described as having a "speckled trout," another "chub," or any variant of vernacular labels that either do not survive to the modern period or were perhaps misapplied in the 1930s. Other ambiguities arise from temporal conventions of "late summer" or "early spring," and nowhere is there a simple accounting of how many pounds of fish were taken at a place or how long it took to attain that goal.

These ambiguities do not simply arise from the dimming memories of the elderly; my own Kalispel mentor had participated at the mountain whitefish fishery as a young girl, and she recounted that the activity had been discontinued because of the zealous enforcement of state fish and game regulations in the 1930s (Lyons 1999–2008). The lack of precision and the data gaps that arise within the primary ethnographic literature are the result of a complex process in which local fish ecology was rapidly changing *and* the community that used these resources was becoming increasingly removed from their ability to access them. Despite ambiguities that persist in the following ethnographic accounts, a credible and reasonable argument for what was being harvested and the ways in which this activity may have left recognizable evidence can be derived from both the environmental and cultural contexts.

Substantiating oral traditions by adequately anticipating their patterns, verifying their presence in the real world, and properly interpreting the material record of these behaviors can only serve to aid in the restoration of threatened and endangered species. The primary literature cited within this section is from Allan H. Smith's (1936–1938) dissertation fieldwork at Yale. Over the course of three summers he visited the Kalispel community near Usk, Washington, interviewing the gentlemen named above and typing up notes of those transactions in the evening.

But for the physical evidence of the flowage entrapment system observable at that time about the old village site (now powwow grounds), Smith had to visualize the technologies and their contextual descriptions through narrative. Occasionally he was able to solicit a demonstration of fishing-related technologies (e.g., the manufacture of cordage), but by and large, use of many of the places and methods described had been discontinued during the lifetimes of One-Eye Tom and Blind Paul, the latter born circa 1850.

In the 1880s, the upper bands of the Kalispel people (those who lived about Lake Pend Oreille) would emigrate to the Flathead reservation in Montana, while the lower Kalispel bands doggedly resisted resettlement only to eventually realize their own reservation by 1914. By then, the railroad and diking districts of the Lower Pend Oreille Valley had isolated the river from its floodplain, altering the normal hydrology and perturbing local fisheries. This, coupled with ever-increasing immigration, settlement, and further agronomic development and industrial resource extraction by Euro-Americans, not only reshaped the surrounding ecology but socially circumscribed the Kalispel people onto "the little reservation between the mountain and the river,"[6] a ten-mile-long reserve within their traditional range. Inasmuch as modern ichthyologists chafe at missing connections within the ethnographic record, I marvel at what was salvaged by Smith and his mentors—and thus can forgive them the fact that they were not fishery biologists and credit them with the faith that they did not "make something up."

Indiscriminate Fishing Methods

In reading the ethnographic materials I have come to the conclusion that Kalispel people employed two general strategies when it came to fishing: active and passive harvest methods. The former were deployed against specific targeted species and occasioned considerable logistic organization in terms of the division of labor, prepositioning of material, scheduling, and social (if not equitable) redistribution of the harvest. In short, active harvest methods are common to communal fishing under the direction of a situational leader.

Passive methods were largely incidental to other provisioning activities or were used without a particular species in mind. Passive strategies would result in differing potential faunal assemblages within excavated site contexts and perhaps can be used as seasonal indicators of site use/occupancy. Moreover, passive methods appear to have been employed to augment other hunting and gathering tasks conducted at the same time and thus functioned as a hedge against risk. If for no other reason, we should examine these data to anticipate the associated fishing tool kit, the archaeologically visible elements of that kit, and the locations on the landscape where we should expect its occurrence.

Flowage Traps

Flowage traps were indiscriminate as to intended species and likely produced a catchall harvest reflecting the species composition within the river. But for the initial construction of the dike at a slough outlet that would have been reinvested in either annually or as hydrology would permit, this method was a pragmatic, low-cost adaptation to periodic landform inundation that occasionally yielded high returns. The nominal effort of corralling the catch, initial construction, and annual maintenance activities would have made this practice highly cost effective.

Flowage traps have been tentatively identified at three locations thus far in the Lower Pend Oreille Valley, two based upon ethnographic designation as to physical attributed functions observed and a third case independent of those data but physically similar to the attributes described:[7]

> A long time ago when the water began to go down in the summer after the summer flood, men built up dirt dams or dykes (no stones were used) all over the meadows so that the fish are left stranded when the water is low or gone by sinking into the ground, when they pick them up with hands. These dykes are about 2 feet high.... They kept doing this every year and each year it sods over and so they just kept putting a little more dirt on each year.... This method of damming the fish up as the Kalispel do is called sqwLt'IC'm, "corralling fish."...The Kalispel also built these dams of dirt in some other place; a slough in a meadow on the east side of the Pend Oreille about one mile below Basil's. The slough is called sc'qamI, where they have a brush weir.... This method [at that location] is done only on certain years for the two meadows do not flood every year.... When the water is real low in the sloughs where they have their brush weir, many Kalispel men (8 or 10 at least) go into the water at the upper end of the slough. They tie many tent poles into a big "log" and they roll this down the slough. As it went it gathered weeds [etc.] and it became bigger slowly driving the fish before it. When they got close to the weir, the men get in front and throw the fish ashore with the hands.... This method of fishing is called

> sinSEl'C'm, "rolling something down in a long depression with very shallow water." (Smith 1936–1938:376–377, 379)[8]

Contrary to the ethnographic description, all three observed cases of a flowage trap on or near the Kalispel Indian Reservation show evidence of fire-cracked rock within the matrix of the remains of the earthen and sod dams at the outlets of these sloughs. As an archaeological signature during initial surveys, these features are present as a perpendicular sod-covered "earthen thumb" jutting into the medial line of the drainage from either side of the slough. As previously mentioned, fire-cracked rock comprising low-density (≤ten pieces/one square meter) fist-size cobblestones has been observed.

As yet, no subsurface archaeological sampling of these features has been conducted, and their additional cultural material associations are still to be determined. I posit as an expectation that, given their seasonality of use, the catch was consumed in season and that evidence of on-site butchery might be scant. Moreover, this could be no more than an opportunistic dip net method, albeit on a grander scale, and there may likely be a broad spectrum of prey species represented in the faunal assemblage of such sites. The cultural selection of fauna in an archaeological site should be verified through sampling of "nonsite" locations to differentiate the assumed assemblage from natural fish-stranding events. The natural matrix sampling effort would have additional benefit in defining the resource mosaic that was available in the valley at mid-season. This type of information may prove valuable in assessing if there were diachronic shifts in cultural prey selection that could have included lower-ranked foods.

Waterfall Traps

The ethnohistoric case of fish harvest below asserts that waterfall traps were used only at one location within the watershed and that they were specifically used to target rainbow trout. As to the latter assertion, rainbow trout are sadly scarce in the Pend Oreille system, and it is far more likely for the given stream that this type of trap was used to attain WCT, which also spawn in April and are associated with that creek. The apparent effectiveness of this method being limited to one particular stream when good conditions for this type of harvest are common throughout the watershed requires a better explanation than current ethnographic materials provide.

It is counterintuitive that a simple and effective fishing method of "set and forget" that allows an individual to attend to additional tasks was confined to only one location.

According to Smith, the waterfall trap harvest method is as follows:

> In the spring, in April, when the rainbow trout was going [upstream] to spawn, the Kalispel used a trap in a creek coming into Priest River about 8 miles above the town of Priest River; it comes in from the west. Quite a ways up the creek from the river, right where the road crosses it, they hung a basket with a projection under the falls in a practically vertical position so the trout, trying to jump the falls, hit the projection and fall back into the opening and the basket. The basket is about 4 feet deep from the hoop at the opening and the projection is about 2 feet long.... When it is full it is taken down and emptied out at the mouth. The basket was hung up so the hoop was about 2 feet below the edge of the falls. It hung almost vertically. At each side of the falls right on top was one fir tree growing. They fastened a log across from one to the other just above the falls. From this they hung the basket by wrapping the two outside sticks of the flat part around the log and tying them there. The log was about 3 or 4 inches above the water. These side sticks were a little heavier (that is bigger round) than the rest and extended longer than them. It was a pretty productive method of fishing. Anybody can go there and do this; Paul himself has gone there and done this. They hang this up at night and empty it in the morning, by which time it would be full. The top half hoop is about 18 inches in diameter.... This was the only place in Kalispel country where this trap was used. (1936–1938:350–351)

This account prompts the following thoughts. All harvest technologies are overengineered to meet service life expectations and scaled to accommodate encounters with a robust specimen of a targeted species. The basket trap described had a maximum aperture of 18 inches and a maximum length of four feet, which indicates the maximum specimen range. We may also infer that, while a basket trap was hung under a falls, the resource patch was individually owned while in use but, given the passive harvest method, was likely not purposefully attended to but used when a work group was in the vicinity while engaged in other tasks (e.g., checking traplines). But for placing the trap within a spawning stream, this method is indiscriminate, in that it does not select for size or species. This particular method is not likely to be distinguishable archaeologically, as all the associated technologies that it uniquely represents are composed of cordage and wooden materials.

Setlines

The description of the setline method holds sufficient detail to anticipate portions of an individual's fishing kit and the tools used to manufacture and/or maintain its elements:

> Set hooks [were called] Ca/acqE, they were [placed] 14 to 15 inches off the [river] bottom. They take a 3 foot stick, tie the hooks with the bait on at each end so they come about 1 foot off the bottom. The stick was momoE because it won't break so easily, or a service berry, or some other leafy tree but no evergreen because it is not heavy enough.... From each end [of the stick] a string with a hook hangs. From the center of the stick a line goes to a rock on the bottom and from the same place the line goes to the surface. They anchor it to keep it close to the bottom where the big fish travel. The string went to the surface where it is tied to a bundle of tules, which were light and couldn't be pulled under the surface. The tules were tied in a bundle with willow bark or rarely Indian hemp. (Smith 1936–1938:341–342)

The description includes the manufacture of fishing hooks by shaping splint long-bone fragments from a deer foreleg with sandstone abraders (locally attainable) to build a composite barbed hook. The hook comprises two elements: a shank and the barb. The shank is roughened into a wedge configuration against which a similarly roughed wedged barb is lashed. On the opposite (top) end of the shank two parallel notches are incised to lash the hook to the leader material in the rigging described above.

When fishing in this manner an individual would have four to five sets deployed while camped nearby. This method was used in the main stem of the river in moving water, typically at night when big fish were said to bite. In the foregoing, no description of bait or any indication as to season was provided, but in spite of these omissions the following insight may be derived: the setline anchors (see discussion below), fishhook fragments, and abraders (equipment-maintenance tools useful in both wood- and bone-working industries) may have been included in a individual's personal gear, as these people were primarily canoe-borne for much of the season. Preferred hunting and gathering encampments were visited annually, which could allow for caching of anchors and other less portable gear (negating the need to haul them about the valley).

As such, these tools could as easily be classed as camp or site furniture. Again, but for setting the rigging and periodically inspecting their success, this method is passive and allows an individual to engage in other activities. Other than selecting for a size class common to bottom-dwelling species, this method is also indiscriminate as to its take and potential contribution to the faunal record. Big fish, if live bait was used, would have included BT, burbot, and northern pike minnow.[9]

Targeted Fishing Methods

Reminiscent of the intensive communal fisheries of Celilio or Kettle Falls, the weir fisheries of the Lower Pend Oreille River and circum–Priest Lake margin constituted significant expenditures of labor and intellectual capital by Kalispel families. Each location (far too many to enumerate here) was under the administration of a "fishing chief," who not only ensured magico-religious sanction but also administered the redistribution of the catch for families (either present or absent) at each of the weir locations. One key attribute that should be remembered is that all technologies described below were extensively overengineered to withstand the rigors of variable flow, debris encounter, and the potential of encountering numerous and/or large prey specimens.

Weirs

Despite the variability and ingenuity of the various fishing methods employed by the Kalispel, no less than two-thirds of the fish caught and consumed by Kalispel families was the result of weir fishing (Smith 1936–1938: 345). Given this fact, in terms of caloric intake it must be recognized that Kalispel fishing was a corporate endeavor subject to prescribed ritual and regulation.

Smith and his mentors made a classificatory distinction between the trout weirs of the Lower Pend Oreille River and those used to catch mountain whitefish along the margins of Priest Lake. The former were "brush/balsam weirs," and the latter were "stick weirs." Aside from these differing labels, they were decidedly dissimilar methods of attaining the same objective while targeting different prey. The following is an account related to a brush weir commonly used in late summer and early fall in the Lower Pend Oreille River:

> When it comes time to build the weir across the slough, the [fishing chief] announces to the people that they are going to build the weir across a certain slough. The [fishing chief] has much more power [than] the rest, is a more powerful medicine man then [*sic*] the rest. This is the reason he was chosen for this. No common man could make the weir hold; a big fish would come along and break it. It would only be a huge fish that broke it, not a floating log or anything else. Then he goes out, tells them what kind of tree to cut down first and not let it fall carelessly on the ground but they must catch it, prop it up carefully and then let it down easily to the ground. This is the first pole to be cut. Then on, they can cut the poles anyway it is the handiest.
>
> The [fishing chief] strikes the first lick of the chopping. Then all the men who want to help cut down any kind of poles and only balsam for the boughs because they lay flat. Then the women carry them on horses or on back to where they are going to build the weir. When they get everything ready and down to the bank they build the weir today and right away lest boughs wilt.
>
> To build this weir they use small sticks about an inch in diameter and as long as possible. Lay this stick on the ground, put a [six] or [eight] inch layer of boughs on it, then another stick on top right above the other stick and then they tie the [two] sticks together through the boughs with willow bark cord. Tie this every [six] or [eight] inches along the pole. The butts of the boughs are at the top when in the water. They lay the whole thing out on the ground first so it won't be unequal in thickness and have poor joints.
>
> Then when all is layed [*sic*] out, then one man begins at the end of each pair of sticks and ties them. Its hard work but all done in one day, else boughs wilt. At the same time some men are building the frame in the water and others, generally the women, and a few men not doing anything else, were peeling sod off the ground....

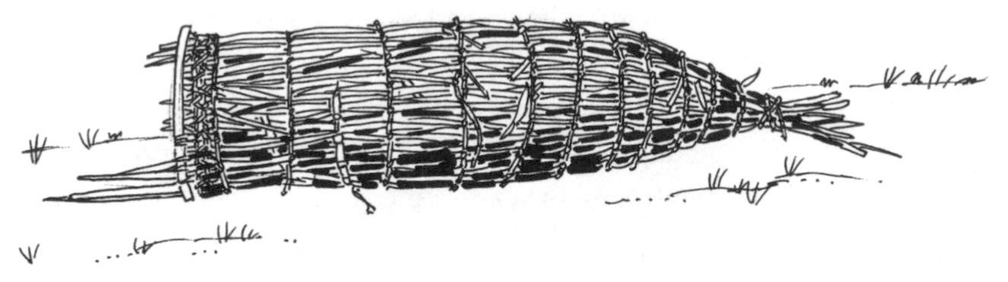

FIGURE 4.3. Typical Kootenai basket trap ca. 1860, comparable to those used by the Kalispel bands. Illus. by P. Yu.

> Where they can find rocks they use those instead of the sod. The sod is cut in square pieces, carried out in canoes and fastened to the top of the fir boughs (or the bottom of the weir). Space is left at each shore for the trap or basket, so the weir doesn't go clear across the river; probably a [six] or [eight] foot space is left at each end. (Smith 1936–1938:324, 326)

As demonstrated in the above account, considerable thought and effort went into the design and construction of these weirs. The fact that these efforts were officiated by a specialist who had technical knowledge of the appropriate methods and also imbued activities with religious ceremony marks tribal weir construction and use as an economically important activity to the entire tribal membership.

Another telling fact is that the design of these weirs allowed for two lateral basket traps with a minimal diameter of six feet; a representative example of this part of the weir is illustrated in Figure 4.3. In addition to this, very large fish were considered potentially injurious to the successful operation of the weir, in that they could topple the structure. Thus it had to be overbuilt for this consideration.

The stick weir was commonly used in the mountain whitefish fishery of Priest Lake, Idaho. It differs from the brush weir apparently in response to adfluvial MW spawning behavior. The method was described as follows:

> When whitefish begin to run in the beginning of October, they [Kalispel families] gather again. A few built a weir across one of the mouths of the Pend Oreille River, about 150 feet across. It is a stick weir on real tripod foundations. The whitefish won't go into the basket trap and so [they] built a trap on the downstream side into

> which a hole leads. When there are enough inside they close the hole and spear them out. The pen was of sticks woven together; the bottoms are pushed into the mud and all holes at the bottom of the trap and along the weir are closed with rocks. The trap here was 12 feet in diameter; they were smaller for smaller creeks. The hole was about 6 inches square and was cut in the pen; it was closed with a piece of stick woven together which was slipped in. They spear the fish out from the shore and by walking out on the weir. There was no top to the pen but the sticks extended about 1 foot above the water, i.e. just as high as the weir. (Smith 1936–1938:364)

Spearfishing

A piece of personal gear typically used for three to four years until lost or replaced was the two-barbed fishing harpoon point called *sxO/l'/qn* (Smith 1936–1938:353). Fashioned from deer antler, this composite harpoon had a conical central shaft with parallel lateral tangs that were both wedge-shaped at the base of their hafting with the central shaft. The basal portions of the tangs were intentionally left rounded or blunted to facilitate fish capture, and the hafting was roughened to accommodate for sinew lashing. This harpoon was pressure fitted to a cedar pole 12 to 14 feet long (when in the context of platform fishing), and the head was also tied to this pole with a leader.

This harpoon was used in salmon, trout, northern pike minnow, and sucker fisheries. Although the cedar pole was often cached at a fishing site, the harpoon would always travel with its owner. The entire apparatus (including the pole) was called *Lu/mIn*. Combined with a torch, it formed an effective fishing technology in the Kalispel arsenal. During low flow periods in the local hydrocurve (see Figure 4.2) and when ice had not formed, fishermen would place a torch in the bow of their bark-hull canoes extending three to four feet over the water.

Smith recounts that two men, one paddling aft and the other manning the torch and spear, could bring in two canoe loads in a night, and it "was the most important method of fishing at this time of the year" (1936–1938:331–332). It bears mention that burbot's reproductive behavior during the later end of this window of opportunity made it a highly susceptible species for this form of fishing. This method was used to augment stored foods with a fresh catch.

Seine and Torchlight Fishing

Seine and torchlight fishing methods were used on Lake Pend Oreille specifically for BT and executed from canoes in close proximity to the Clark Fork Delta. The first accounts for one archaeological visible artifact type (i.e., net weight sinkers), whereas the other is unlikely to be differentiated from other forms of fishing in terms of its material record. Nighttime seining between two canoes occurred in the spring when there was an increase in inflows and an increase in sediment load. Why this was conducive to fishing, other than making the tributary mouths of streams entering the lake more navigable, is unclear. Primarily both methods caught "char," a vernacular name for BT in the 1930s; secondary to this catch was an unspecified trout species:

> Early at night, two canoes, one at each end of a big net (the size of which is unknown), would go out and move in and thus catch the fish. They moved up into the creek. The bottom was weighted down with stone sinkers. It was emptied on the shore. Probably they had floats in the center; and if they had them they would be of cedar. They get lots of fish in this way. They pull the net out onto the shore to empty it. Then they warm themselves at the big bonfire because they get wet and cold and they give the fish time to come in again. Then they do it again; they do it about 6 times on one night. They work all night. (Smith 1936–1938:367)

This particular harvest method was practiced within a two-week window sometime during the spring freshet. The task group comprised two to three men per canoe, and the catch was redistributed to the families back at a residential base camp, where it was consumed as an in-season staple (rather than smoke-cured and stored for winter provisioning).

In addition the ethnographic materials assert that this practice was only used in this vicinity and at that season of the year. Although they are not found ubiquitously throughout the watershed, the archaeological recovery of net weight sinkers from a surface context casts some doubt as to the absolute reliability of that caveat.

Later in the season, during the week of the new moon in September and as the lack of light allowed, the torchlight method was used just south of the Clark Fork Delta:

> They [a task group] sit on the rocks until they hear a little rustling noise, made by the tail probably or possibly by the fins or the movement of the whole body. Maybe they are spawning but they don't just know what they are doing there. The fins and part of the tail are out of the water and the fish are practically motionless: they wiggle only a little. There are never fewer than three fish.... Probably all the canoes of the encampment would be out there. Only one canoe would go out after each sound. This took place in a cove made by a basin, and the fish might be anywhere in here for one half of a mile along the shore and to 300 yards out from the shore.... When they got out to the noise, they would spear them with a wecC spear. There were three men in each canoe: one holds the torch in the middle of the canoe, one mans the canoe in the stern, and a spear man is in the bow. When they spear one fish in the water they get the fish off and spear another and in the same way get still a third; for the fish, when they are disturbed they sink slowly and go horizontally and do not dive. So they can spear 3 or 4 before the others are out of sight. And then they return to the shore and put the torch out and wait again for the noise. The various canoes would be 300 to 400 yards apart so the noise of one would not interfere with the others. (Smith 1936–1938:371–372)

The account tells that at the end of each night's fishing the catch was redistributed among the families back at the residential base camp. The notes are mute as to if this catch was an in-season or winter-over store, but inferring from the season to which the behaviors are attributed (fall), these activities suggest that this fishery was for winter stores.

Summary of Fishing Methods

The wealth of ethnographic data pertaining to historic Kalispel fishing behaviors falsifies the notion that the absence of salmon in the Pend Oreille is a sufficient condition to "class" their settlement and subsistence patterns as different from those of their contemporaries. Differences certainly existed in their larders but not in terms of their residency patterns, task grouping, harvest schedules, or technological capabilities. In fact, the examination of ethnohistoric fishing practices indicates very few probative differences that can be recognized archaeologically.

Furthermore, despite its many merits, the ethnographic record is frustratingly vague in terms of specific fish yields or indeed species targeted, particularly with regard to modern efforts to restore bull trout as a viable species in these waters. I have previously argued (Lyons 2002) that the brush weirs of the Lower Pend Oreille River were used to catch bull trout; the logic of that position is as follows: The economic activity was a corporate duty, its output was equally redistributed, it occurred in late summer, and the target catch was a "spotted" trout that was spawning at that time of the year. Furthermore, the technology was designed to catch large and vigorous specimens.

These individual threads collectively point to only one species native to these waters, and that is bull trout. As the seasonal flood abated in the valley (see Figure 4.2) and ambient air temperatures rose in late summer, these temperature-sensitive fish migrated out of the main stem of the river back into their cold-water natal creeks. Many of these tributaries transected one of the most productive root grounds within the interior Pacific Northwest, where resident and visiting Indian bands were already engaged in family provisioning tasks—namely, root digging.

What remains for archaeological science is confirmation of this oral history with an eye to its historic variations and ramifications for hunter-gatherer adaptation strategies. The prehistory of the Columbia Plateau is replete with numerous climatic changes that have impacted the reliability and abundance of key resources. Locally, bull trout, large fish with very narrow habitat requirements, are an important indicator species of watershed health and a subtle gauge of hunter-gatherer predation patterns. As the necessary habitat conditions of bull trout deteriorated through time, what other resources would be available to dependent human populations? If the resource was stable and hunter-gatherer subsistence technologies and/or efficiencies improved, then how would the hunter-gatherer prey spectrum broaden? These are among the midrange theory research questions that immediately come to mind from this recounting of oral traditions.

Archaeological Expectations and Observations

At present there are two forms of archaeological evidence confirming prehistoric fishing within the valley: site placement and artifact recovery. Generally, the former is open to debate without the supporting evidence of the latter. In a local case where a traditional trout weir fishery is known to have been placed (Lyons 2001), the "ground truth" of this history presents as a series of fire-cracked rock couplets on either side of the tributary creek outlet. Rather than being located at precisely one spot within the wetted margins of the creek's flanks, these couplets appear to have followed the annual variation of the hydrologic curve, resulting in multiple parallel activity areas that used fire features.

Testing these sites' economic functions and their antiquity, and if indeed they were related to fishing, is still pending—yet a number of fishing-related activities suggest themselves. If the multiple fire-cracked rock scatters on the littoral margins of the creek represent fishing stations that moved from season to season relative to the hydrologic curve, they should have a homogeneous assemblage of tools and waste categories dominated by generalized and expedient tool forms. Additionally, smoke-curing seasonal surplus was ethnographically the preferred method for postcatch treatment—such smoky, low-temperature fires would provide some relief from the insect clouds attracted to the gut piles no doubt present at the fishing station; yet they do not explain the presence of fire-cracked rock at these locations, as boiling or roasting features are not needed for smoke-curing fish.

Broadly, the material record of fishing may consist of four artifact types as well as the faunal record. The artifacts less likely to be disputed as fishing-related tools, or their elements, are worked bone (specifically spatulated and/or incised), bilaterally notched tabular cobbles commonly called fishnet sinkers, tabular knives (an expedient butchery tool), and the problematic case of girdled stone. This last tool form (Figure 4.4) has been typed as "mauls" and alternately as "set-weights," and there is a credible case for either interpretation. In the argument for mauls, heavy bipolar pecking is often but not always evident and is clearly associated with repeated and heavy pounding actions. Also, these artifacts are found within residential or in near proximity to assumed residential encampments. Although it is not universally the case, a significant fraction of the girdled stones of the Pend Oreille Valley have a highly ground and polished "waist" that has been crafted for hafting.

The case for "set-weights" is more a form-follows-function argument that does not account for the bipolar pecking observed on those pieces classed as mauls and is most defensible when specimens lack heavy bipolar pecking wear. Based on the ethnographic description, a set-weight should

FIGURE 4.4. Girdle stone: maul/set-weight anchor.

be found within or near a residential camp; in fact the occupants of semipermanent encampments likely treated such objects as camp furniture, given their daily use. Similarly these objects could have been classed as canoe gear when out on a foraging trip. In some cases, particularly large specimens (far too large for the purposes of a handheld maul) have been classed as canoe anchors (Miss 2001:84; Figure 4.5).

In our emerging classificatory schema we still have work to do in resolving these interpretive disparities and negating some of the contextual/subjective interpretations that still persist in artifact analysis. If indeed these objects were set-weights, then their relative mass (one example being 1.6 kilograms [Miss 2001:84]) is substantial and indicative of catching big fish—and thus consistent with rational provisioning behaviors.

Discussion

Ultimately, current lines of evidence for fishing in the form of tools (such as net sinkers, pictured in Figure 4.6) and faunal remains will always lack the probative weight to compel the restoration of endangered species' habitats on their singular merits. The limited data sets that cultural resource management provides are at best supporting contextual evidence for ongoing industrial and intergovernment negotiations over the biodiversity and biodensity of the western North American river systems. Although

FIGURE 4.5. Girdle stone: canoe anchor.

I am mindful of archaeology's political and pragmatic limitations, I hold great optimism in the development of paleo-DNA studies. Protein residue analysis is presently within the grasp of the modern archaeological arsenal, but we still cannot differentiate salmon from trout blood proteins; if this could be corrected, it follows that if blood proteins persist on butchery tools, then the propagation of prehistoric DNA from tools derived from dated contexts holds considerably superior potential to simple presence/absence analyses of blood protein assays.

Contemporary fishery biology is heavily invested in mapping the historic spatial distribution of native trout species throughout the Columbia Basin. With modest effort on the part of archaeology we could add considerably more depth to these studies, which would lend the political and pragmatic weight necessary in multibillion-dollar restoration efforts currently being debated.

Acknowledgments

Not a noun or verb above would have been possible without the gracious allowances provided to me by the Kalispel Tribe of Indians Business Council, its leadership, and the support that I have received from the Kalispel community. In these ten-plus years I have been given much by my dear friend Alice Ignace, now no longer among us, but her lessons and those of the generations of Elders before her still carry on in the efforts of this community: tell truth and work hard. These

FIGURE 4.6. Bilaterally notched tabular cobbles: fishnet/fishline sinkers.

values and directions continue on among the dedicated women and men of the Kalispel Natural Resources Department, who actively seek many ways of bringing these first foods back from the brink and through those efforts ensure that the purposes of the little reservation between the mountains and the river continue to be met: to provide a homeland filled with opportunity and free from want.

Notes

1. I assume from precedence that this was a maximum annual individual take rather than a daily take; regrettably the primary citation is unclear as to this fact.
2. At the interwatershed scale the terminal spawning period of BT and the spawning window for MW do overlap, yet locally, particularly in the Lower Pend Oreille Valley, BT migrate out of the main stem very rapidly when peak flows within the river abate and ambient air temperatures are at their seasonal highs.
3. It is the seasonality of this fish behavior that was important for hunter-gatherer risk/reward analysis.
4. Smith (1936–1938:350) recounts a rainbow trout fishery in the Priest River basin, but the scarcity of this resource indicates to me and several fishery biologists that this may well be a case of misidentification on Smith's part and is generally discounted by modern fishery biologists.
5. Despite this sparse mention there are numerous incidental comments about how these species were incidentally caught and processed.
6. This was a common phrase in local sweat lodge prayers describing the Kalispel Indian Reservation (Lyons 1999–2008).
7. At the time of this writing a fourth locality had been identified within the lower

valley with the use of high-resolution air photography coupled with a lidar data set.

8. Confirmation of Smith's Salish orthography, identification of lexical roots, and relationship to cognate Salish languages has not yet been completed, thus the place-names presented herein are tentative but fair approximations of the lexemes (words) that were and are recognizable to competent Kalispel Salish speakers.
9. Burbot (*Lota lota*), often cited as a native to these waters, exhibits both an artificial distribution and a copious "planted" record from the mid–19th century and if availed of by the Kalispel, was a late historic adaptation to changes in the local fish ecology.

References Cited

Binford, L. R.

2001 *Constructing Frames of Reference: An Analytical Method for Archaeological Theory Building Using Ethnographic and Environmental Data Sets.* Berkeley: University of California Press.

Chance, D. H.

1993 *Cabins in Clearings: Homesteading in the Pend Oreille Country of Washington.* Moscow, ID: David and Jennifer Chance and Associates.

Connor, J. M.

2010 Pend Oreille River Fisheries Management: The Past, Pike, and Future. Paper presented at the Lake Roosevelt Forum 2010 Conference, Spokane.

Fisherman Review

2010 Trophy Record for Bull Trout. Electronic document, http://www.Fishermanreview.com, accessed May 15, 2010.

Fraley, J. J., and B. B. Shepard

1989 Life History, Ecology, and Population Status of Migratory Bull Trout (*Salvelinus confluentus*) in the Flathead Lake and River System, Montana. *Northwest Science* 63:133–143.

Goetz, F.

1989 *Biology of the Bull Trout* Salvelinus confluentus*: A Literature Review.* Eugene: Willamette National Forest.

Holton, G. D.

2003 *A Field Guide to Montana Fishes.* Helena: Montana Department of Fish, Wildlife and Parks.

Lyons, K. J.

1999–2008 Kalispel Ethnographic Field Notes. Unpublished MS on file at the Kalispel Natural Resources Department, Kalispel Tribe of Indians, Usk, WA.

2001 *A Cultural Resources Inventory of the Pend Oreille County Public Utility District Number One's Bryant Property Acquisition, Pend Oreille County,*

Washington. Kalispel Natural Resources Department Reports on Cultural Resources no. 01-06. Usk, WA: Kalispel Tribe of Indians.

2002 *Kalispel Aboriginal Fisheries of the Lower Pend Oreille Watershed: Ethnographic Data Analysis Supporting the Presence and Use of Bull Trout by the Lower Kalispel Bands*. Usk, WA: Kalispel Natural Resources Department, Kalispel Tribe of Indians.

Miss, C. J.

2001 *Report of National Register of Historic Places Site Evaluations for the Albeni Falls Dam Reservoir Bonner County, Idaho*. Seattle: Northwest Archaeological Associates Inc.

Northrop, Devine, and Tarbell, Inc.

1996 *History of the Diking Districts of Pend Oreille County (Draft Report)*. Bothell, WA: Northrop, Devine, and Tarbell, Inc.

Pratt, K. L.

1992 A Review of Bull Trout Life History. In *Proceedings of the Gearhart Mountain Bull Trout Workshop*. P. J. Howell and D. V. Buchanan, eds. Pp. 5–9. Corvallis: Oregon Chapter of the American Fisheries Society.

Rieman, B. E., D. C. Lee, and R. F. Thurow

1997 Distribution, Status, and Likely Future Trends of Bull Trout within the Columbia River and Klamath Basins. *North American Journal of Fisheries Management* 17:1111–1125.

Rieman, B. E., and J. D. McIntyre

1993 *Demographic and Habitat Requirements for Conservation of Bull Trout*. U.S. Department of Agriculture Forest Service, General Technical Report INT-302. Washington, DC.

Scholz, A. T., and H. J. McLellan

2009 *Field Guide to the Fishes of Eastern Washington*. Cheney, WA: Eagle Printing.

Sims, C.

1999 *Archaeological Excavations at Priest Lake, Idaho*. Coeur d'Alene: Panhandle National Forest, U.S. Forest Service.

Smith, A. H.

1936–1938 Kalispel Ethnographic Field Notes. Lewis Clark State College Archives, Lewiston, ID.

Stasiak, R. H.

2006 *Lake Chub (*Couesius plumbeus*): A Technical Conservation Assessment*. Golden, CO: U.S. Department of Agriculture Forest Service, Rocky Mountain Region, Species Conservation Project.

U.S. Fish and Wildlife Service

2002 Introduction. In *Bull Trout (*Salvelinus confluentus*) Draft Recovery Plan*. Pp. 1–137. Portland, OR: U.S. Fish and Wildlife Service, U.S. Department of the Interior.

Intensification of Secondary Resources along the Lower Spokane River and the Role of *Margaritifera falcata*, the Western Pearlshell

JASON M. JONES

Readily emphasized in the wealth of ethnographic and archaeological literature of the Columbia Plateau is the importance of riverine resources to semisedentary populations. Both permanent and temporary villages were constructed in proximity to procurement areas along the Columbia River and its tributaries, commonly at river rapids. Accounts of traditional fishing practices shed light on the variety of devices and adaptable technologies employed in the harvest of aquatic resources. A primary resource of such harvests was salmon, whose migration pattern is relatively dependable and which are vulnerable to capture in the streams where they breed, including the Spokane River.

The ethnographic literature supports the collection of freshwater mussels, in addition to fish species, for sustenance by the indigenous Spokane people. The archaeological record substantiates their importance, as shell midden deposits are still evident on the Spokane River and are typically located where traditional fishing villages once were. Beds of freshwater mussel species were exploited throughout the year but primarily during the late spring through fall, also a usual time frame for the harvest of local anadromous fish species. The seasonal exploitations of salmon and freshwater mussels do not appear to have been mutually exclusive.

Rapids and falls were the most common places for indigenous Spokane populations to employ their extensive repertory of fishing strategies.

The western pearlshell's habitation preference is the natural rapids of rivers and streams. Focused fishing at rapids enabled indigenous peoples to efficiently procure another important food: freshwater mussels, whose nutritive values greatly outweigh the cost of their harvest, while situated within a habitat ecologically perfect to take advantage of the migratory fish. The following explores the importance of a specific freshwater mussel, the western pearlshell, to traditional Spokane groups inhabiting the Lower Spokane River.

The Western Pearlshell as a Resource: Habitat and Life History Characteristics

The western pearlshell (*Margaritifera falcata*) is found in Pacific drainages from California to British Columbia and southern Alaska and east to western Montana and northern Utah (Ross 1969:31). Their primary habitat is the location of natural riffles in the river system. A riffle occurs in a shallow stretch of river or stream where the current is above the average stream velocity and where the water forms small rippled waves as a result. It often consists of a rocky bed of gravels or other small stones. This portion of a stream is often an important habitat for small aquatic invertebrates, freshwater mussels, and juvenile fish (Chasse 2007; Nedeau et al. 2009).

In ideal ecological habitats western pearlshell can "attain very high densities (>300 per square yard)" (Nedeau et al. 2009:34). Empirical evidence suggests that this mussel prefers cold and clean creeks and rivers and most importantly, those streams that support salmonid populations. *Margaritifera* prefer gravelly streambeds. This is in contrast to different genera such as *Gonidea* and *Anodonta,* which prefer the muddy bottoms of Columbia Basin streams and lakes (Lyman 1980; Nedeau et al. 2009).

The ultimate western pearlshell beds are those where large boulders can weather from rock outcrops and enter the stream system. These boulders can enhance the riffles and act as protectants for mussels to shelter behind. Western pearlshell are absent from deep pools except in instances where there are large boulders in the riffles, which stabilize the substrate and enhance the growth of the mussels. These locations are habitats for large populations of the western pearlshell and are "crucial for long term recruitment... in areas where there is periodic scour" (Vannote and Minshall 1982:4105). In addition, studies of western pearlshell populations indicate that a downriver gradient may be a preferred characteristic of beds containing larger individuals. Moreover, these mussels are best suited for streams that drain mountains of granitic bedrock with little to no deposits of lime (Murphy 1942:90; Vannote and Minshall 1982).

Although some species of freshwater mussel have separate sexes, hermaphrodites exist in certain North American species, including western pearlshell (Nedeau et al. 2009:3). *Margaritifera* can reproduce throughout their entire life span (Murphy 1942:95). During early spring, eggs of the western pearlshell begin to develop in female or hermaphroditic mussels. The eggs pass from the ovaries of the parent into the gill chambers. The development of the embryo takes place there, where they transform into tiny bivalve organisms. The tiny bivalve is discharged from the parent upon complete development, but it must find a host to survive. More specifically, nearly all species of freshwater mussel require a host during the beginning stages of their life cycle. Hosts are usually fish species, and as larva, the tiny mussels situate themselves on the gills of host fish for dispersal to a suitable habitat (Murphy 1942:89). These larvae, termed *glochidia,* are "external parasites of fish that clamp onto fins or gill filaments" (Nedeau et al. 2009:4).

More specifically, "the glochidium (larval stage) of the pelecypod [bivalve] attaches itself to the trout [host]. After embedding itself in the trout in the form of a cyst, the glochidium becomes parasitic and remains so until the young adult forms" (Ross 1969:31). Glochidia must attach to a suitable host soon after being released into the stream. If one does not, it dies in the streambed or in the stream current (Murphy 1942:94). During this attachment period, particular species of fish (i.e., migratory species) may swim multiple miles from the location where they encountered the glochidia. This can contribute to a mussel's dispersal within a stream (Nedeau et al. 2009:5).

Once the mussels find a host and are carried to a suitable habitat, they root themselves into the sediments. During their lives they may move only a few yards from the spot where they first landed. Consequentially, mussel beds are maintained over centuries in prime habitats such as in or near the aforementioned riffles (Nedeau et al. 2009:5–6).

Only a small portion of the glochidia survive. Yet, once mature, some species of freshwater mussels can live longer than 100 years. *Margaritifera falcata* and the closely related *M. margaritifera* are the longest-lived freshwater mussel species and also among the longest-lived animal species on earth (Nedeau et al. 2009:6). The largest shell hinge ever recorded for *M. falcata* was 16.2 centimeters in length. Scientific analysis indicates that hinges ≥11 centimeters in length range in age from 60 to 100 years old (Vannote and Minshall 1982:4104). As a result of their impressive life span, *Margaritifera* species retain nutrients and minerals for a very long time (Nedeau et al. 2009:7).

Western pearlshell were important to the traditional Spokane people but also to the ecology of the Spokane River. Mussels are very essential to "food webs, water quality, nutrient cycling, and habitat quality in freshwater ecosystems" and can filter bacteria and algae as well as zooplankton and sediment from the water (Nedeau et al. 2009:7). As the mussels eat through filtration, a portion of the digested material is laid down onto the riverbed. This digested material is food to other riverine invertebrates, and the mussels themselves feed riverine mammals such as otters and minks (Tennant 2010:8–9).

Prior to reservoir development, common hosts for western pearlshell in the Northwest were particular species of trout and salmon, including cutthroat trout, rainbow trout, Chinook salmon, Coho salmon, redband trout, sockeye salmon, steelhead trout, brook trout, and brown trout (Nedeau et al. 2009:33). The presence of the western pearlshell in a stream indicates that representatives of these fish species inhabited the same waterway (Ross 1969:31). Since mussels rely on fish to reproduce and replenish populations, changes in host populations concomitantly threaten the western pearlshell (Nedeau et al. 2009:1). These simple little creatures, only about three inches long on average, are the lungs of the river. They breathe in particulate matter, dissolved pesticides from upriver agriculture, and liver toxins borne of the algae produced in man-made reservoirs and breathe out pure clean water, the kind that salmon and sturgeon cannot do without (Tennant 2010:8).

The Spokane River

The Spokane River measures approximately 110 miles in length and is a tributary of the Columbia River. The Spokane headwaters drain the northern portion of Lake Coeur d'Alene in northern Idaho (post-dam elevation 1,994 feet above mean sea level [amsl]). The Spokane River then flows west through the city of Spokane in eastern Washington to its discharge into the Columbia River (post-dam elevation 1,293 feet amsl). It is recharged just

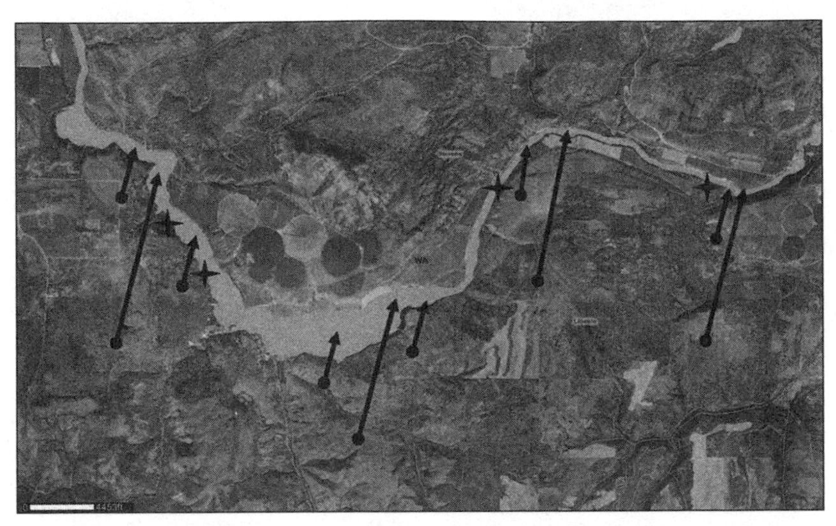

FIGURE 5.1. Stretch of the Spokane River of interest to the study. Long arrows = riffles in the river that are still visible today, primarily during the drawdown of the reservoir; short arrows = natural shoals, which are the ethnographic locations of mussel beds; stars = archaeological sites discussed in the study: right (upstream) to left (downstream) = 204, 219, 412, 401 (map adapted from U.S. Department of Agriculture 2007).

west of the Idaho–Washington state line by the Spokane Valley–Rathdrum Prairie Aquifer, and its current average annual temperature is 53 degrees Fahrenheit (Northwest Power and Conservation Council [NPCC] 2012).

The Spokane River has three major tributaries located in the middle to lower part of the river valley. Currently there are seven hydroelectric developments along the length of the river, which have impeded its natural flow, temperature, and ecology. The lower 29 miles of the Spokane River are known as the Spokane Arm of Lake Roosevelt, a portion of the reservoir created with the construction of Grand Coulee Dam. Not only is this impoundment an obstacle to salmonid migrations, but hydroelectric development has been linked to decreased numbers of freshwater mussels and in most cases complete destruction of the population (Bogan 1993).

The upper ten-river-mile stretch of the Spokane Arm of Lake Roosevelt is the area pertinent to this discussion (Figure 5.1). In this stretch the pre-dam river elevation is at a gradient, east to west, from 1,265 to 1,235 feet amsl (U.S. Geological Survey 1915). Most of this ten-mile stretch remains moderately turbulent, regardless of the impoundment from Grand Coulee Dam (Jones 2012).

TABLE 5.1. Characteristics of *Margaritifera falcata* Habitat and the Spokane River.

Favorable Conditions for *M. falcata*	Original Spokane River Conditions
Cold, clean creek	√
Gravel bottom	√
Gradient or incline	√
Large boulders present in the river	√
Natural riffles	√
Granitic highlands/mountains	√
Presence of salmonid populations	√

Note: Checkmark = present in the ten-mile stretch discussed in this chapter.

It is important to note that although the dam at Grand Coulee impacts this ten-mile stretch of the Spokane River, this upper portion of the reservoir remains narrow, moderately shallow, and reminiscent of its original appearance prior to dam development. These characteristics make it unique versus the remainder of the Spokane Arm and the Lake Roosevelt reservoir in general (Jones 2012). At least four locations of increased turbidity—riffles—are known in this stretch, and at least two large rock outcroppings important to traditional Spokane people are present; one of these riffles may be artificial (Jones 2012). These riffles were primary locations for fish traps, the placement of weirs, and spearfishing (Ray 1933; Ross 1993, 1995) and based on geomorphology, highly suitable for *Margaritifera falcata* (Table 5.1).

Traditional Cultural Context

The traditional cultural setting for the Spokane River shares a number of similarities with much of the Upper Columbia River region. It was centered on a subsistence pattern dependent upon the seasonal succession of resources, which included identified game animals, fish, and a wide assortment of plants. These economic activities were extensive and complex prior to non-Indian settlement. The traditional annual economic cycle was composed of two primary phases: winter life along the major river systems and summers spent on the plateaus and higher ground in search of productive resource areas for roots, medicines, and berries. Interspersed were visits to the river fisheries for the major anadromous fish runs (Hunn 1990).

Historically the Spokane River was a salmon river, and the Spokane Tribe of Indians was a salmon-fishing tribe. Well into the historical period the diet of the Spokane people was largely dependent upon salmon. Before hydroelectric development, "at least five species of fish went up the [Spokane] river—summer Chinook; fall, winter, and spring steelhead; Coho, and a small silver fish that could have been sockeye or mountain whitefish" (NPCC 2012). Additionally, species of trout, lamprey, sucker, and sturgeon were also available. Some of the largest salmon ever caught in the Columbia Basin were fall Chinooks from the Spokane River (NPCC 2012; Ross 1995:72, 83–90).

Spokane groups would commence food-gathering activities in the early spring. By early April it was common to gather freshwater mussels, and men, women, children, and the elderly were known to participate (Erlandson 1988; Ross 1995:60). Ray (1933) notes that traditional peoples in the general area of the Lower Spokane River valley exploited the freshwater mussel year-round, and the Spokane specifically "claim that they gathered river mussels from mostly during the late spring through fall, but also frequently during the winter" (Ross 1995:73). When wading was not an option, mussels were often collected "with a forked stick through holes in the ice" (Post 1938:29).

The Spokane people had designated camping sites for freshwater mussels, known as "clamming sites." Note, the traditional terminology of the Spokane people for freshwater mussels is historically and ethnographically interchangeable among *clam*, *mussel*, and *oyster* (Spokane Tribal Elder Ann McCrea, personal communication, June 2010–January 2012; see also Ross 1993, 1995). Prior to reservoir development, shell midden deposits (see Figure 5.2, for example) were nearly one meter thick for several hundred meters along the portion of the Lower Spokane River discussed here. Spokane people baked, boiled, or steamed the mussels, and some groups dried and traded them (Ross 1993, 1995:73–74; Spinden 1908:36).

The western pearlshell was useful to prehistoric people for food, technology, and trade: "This mollusk provided a possible source of protein and decorative or useful shell" (Ross 1969:31). Recent studies have indicated that minimal energy is required for gathering freshwater mussels,

FIGURE 5.2. Example of a shell midden feature uncovered during the 2006 excavation at Site 204.

especially in areas of high densities (locations of natural beds, for example). Although there is "but a minimal, edible portion of the creature, their harvest still weighs heavier for positive consequences" (Glassow and Wilcoxon 1988:36).

Shellfish resources may have supplied subsistence needs comparable to the protein-rich fish and game, and the latter reasonably involved relatively higher efforts. Studies have estimated that there is 4.26 to 9.06 grams of edible meat per mussel (Glassow and Wilcoxon 1988:42), and approximately 40 grams of protein was likely the necessary minimum per individual per day (Erlandson 1988:103). These data indicate that individuals could obtain their daily protein needs with the consumption of only four to ten freshwater mussels, which may only take minutes to collect at a high-density mussel bed. As noted, this easy-to-procure resource also did not require complex processing.

Spokane tribal Elders support the idea that the shells were used as soup spoons and for scraping small hides (McCrea, personal communication, December 2011). Along with some imported shell (dentalium, for example), *Margaritifera falcata* were fashioned into beads and have been found with human remains in the Spokane River valley and along the Middle Columbia River (Ross 1969; Ross 1993). Shell middens made by prehistoric Native Americans in the Columbia Plateau indicate that western pearlshell was harvested as early as 9,500 years ago (Nedeau et al. 2009:9) and as late as the 1890s (Ross 1993:2035).

Another important factor in this foodstuff pursuit is that the tools needed to process shellfish are minimal. Therefore it is expected that at optimal processing localities, a minimal diversity in tool assemblages and limited quantitative inventories will be common. During the Chief Joseph Dam Cultural Resource Project on the Columbia River, the most common deposits at sites with shellfish remains were hide-preparation tools, signifying winter habitation. This supports the finding that at spring and summer camps little besides the shellfish refuse is common, similar to archaeological contexts of sites along the upper ten miles of the Spokane Arm (Campbell 1985; Glassow and Wilcoxin 1988; Lohse 1985:125; Ross 1993).

Goals of Discussion

The remainder of this chapter will introduce interpretive data gathered during recent archaeological investigations within a select reach along the Lower Spokane River. The goal of this study is to demonstrate that traditional subsistence was more complex and diverse than salmon-and-roots stereotypes and the western pearlshell was a common food source for traditional Spokane populations. This has interesting implications for understanding the Late period incorporation of mussels into the diet and the transformation in which an ever more diverse suite of river resources was comprehended, incorporated, and maximized by the people of the Spokane River.

Each of the areas discussed in this chapter contains valuable archaeological deposits. As it is common for fish remains to be absent in the archaeological record, and since much of the fishing tool kit was constructed from animal bone and other carbon-based materials, the preservation of fish remains or fishing equipment is poor in the study area. However, artifacts such as net sinkers provide indirect evidence of the fishing technology, and by the same token western pearlshell midden features provide evidence of their harvest by indigenous people. In several instances during surface inventory of sites in this ten-mile stretch, I noted notched pebbles in the shell middens. Notched pebbles are locally designated as net weights or net sinkers; these net weights/sinkers are ubiquitous along certain stretches of the Spokane River, from downtown Spokane west to its confluence with the pre-dam Columbia River (Jones 2012). The presence of these implements *within* a midden provides great support to the notion of the freshwater mussel being collected during the habitation and use of important fishing grounds.

The four archaeological sites discussed below are representative of the aforementioned "clamming sites." This stretch of the Spokane River system is remarkable in that it contains some of the richest mussel beds within the Spokane River valley. In addition to the four archaeological sites, 29 ethnographic locations in this ten-mile stretch are representative of shell-processing locations (Ross 1993).

During the test excavations at the four precontact sites discussed in this chapter at least one cooking feature was discovered along with western pearlshell midden features. Data for both the on-site cooking features and shell midden features are important to this discussion. A comparative analysis of these features appears to indicate variability in the preparation of the western pearlshell. In general, the midden features are characterized by being small and thin, representative of individual meals of relatively simple strategy. They are different from coastal shell middens that are much larger and represent evidence of long-term, focused areas for shellfish processing. The shell midden deposits in the study area are a common occurrence but are most dense at the locations of rapids and riffles in the original stream.

Overview of the Archaeological Sites

This summary of site and feature information is used to demonstrate diversity in and adaptation of strategy for the processing of western pearlshell based primarily on cooking feature morphology. It is possible that, through time, Spokane populations adjusted to climatic variation by using alternative means of meeting subsistence needs; yet it appears that, based on the study sample, this mussel was a common staple over several thousand years. Most of the sites discussed in this chapter date to within or near the transition into the Chief Joseph Dam Cultural Resource Project's Coyote Creek phase (ca. 150–2,000 years before the present). The criteria used in selecting sites for this discussion were (1) rich *Margaritifera falcata* midden deposits exposed on and below the surface, (2) the demonstrated subsurface integrity of features, (3) readily comparable data based on the spatial proximity of sites, and (4) the consistent fieldwork techniques and strategy I employed.

It is understood that shell midden deposits may represent remnants from natural predators such as river otters and other rodents, yet it is certain that the shell middens discussed here are cultural based on their relative association with definitive cultural deposits. The interesting thing is the minimal volume of sediment excavated relative to the number of mussel-related discoveries. Although a limited number of excavation units and shovel test probes were used, intact midden and cooking features were found each time.

Finally, in reference to differential preservation techniques, it should be stated that heavy deposits of *Margaritifera falcata* are not ubiquitous along *all* banks of the Spokane River. In some places where they were expected, none were found (see Jones 2009). Since the shells are typically better preserved than other foodstuff remains (State Government of Victoria 2008), and shellfish were typically consumed near the area where they were collected (Stevens 2000:73), the lack of shell middens just outside the bounds of this river stretch further supports that it was indeed a specialized "clamming" location.

Although an overview of the data is presented in tabular form (see Tables 5.2, 5.3), it is beneficial to provide a brief discussion of each site. This information supports observations made during fieldwork in reference to the processing of *Margaritifera falcata*. While the sites exist in a relatively homogeneous geographic corridor and the qualitative data regarding artifact assemblages are comparable, there are some differences in site features. The variance in cooking feature morphology for a single resource type may indicate (1) a certain technological stage of a people, (2) a specific food-preparation method, (3) the preparation of a specific food, or (4) the season of occupation. Therefore, the dynamic characteristics of shell features offered here may signify the adaptive strength of the Native people.

This study arose from my work conducted with the Spokane Tribe of Indians (STI) on Lake Roosevelt between spring 2006 and fall 2011. As the STI desire to maintain confidentiality for site data on their reservation, only National Park Service site information is discussed here. All locational and sensitive information is intentionally redacted. General information was derived through several years of research with the STI and personal consultation with knowledgeable STI members and Elders fluent in the traditional Spokan(e) dialect of Interior Salish. These individuals deserve

TABLE 5.2. Summary of Select Site Data.

Site No.	Site Type	Year of Phase II Investigation (Reference)	Approximate Feature Elevation (ft amsl)	Approximate Original River Elevation (ft amsl)	Midden Feature Thickness (cm)	Midden Feature Hinge Size (cm)[a]	Midden Feature Depth below Surface (cm)
204	Village	2006 (Jones 2006a)	1,290	1,265	10	5–7	38–48
219	Fishing station	2009 (Jones 2010)	1,290	1,262	5	6–7	70–75
401	Camp	2007 (Jones 2008)	1,290	1,235	14	10–11	30–44
401	Camp	2007 (Jones 2008)	1,290	1,235	5	8–9	35–40
412	Camp	2011 (Jones 2011)	1,240	1,235	14	Both 4–6 and 8–9	4–18
412	Camp	2011 (Jones 2011)	1,240	1,235	6	6–7	37–43

Note: All features were intact; per site, cooking and midden features included in the same row were found at similar elevations and in similar matrix with comparable ground cover (the slight variance in 204 feature depth may be representative of the cooking element's discovery in the floor of the house pit), reasonably signifying their temporal relation. FCR = fire-cracked rock.

[a] Both valves present (size of shells in the middens may be indicative of the intensity of resource exploitation at a given time, since small shells in middens would indicate that traditional groups were not

Midden Feature	Cooking Feature					
Associated Artifacts[b]	Type	Depth below Surface (cm)	Distance to Shell Feature (m)[c]	Associated Artifacts	Radio-carbon Dates (BP)[d]	Possible On-Site Processing Method(s)
33 FCR	Shallow oven	Contained within 22–42	180	Biface fragments, debitage, 330 faunal bone fragments, shell, FCR	None	Surface fire, shallow pit roasting
12 FCR	Multiuse hearth	Contained within 12–40	15	Flaked tools and debitage, pebble tool, faunal bone, shell, FCR	150 ± 40, 270 ± 40	Surface fire, stone boiling
1 flake, 3 bone fragments, 11 FCR	Oven lid	Contained within 24–30	35	Flakes, shell, FCR	Midden: 1420 ± 40	Baking, steaming
	Intact baking oven	Contained within 80–96	35	Flakes, biface, FCR	2510 ± 40	
1 flake, 1 modified flake, 7 FCR	Oven lid	Contained within 24–30	30	Flakes, biface, FCR	Midden was not radiocarbon dated	Baking, steaming
	Intact baking oven	Contained within 80–96	30			
1 flake tool, 2 spent cores, 13 flakes, 3 bifaces, 251 FCR, faunal material	Hearth	Contained within 4–18	Immediate	Directly associated with midden	Hearth and midden: 2540 ± 30	Surface fire, stone boiling
3 FCR	None found to be in association in 2011			—	Midden: 4480 ± 30	Surface fire, stone boiling

allowing the creatures to grow [per Lyman 1980]); all horizontal feature dimensions are unknown, as each was discovered during limited test excavations.

[b] "What is in the midden is direct evidence of contemporary behavior at each site" (Wessen 1982).

[c] All cooking features contained only specimens of *Margaritifera falcata*.

[d] Conventional radiocarbon from charred material (except the 4480 ± 30 BP date, from acid etch, shell).

TABLE 5.3. Site Artifact Assemblages.

Lithic Artifact[a]	Site 204 (6.14 m³ of Excavated Sediment)	Site 219 (9.65 m³ of Excavated Sediment)	Site 401 (13.07 m³ of Excavated Sediment)	Site 412 (9.2 m³ of Excavated Sediment)
Debitage count	485	229	254	69
Bifaces	2	10	5	8
Unifaces	1	8	2	2
Net weights	6	1		0
Ground stones	1	1	1	0
Expedients (cobble/ pebble tools)	6	8	0	1
Projectile points[b]	16	7	1	2
Tabular knives	0	1	1	1
Cores	1	1	1	4
Flake tools	0	6	5	10
Cooking stones[c]	0	2	0	3

Note: Sediment volume shown here includes shovel test probes and test units.

[a] Does not include fire-cracked rock or miscellaneous subsistence refuse.

[b] Projectile points discovered as a result of these four excavations indicate that a wide range of typologies is present at "clamming sites" on the Spokane Arm of the reservoir: Plateau side-notched and basal-notched relative to the Coyote Creek phase of the last 1,500 years (per Lohse's [1985:347] sequence); corner-removed types comparable to points found near Kettle Falls representing the Sinaikst period (600–1,700 years before the present) (per Chance and Chance 1985; Roulette et al. 2000:32); Columbia corner-notched type B of the last 2,000 years (Lohse 1985:351); Rabbit Island Stemmed type B, confined to the latter part of the Hudnut cultural sequence (approximately 3,000 years before the present) but occurring in the early Coyote Creek phase (1,500 years before the present) (Lohse 1985:349); Cascade C variety, extending from 8,000 to 4,000 years before the present (Lohse 1985:345); Columbia stemmed type B, which is confined to the Coyote Creek phase of the last 2,000 years (Lohse 1985:354); and Columbia Corner-notched A (ca. 2,000–4,000 years before the present).

[c] Signifies "stone boiling" as an on-site food-preparation method.

acknowledgment, and their assistance was crucial to the development of this document.

All pertinent feature information has been included in tabular form (Table 5.2). All shell midden features had both valves represented and included only *Margaritifera falcata*. A majority of the valves were complete and available for measurement. This is important since the size of each valve may be indicative of the intensity of resource exploitation at a given time. More specifically, small shells may indicate overexploitation since groups were not allowing the creatures to grow and reestablish the mussel population (per Lyman 1980). In addition, Table 5.2 includes material found with the individual shell middens (e.g., fire-cracked rock) to support "contemporary behavior" at each site (per Wessen 1982).

Cooking and midden features included in the same row in Table 5.2 were found at similar elevations and in similar matrix with comparable ground cover, reasonably signifying their temporal relationship. The slight variance in Site 204 feature depth may be representative of its discovery in the floor of a house pit. Finally, all horizontal feature dimensions are unknown, as each was discovered during limited test excavations, and the conventional radiocarbon ages are from charred material. The only exception is the 4480 ± 30 BP date, which was collected from a shell acid etch.

The complete artifact assemblage at each of the four sites has been included for reference in Table 5.3. Projectile point data are significant, as it has been suggested that the Coyote Creek phase has the widest variety of projectile point forms (Lohse 1985:355). This is supported by feature data at the four sites discussed in this chapter. Projectile points are used in this discussion as time markers and indicators of hunting activity.

The artifact assemblages offer little evidence that a specific tool was always associated with the shell middens discussed below. However, it does appear that at the four "clamming sites," (1) expedient-type tools and flake tools (modified and utilized debitage) are more common, and (2) there are many fewer formed flaked- and ground-stone artifacts present.

Site 204

The expansive Site 204 is situated upon the first terrace above the floodplain of a small creek and contains at least 19 house pits (Larrabee and Kardas 1966). The site is approximately 1,500 meters west of the traditionally important Little Falls, a principal salmon-fishing village of the Spokane people and likely the most populous (Ray 1936:134–135). One shallow oven was found in the central portion of one partially excavated house pit at Site 204. This feature consisted of oxidized and charcoal-stained matrix with a mixture of intensively fragmented fire-cracked rock (Jones 2006a).

The number of projectile points, both incomplete and intact, coupled with the amount of processed bone and the shell midden (Figure 5.2), is a definitive indication that residents of this site, although close to a significant fishing ground, maintained steady procurement of complementary food resources. Although no radiocarbon samples were obtained, a relative chronology based on the projectile point assemblage suggests that the site was occupied between 2,000 and 200 years before the present (Jones 2006a). The discovery of mussel shell refuse intermingled with debitage and, more importantly, diagnostic projectile points during deep excavation is a good indication that freshwater mussels were consumed here for at least several thousand years (Jones 2006a).

Site 219

Site 219 is located at the base of a draw between two steep slopes, approximately one mile downriver from a second large salmon-fishing village (see Ray 1936). Site 219 is situated at a southerly bend in the river, which is increasingly turbulent, with steep cobble-laden terrace risers. This site may be best defined as a satellite location to a large residential base (or in the classification scheme for Lake Roosevelt, a short-term occupation camp [Site type 2 per Galm 1994:10.70; see also Jones 2010]).

The shell feature discovered at Site 219 is a good indicator of processing and associated consumption on-site. The small amount of refuse was not dumped into a prepared pit but, instead, onto the site's surface, which supports the notion of a small meal (Jones 2010). The associated hearth feature was vertically discontinuous within 28 centimeters. This hearth feature was interpreted as a surface cooking area used on at least two occasions, evident from two lenses of oxidation (Jones 2010). The discontinuous oxidation likely indicates a multiuse hearth as opposed to an oven (Stan Gough, personal communication, September 29, 2009).

Each defined cooking surface was estimated at 50 centimeters in diameter and composed of oxidation with black, greasy, charcoal-stained earth intermingled with fire-cracked rock and mussel shell fragments. It has been suggested that the bulk processing of edible plant foods necessitated large cooking features (1.5–3.0 meters in diameter), while cooking/heating features approximately 50 centimeters in diameter were constructed for the preparation of shellfish (Thoms 1998).

The presence of cooking stones (see Table 5.3) may support stone boiling (water would be placed in woven baskets and the hot stone would be placed inside). All data suggest the expedient preparation of the western pearlshell, either directly on the ground surface or by boiling, on two occasions during the Protohistoric period (Jones 2010).

In addition, three girdle-pecked cobbles (10–12 centimeters in size) were observed on the cobble-laden terrace riser during low reservoir pooling at this site. This type of artifact is classified as a traditional canoe anchor. On the Spokane Arm of the reservoir, these anchors have only been found at Site 219 and for 1.5 miles downriver from the site. These canoe anchors are not commonly found in other locations along the Spokane Arm of Lake Roosevelt (Jones 2012). Interesting to note, within this 1.5-mile stretch the ethnographic information describes men diving from anchored canoes or boats to gather quantities of freshwater mussels, which were placed in baskets (Ross 1995:73).

Site 401

Site 401 is on a relatively flat bench that is bisected by a small tributary to the Spokane River. Here, two shell middens and two different cooking feature remnants were discovered in 2007. One of the two shell middens was radiocarbon dated. The morphological characteristics of the dated shell midden are readily comparable to those of the midden discovered at Site 204, seen in Figure 5.2 (Jones 2008).

Near the dated shell midden, my excavation team and I found a tight clustering of fire-cracked rock in an ashy matrix. It is likely that this feature was not a cooking element in itself due to its random pattern and lack of intact, intensively heated (oxidized) or charcoal-stained sediments (Pei-Lin Yu, personal communication, September 7, 2007). It is quite possible, especially when the intensive fragmentation of the rocks and their associated matrix is accounted for, that this feature is the "cap" or "lid" of a type of roasting oven (sensu Black 1997:259). Based on similarities in provenience and stratigraphic context as well as spatial proximity to the dated shell midden, it is likely that this "cap" was contemporaneous with shellfish processing.

In addition, and most important for this site, is the discovery of a unique oven feature (Figure 5.3). This feature was composed of 11 large cobbles arranged in an ovoid fashion (40 × 85 centimeters) surrounded by more than 100 highly fragmented fire-cracked rocks. Besides a few minor cracks visible on the rock surfaces there was little breakage, which suggests a feature unlike the standard pit-roasting oven. Upon removal of the cobbles a distinct circle of charcoal staining was visible (65 × 65 × 6 centimeters). This feature, which includes both the ovoid concentration

FIGURE 5.3. Intact baking oven at Site 401 as it first appeared once completely exposed.

of cobbles and the circle of charcoal staining, was classified as an intact baking oven.

Archaeological features discovered at Site 401 strongly suggest pit roasting *and* baking as methods of shellfish processing. It seems reasonable to assume that these remnant cooking features are representative of different preparation methods of a similar resource at differing times.

This site had been previously excavated on two occasions (Arneson 2000; Jones 2006b), both of which turned up a variety of shell features spanning the last 4,000 years. This is a primary shell-processing site, one of the biggest excavated on the Spokane River to date.

Although morphological variation of a feature may be indicative of the processing of different foodstuffs, it is possible that the variance marks a distinction in the preparation technique of the same resource over time, for a distinction in form does not necessarily reflect a change in function (Sammons-Lohse 1985:478). More specifically, "changes in shellfish assemblages through time...can be interpreted as changes in culinary preference" (Wessen 1982:43).

The anthropological and archaeological record of aboriginal populations worldwide indicates striking similarities to the processing techniques discovered at Site 401. From the southeastern United States I have selected a case from a publication by Parmalee and Klippel:

> The mussels were steamed open for eating, as proven by the quantities of *water-cracked* rock fragments.... [T]hese rocks were river cobbles, brought in by the Indians, and heated by them in a fire, before the mussels were placed over the rocks for cooking. (1974:421; italics added)

And the oven found at Site 401 (Figure 5.3) was likely used for baking, not roasting. Clam pit baking was recorded on the Northwest Coast in the early 1900s:

> A pit was usually dug to hold the clams and dug in proportion to the clams secured. A large pile of wood was heaped over the pit and ignited and when it had burned down to the charcoal state thick wet rushes, or wet boughs, were placed hurriedly over the heated mass and the clams poured in a heap over this.... *Often, instead of a pit to hold the clams, a layer of stone was placed on the ground* and occasionally not even that was used. (Reagan 1917:27–28; italics added)

In addition to these three features at Site 401, a second shell midden was discovered (see Table 5.2). Within this generalized midden one broken tabular quartzite biface of a type commonly linked to the processing of fish (see Chance and Chance 1985) was found along with *Margaritifera falcata* valves, one salmonid vertebra, and miscellaneous faunal specimens. The salmonid vertebra "could represent an anadromous salmon or steelhead, or a catadromous trout or whitefish," and one of the faunal specimens is a deer-size "radius shaft displaying flake scars that likely were made by a hammerstone-wielding human who broke the bone in order to extract marrow" (Lyman 2007:1–2). These data suggest that the western pearlshell was intensively harvested along with other food resources at Site 401.

Site 412

Site 412 is located on the floodplain of the original Spokane River, and its site stratigraphy demonstrates that it was buried sometime around 2,300 years ago (Jones 2011). Its charcoal-flecked shell midden was associated with a roughly circular patch of oxidation containing fire-cracked rock. This shell midden and the associated oxidation represent the actual location of a cooking area, complete with intact sustenance refuse. In a majority of cases, shells in this midden are represented by both valves (212 left valves, 194 right valves), signifying the intact nature of the archaeological deposit. Within the shell midden matrix two fish vertebrae were collected, one possibly from a chum/dog (*Oncorhynchus keta*) or coho/silver salmon (*O. kisutch* [Lyman 2011]). Traditionally, chum and coho salmon were a late-summer/early-fall food (Ross 1990:51).

Recent studies of freshwater shell middens in the western United States indicate a variety of characteristics in what some may assume are homogeneous features. In actuality, these middens may be distinguished by specific characteristics. The midden at Site 412 indicates (1) an accretion midden—one defined by small overlapping shell heaps derived from a short-term event; (2) a primary shell deposit—suggesting that the midden has not moved from the processing location; and (3) a limited-activity midden—characterized by a concentration of low density and low artifact diversity (per Stevens 2000:10–11).

Finally, a second shell midden was discovered at this site in a shovel test probe 40 meters south of the shell midden discussed above. This second midden dated to almost 4,500 years old (Table 5.2), emphasizing the antiquity of these "clamming sites."

These archaeological cases strongly suggest that traditional Spokane populations did not limit their resource pursuits at any given time to any singular species. The traditional ecology of this river corridor, based on archaeological data, indicates that freshwater mussel harvests were not secondary but a valued resource incorporated into the more common regional subsistence pursuits of fishing and hunting game animals. Mussels as a resource were complementary to anadromous fish, in that their habitats and life histories overlapped, making them readily available, but unlike migrating fish, mussels could be procured year-round.

Data Gaps

Landslide evaluations may be of strong benefit to this study. The unstable terrace risers composed of noncoherent glacial deposits in the Lower Spokane River valley have undergone mass wasting events (see Kiver and Stradling 1995). These mass wasting events were large enough to block the pre-dam river and therefore limit the upstream travel of migrating fish species. A possible consequence was increased harvesting of freshwater mussel species, which could lead, in time, to temporary overexploitation.

Also of interest is a suggested relationship between pictographs and mussel shell beds (Vannote and Minshall 1982). The evidence indicates that, due to the habitation preference of large *Margaritifera falcata* populations for rock outcrops and the use of these outcrops by Native Americans for rock art, one may indicate the presence of the other. These data have research potential for Columbia Plateau land use.

Additionally, the presence of *Gonidea* and/or *Anodonta* would indicate shifts in the energy level of the river, since these two species prefer muddy bottoms and minnow rather than trout as a host species (per Lyman 1980). To date, no extant archaeological data reference the presence of either of these two genera in midden deposits in the Lower Spokane River. Therefore it is reasonable to assume that *Margaritifera falcata* was the only shellfish present, as opportunistic hunter-gatherers would not have overlooked *Gonidea* or *Anodonta*. However, field reconnaissance within the study area recorded the presence of live specimens of *Anodonta* and Asian clam (*Corbicula fluminea*), likely related to changed river conditions as a result of dam construction and reservoir formation (Jones 2012). These data may be of interest to Spokane River ecology.

Last, a 1940–1941 study of *Margaritifera falcata* on the Truckee River of northern California concluded that mussel glochidia were linked to infections of the host fish. Characteristics of the Truckee River are comparable to those of the Lower Spokane River. The Truckee River studies determined that there are "some differences in the susceptibility of the fishes found...to infection by these glochidia" (Murphy 1942:94). The fish most commonly found to be infected were rainbow trout (*Salmo gairdneri*) and brown trout (*Salmo trutta*), which are two of the most successful hosts to *M. falcata*. During experimental work, infection could not be induced in mountain whitefish (*Prosopius williamsoni*). According to these results, many of the fish must have perished, and most glochidia did not reach full development (Murphy 1942).

The conclusions of the above study were limited but intimated that abundant infestation on host fish can take place naturally and may be linked to a high density of glochidia and low density of host fish at a given time. If these data can be extrapolated to the traditional environment of the Spokane River, then the regular harvest of the western pearlshell may have not only assisted indigenous populations to meet their nutritive needs but enabled fish populations to develop in healthy quantities.

Concluding Thoughts

During the earliest archaeological investigations of the Upper Columbia River region and particularly the Lower Spokane River (Collier et al. 1942), archaeologists categorized sites encountered into three types: habitation sites, temporary camps, and areas used to obtain river mollusks during times of subsistence stress. A number of studies for the next 40 years also introduced the freshwater mussel as a starvation food (see Parmalee and Klippel 1974; Rice 1975:35). Was the western pearlshell harvested in times of resource stress, or was it a preferred resource? It may have been that this abundant resource, which requires little energy to procure, was regularly harvested simply because people ate what was available (Lyman 1980).

However, by the early 1980s, researchers began to theorize that mussels may have had more importance than previously thought, especially when environmental circumstances are considered (Erlandson 1988). Could climatic variances that limited the availability of game in winter months have been offset by focusing on freshwater mussels? Cultural adaptations were likely more complex than is generally accepted and may have included varied subsistence strategies based on population needs and/or local environmental complications at a given time. It is likely that Native American populations in the Spokane River valley had adaptive technologies in place to counter unplanned resource deficits, which would not necessarily indicate "distress" or starvation but, rather, planned tactics to offset scarcity of other resources. This is an excellent example of successful resource intensification rather than resource stress.

The shell midden is a definitive indicator of the harvest of the freshwater mussel, and the variety of site types and preparation methods, examples of which I have shown here, may suggest that this resource was harvested throughout the year and processed alongside "higher"-ranked food resources. Excavations along the Chief Joseph Reservoir revealed that shellfish collecting and hunting were the primary economic pursuits 2,500 years ago, not fishing (Lohse 1985:116).

Based on the sample collected along the upper ten-mile stretch of the Spokane Arm, it appears that similar subsistence strategies were in place along the Lower Spokane River. These data suggest that sometime around 2,500 years ago traditional groups in the Columbia Plateau were placing themselves at vital locations along the major river systems where little movement was necessary to secure foodstuffs year-round. If this is the case, inhabitants of these locations would have had little need for storage. Additionally, harvested freshwater mussels remain fresh if buried in damp soils for up to two years (State Government of Victoria 2008).

It may be premature to state that oven and hearth features of the Lower Spokane River are always evidence of freshwater mussel processing, but it may also be equally erroneous to state that oven features in the Spokane River valley were primarily used for processing fish, terrestrial prey, or edible plant foods. Globally, foraging peoples seeking to broaden their subsistence repertory will, in the absence of terrestrial animal foods, use technological means to harvest aquatic resources before and in preference to intensifying the harvest of wild plant foods (Binford 1983:211–212).

Data suggest that there may be "certain cultural or environmental circumstances in which shellfish may represent a viable alternative to terrestrial resources," and although shellfish may be a limited source of necessary carbohydrates, "collection can provide protein yields which compare favorably with deer hunting and other subsistence pursuits" (Erlandson 1988:102–103). Freshwater mussels, abundant in the Spokane River valley, could have supplemented stored foods, lessened the impacts of population expansion, and/or minimized distress but may also have acted as a regular food source regardless of season or situation. The primary supplement to salmonid harvests if the annual run of the fish did not meet the needs of the people would have to have been something that could be harvested and processed in bulk. Pit cooking of supplementary resources was the only alternative. As environmental settings would indicate the type of food sought as the supplement, it is reasonable to presume that riverine populations would intensively harvest shellfish. Shellfish are the only aquatic resource known to be pit-cooked (Yu 2006:148). Complement these data with the predictability of shellfish locations and resource densities, and their intensification seems certain.

In conclusion, the western pearlshell, readily available to traditional Spokane families, may have been the primary resource sought for intensification, comparable to the primary role of the edible root sought by groups farther inland. This should not be interpreted as a statement to reflect the lack of use of root foods by Spokane populations. It is simply a hypothesis that holds that the riverine mussel may have been a more important resource to populations within the Spokane River valley than previously considered. Implications of this study are that over time these people adapted their habitation and resource-procurement strategies to the locations of the western pearlshell, at least partially.

References Cited

Arneson, Kathryn
2000 *Proposal for Archaeological Testing at Cayuse Cove, Lake Roosevelt National Recreation Area.* Report submitted to the National Park Service, Lake Roosevelt National Recreation Area. On file at the Spokane Tribe of Indians Preservation Office, Wellpinit, WA.

Binford, Lewis
1983 *In Pursuit of the Past.* New York: Thames and Hudson.

Black, S. L.
1997 Oven Cookery at the Honey Creek Site. In *Hot Rock Cooking on the Greater Edwards Plateau: Four Burned Rock Midden Sites in West Central Texas.* S. L. Black, L. W. Ellis, D. G. Creel, and G. T. Goode, eds. Pp. 255–268. Texas Archaeological Research Laboratory Studies in Archaeology 22. Austin: University of Texas.

Bogan, Arthur E.
1993 *Workshop on Freshwater Bivalves of Pennsylvania.* Sewell, NJ: Freshwater Molluscan Research.

Campbell, Sarah K., ed.
1985 *Summary of Results: Chief Joseph Dam Cultural Resources Project, Washington.* Seattle: Office of Public Archaeology, Institute for Environmental Studies, University of Washington.

Chance, David H., and Jennifer V. Chance
1985 *Kettle Falls: 1978.* Anthropological Research Manuscript Series 84. Moscow: Laboratory of Anthropology, University of Idaho.

Chasse, Matthew
2007 *Riffle Characteristics in Stream Investigations.* Annapolis: Maryland Department of Natural Resources.

Collier, Donald, Alfred E. Hudson, and Arlo Ford
1942 *Archaeology of the Upper Columbia Region.* Publications in Anthropology 9(1). Seattle: University of Washington.

Erlandson, Jon M.
1988 The Role of Shellfish in Prehistoric Economies: A Protein Perspective. *American Antiquity* 53(1):102–109.

Galm, Jerry R., ed.
1994 *A Design for Management of Cultural Resources in the Lake Roosevelt Basin of Northeastern Washington.* Eastern Washington University Reports in Archaeology and History 100-83. Cheney: Archaeological and Historical Services, Eastern Washington University.

Glassow, Michael A., and Larry R. Wilcoxon

1988 Coastal Adaptations near Point Conception, California, with Particular Regard to Shellfish Exploitation. *American Antiquity* 53(1):36–51.

Hunn, Eugene S.

1990 *Nch'i-Wána, "the Big River": Mid-Columbia Indians and Their Land.* Seattle: University of Washington Press.

Jones, Jason M.

2006a *Results of Archaeological Testing of Four Locations along the Shore of the Lake Roosevelt Reservoir: Part of the Annual Investigations by the Spokane Tribe of Indians, 2006.* Report produced for the Bonneville Power Administration and Bureau of Reclamation under contract no. 24464, amendment 03. On file at the Spokane Tribe of Indians Preservation Program, Wellpinit, WA.

2006b *Salvage Archaeological Investigations at SIR-R4-0001 Cayuse Cove, Lincoln County, Washington.* Report produced for the Bonneville Power Administration and Bureau of Reclamation under contract no. 24464, amendment 03. On file at the Spokane Tribe of Indians Preservation Program, Wellpinit, WA.

2008 *Indigenous Occupation of Cayuse Cove-SIR-R4-0001: Phase II Investigations and Determination of Eligibility, Lake Roosevelt Reservoir Archaeology 2007.* Report produced for the Bonneville Power Administration and Bureau of Reclamation under contract no. 24464, amendment 03. On file at the Spokane Tribe of Indians Preservation Program, Wellpinit, WA.

2009 *The Western Nuclear Oven Site and Jackson Cove Lithic Scatter: Phase II Investigations and Determinations of Eligibility, Lake Roosevelt Reservoir Archaeology 2008.* Report produced for the Bonneville Power Administration and Bureau of Reclamation under contract no. 24464, amendment 03. On file at the Spokane Tribe of Indians Preservation Program, Wellpinit, WA.

2010 *Suyepi Beach-45LI389: Phase II Investigation and Determination of Eligibility, Lake Roosevelt Reservoir Archaeology 2009.* Report produced for the Bonneville Power Administration and Bureau of Reclamation under contract no. 44694 FY10 Task 2B1 ARPA permit no. PWR-1979-09-WA-01. On file at the Spokane Tribe of Indians Preservation Program, Wellpinit, WA.

2011 *Three Oven Site-45LI31 and Mud Flats-45LI374: Phase II Investigation and Determination of Eligibility, Lake Roosevelt Reservoir Archaeology 2011.* Report produced for the Bonneville Power Administration and Bureau of Reclamation under contract no. IGC 49925 FY11 Task 4b3 and 4b4-ARPA permit no. PWR-1979-11-WA-01. Submitted to the Bonneville Power Administration, Bureau of Reclamation, Washington Department of Archaeology and Historic Preservation, and National Park Service, October 2011. On file at the Bureau of Reclamation Pacific Northwest Regional Office, Boise.

2012 Comprehensive Field Notes for the Spokane Arm of the Lake Roosevelt Reservoir: Bonneville Power Administration Drawdown Zone Site Management, November 2005–2012. Unpublished MS in possession of the author.

Kiver, Eugene P., and Dale F. Stradling

1995 *Geology of the Franklin D. Roosevelt Reservoir Shoreline: Glacial Geology, Terraces, Landslide, and Lineaments.* Eugene P. Kiver and Phillip J. Hansen, eds. Report on file at Grand Coulee Power Office, Grand Coulee.

Larrabee, Edward M., and Susan Kardas

1966 *Archaeological Survey of Grand Coulee Dam National Recreation Area, pt. 1: Lincoln County above Normal Pool.* Washington State University, Laboratory of Anthropology, Report of Investigations no. 38. Pullman.

Lohse, E. S.

1985 Rufus Woods Lake Projectile Point Chronology. In *Summary of Results: Chief Joseph Dam Cultural Resources Project, Washington.* Sarah K. Campbell, ed. Pp. 317–364. Report to the U.S. Army Corps of Engineers. Seattle: Office of Public Archaeology, University of Washington.

Lyman, R. Lee

1980 Freshwater Bivalve Molluscs and Southern Plateau Prehistory: A Discussion and Description of Three Genera. *Northwest Science* 54(2):121–136.

2007 Faunal Remains from a Test Pit in the Spokane River Valley. In *Indigenous Occupation of Cayuse Cove-SIR-R4-0001: Phase II Investigations and Determination of Eligibility, Lake Roosevelt Reservoir Archaeology 2007.* Jason M. Jones, ed. Pp. 61–63. Report produced for the Bonneville Power Administration and Bureau of Reclamation under contract no. 24464, amendment 03. On file at the Bureau of Reclamation, Boise.

2011 Faunal Remains from a Test Pit in the Spokane River Valley: Zooarchaeology of 45LI31. In *Three Oven Site-45LI31 and Mud Flats-45LI374: Phase II Investigation and Determination of Eligibility, Lake Roosevelt Reservoir Archaeology 2011.* Jason M. Jones, ed. Pp. 69–81. Report produced for the Bonneville Power Administration and Bureau of Reclamation under contract no. IGC 49925 FY11 Task 4b3 and 4b4-ARPA permit no. PWR-1979-11-WA-01. On file at the Bureau of Reclamation, Boise.

Murphy, Garth

1942 Relationship of the Freshwater Mussel to Trout in the Truckee River. *California Fish and Game* 28(2):89–102.

Nedeau, Ethan J., Alan K. Smith, Jen Stone, and Sarina Jepsen

2009 *Freshwater Mussels of the Pacific Northwest.* 2nd edition. Portland, OR: Xerces Society for Invertebrate Conservation.

Northwest Power and Conservation Council

2012 Spokane River. Electronic document, http://www.nwcouncil.org, accessed January 2012.

Parmalee, Paul W., and Walter E. Klippel
1974 Freshwater Mussels as a Prehistoric Food Resource. *American Antiquity* 39(3):421–434.
Post, Richard H.
1938 The Subsistence Quest. In *The Sinkaietk or Southern Okanogan of Washington.* Leslie Spier, ed. Pp. 9–34. General Studies in Anthropology, no. 6. Menasha, WI.
Ray, Verne F.
1933 *The Sanpoil and Nespelem: Salishan Peoples of Northeastern Washington.* University of Washington Publications in Anthropology 5. Seattle.
1936 Native Villages and Groupings of the Columbia Basin. *Pacific Northwest Quarterly* 27(2):99–152.
Reagan, A. B.
1917 Archaeological Notes on Western Washington and Adjacent British Columbia. *Proceedings of the California Academy of Sciences,* Fourth Series, 7(1): 1–31.
Rice, David G.
1975 *Prehistory of the Western Plateau: Umatilla River to Spokane River.* Report on file at the University of Idaho, Moscow.
Ross, John A.
1990 The Aboriginal and Historical Use and Occupancy of the Spokane River by the Middle and Upper Spokan. March 1990. Unpublished MS on file at the Spokane Tribe of Indians Preservation Office, Wellpinit, WA.
1993 An Ethnoarchaeological Cultural Resource Survey of the Spokane Indian Reservation, vols. I–XVI: 1991–1993. Eastern Washington University, Cheney. Unpublished MS on file at the Spokane Tribe of Indians, Wellpinit, WA.
1995 Spokan Ethnography. In *An Ethnographic and Historical Analysis of the Spokan People.* John Alan Ross and Deane R. Osterman Jr., eds. Pp. 1–151. Report on file at Spokane Tribal Culture Office, Wellpinit, WA.
Ross, Lester A.
1969 *Archaeological Investigation in the Coulee Dam National Recreation Area, Spring 1969.* Report submitted to the National Park Service, contract no. 14-10-4:940-102. Pullman: Laboratory of Anthropology, Washington State University.
Sammons-Lohse, Dorothy
1985 Features. In *Summary of Results: Chief Joseph Dam Cultural Resources Project, Washington.* Sarah K. Campbell, ed. Seattle: University of Washington, Office of Public Archaeology, Institute for Environmental Studies.
Spinden, Herbert Joseph
1908 *The Nez Perce Indians.* Memoirs of the American Anthropological Association 2(3). Lancaster, PA.

State Government of Victoria

2008 Aboriginal Freshwater Middens. Site Identification, Mini Poster 3. Melbourne: Department of Planning and Community Development, State Government of Victoria. Electronic document, http://www.dpcd.vic.gov.au, accessed December 2011.

Stevens, Rebecca

2000 Freshwater Mussel Shell Middens and the Nutritional Value of *Margaritifera falcata* on the Upper Wenatchee River. Unpublished M.A. thesis, Eastern Washington University, Cheney.

Tennant, Cristine

2010 Freshwater Mussels of the Klamath River: A Personal and Scientific Account. Unpublished B.A. thesis, Oregon State University.

Thoms, Alston V.

1998 *Earth Ovens. Archaeology of Prehistoric Native America: An Encyclopedia.* Guy Gibbon, ed. New York: Garland Publishing, Inc.

U.S. Department of Agriculture

2007 Natural Resources Conservation Service, Web Soil Survey. Map of Stevens County, Washington. Electronic document, http://websoilsurvey.sc.egov.usda, accessed June 2008.

U.S. Geological Survey

1915 Plan and Profile of Spokane River: Mouth to Chamokane Creek, Washington. In *Profile Surveys in Spokane River Basin, Washington and John Day River Basin, Oregon*. R. B. Marshall, ed. Pl. 11. U.S. Geological Survey Water Supply Paper 377. Washington, DC.

Vannote, Robin L., and G. Wayne Minshall

1982 Fluvial Processes and Local Lithology Controlling Abundance, Structure and Composition of Mussel Beds. *Proceedings of the National Academy of Sciences of the United States of America* 79, July: 4103–4107.

Wessen, Gary Charles

1982 Shell Middens as Cultural Deposits: A Case Study from Ozette. Unpublished Ph.D. dissertation, Washington State University, Pullman.

Yu, Pei-Lin

2006 Pit Cooking and Intensification of Subsistence in the American Southwest and Pacific Northwest. Unpublished Ph.D. dissertation, Southern Methodist University, Dallas.

Fire, Floodplains, and Fish

The Historic Ecology of the Lower Cosumnes River Watershed

MICHELLE L. STEVENS AND EMILIE M. ZELAZO

Jumping echoes of the rocks;
Squirrels turning somersaults;
Green leaves, dancing in the air;
Fishes, white as money-shells,
Running in the water; green, deep, and still.
Hi-ho, hi-ho, hi-hay!
Hi-ho, hi-ho, hi-hay!
Modoc puberty song

Jump, salmon, jump!
So you may see your uncle dance!
Coyote song to catch steelhead (Chumash), in H. W. Luthin, ed., *Surviving through the Days: Translations of Native California Stories and Songs* (2002)

For thousands of years, the California landscape has been tended and its resources sustainably harvested by its inhabitants. Prior to Euro-American settlement, California Native Americans manipulated the natural environment, particularly plant resources, to meet long-term cultural needs (Anderson 2005; Blackburn and Anderson 1993; Stevens 1999). In fact, indigenous people all over the world have been found to be key factors in influencing biodiversity, sustainability, and optimum resource utilization. Historical ecology focuses on this reciprocal interface between humans and the environment in order to further the understanding of landscape

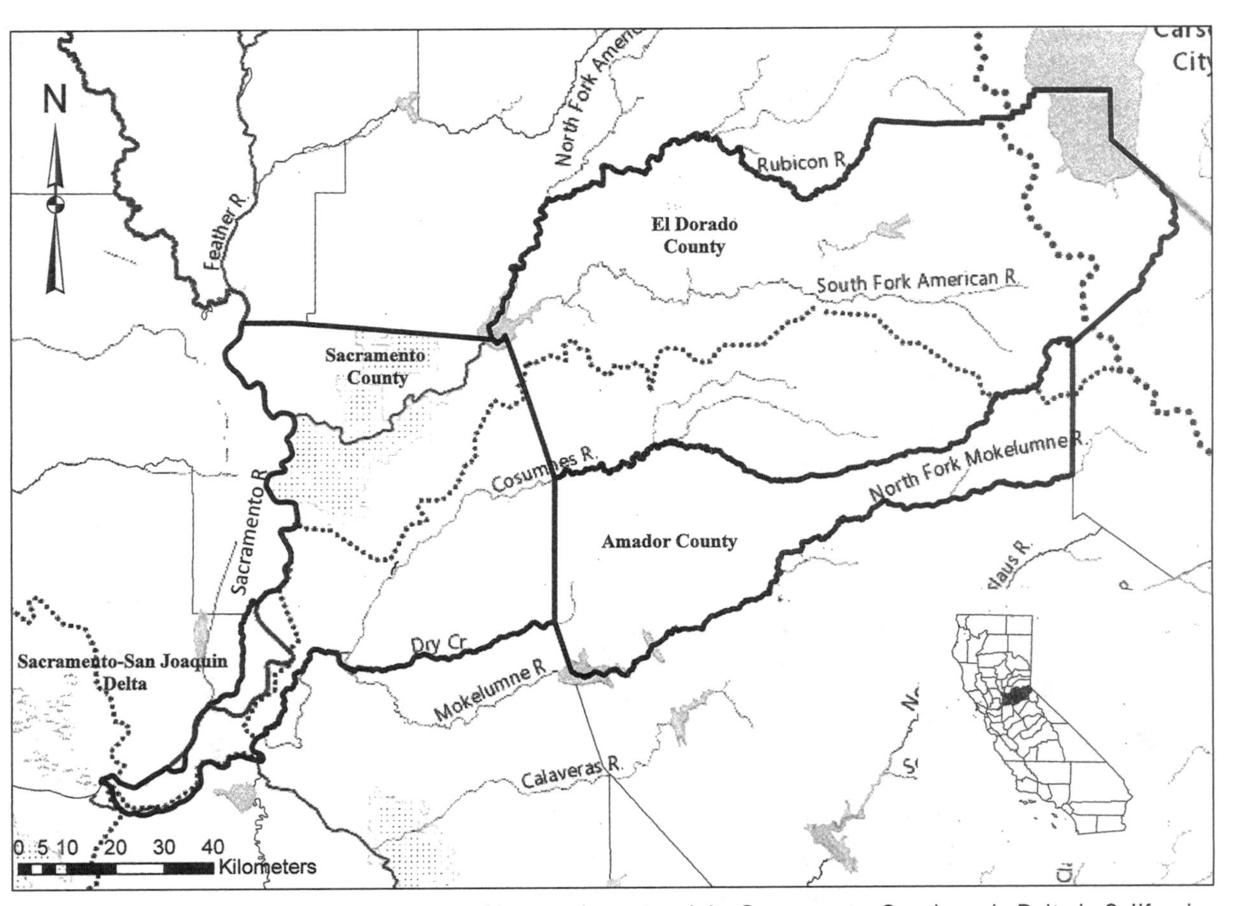

FIGURE 6.1. Overview of the Lower Cosumnes River study area and the Sacramento–San Joaquin Delta in California. Illus. by Emilie Zelazo.

transformations over time (Egan and Howell 2001; Grossinger 2001; Grossinger et al. 2006).

Although historical ecology does not typically incorporate both archaeological data and ethnoecology into an assessment of historic ecosystems, the archaeological record contains not only demographic information not found in most historical texts but also environmental information in the form of material culture, paleobotanical, and faunal remains. This chapter will explore ethnographic data, traditional knowledge, and archaeological fish faunal remains to reconstruct the landscape of the Lower Cosumnes River watershed prior to Euro-American settlement and alteration. The historical reconstruction proposed here will illustrate, within the limitations of the data, how past indigenous traditional management practices influenced both vegetation patterns and probable fish species distributions in the Lower Cosumnes River watershed.

Our hypothesis is that floodplain biodiversity and native fish productivity benefited from burning and other traditional management practices utilized by the Plains Miwok and other Native Californians for thousands of years. These practices may have enhanced floodplain rearing habitats, thereby increasing fish growth and reducing fish mortality. Traditional resource management has been demonstrated to do the following:

- increase habitat interspersion,
- create a more open and parklike riparian physiognomy,
- increase species diversity,
- reduce water lost to evapotranspiration,
- attenuate peak velocities and flood flows,
- increase late-season streamflows, and
- increase the production of desired resources through intermediate anthropogenic disturbance (Anderson 2005; Hankins 2005; Lewis 1973; Martinez 2000, 2002; Stevens 1999).

The Study Area: The Lower Cosumnes River Watershed

The Cosumnes River is located in the northeastern portion of the Sacramento–San Joaquin Delta of central California (see Figure 6.1). The Cosumnes River is 80 miles long. It flows from headwaters in the Sierra Nevada mountain range at an elevation of 2,400 meters to approximately sea level at its confluence with the Mokelumne River (Cosumnes River

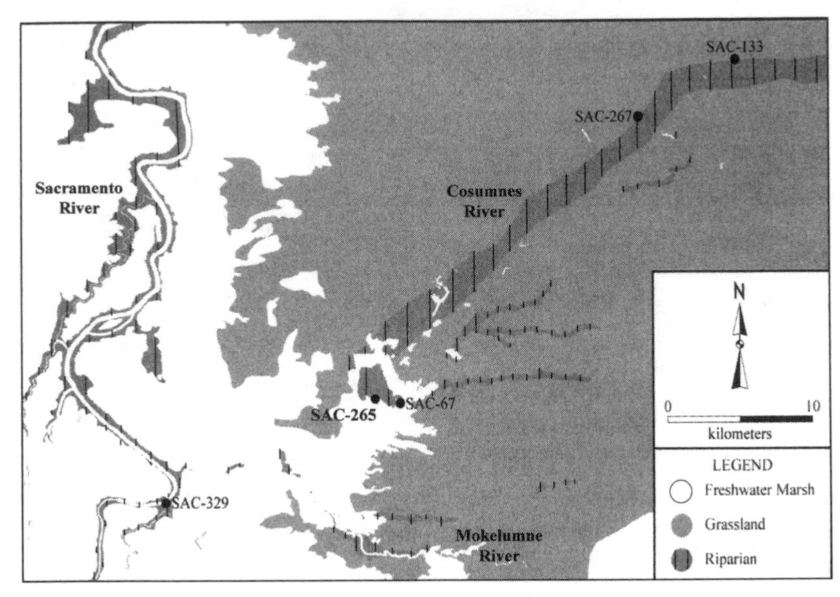

FIGURE 6.2. Pre-1900s California Central Valley historic vegetation map.

Preserve 2010a). The study area is defined as the lower portion of the Cosumnes River, from the edge of the Sierra Nevada foothills just east of Latrobe in the north to its confluence with the Mokelumne near the town of Thornton in the south. The Mokelumne River shortly after this juncture flows westward into the Sacramento–San Joaquin Delta (U.S. Geological Survey [USGS] 1979). The distance covered by the study area is approximately 45 linear miles, encompassing a little more than half of the length of the entire river. The pre-1900s historic vegetation map of the Central Valley is depicted in Figure 6.2, and an overview of the study area appears in Figure 6.3.

In recent years, the Cosumnes River has become a focus of conservation and restoration efforts. The Cosumnes River is the largest watercourse flowing in central California without a major dam on its main stem and has a presumed natural flow regime (Mount 1995; Mount et al. 2001; Moyle et al. 2003). Because of this less altered state, the Cosumnes River hydrogeology more closely reflects historic conditions and is often used as a reference area for the natural process restoration of more modified watercourses. The hydrogeomorphology of the Cosumnes River provides one of the most reliable templates of pre–Euro-American settlement riparian ecologies existing today, providing a facsimile of the world once inhabited

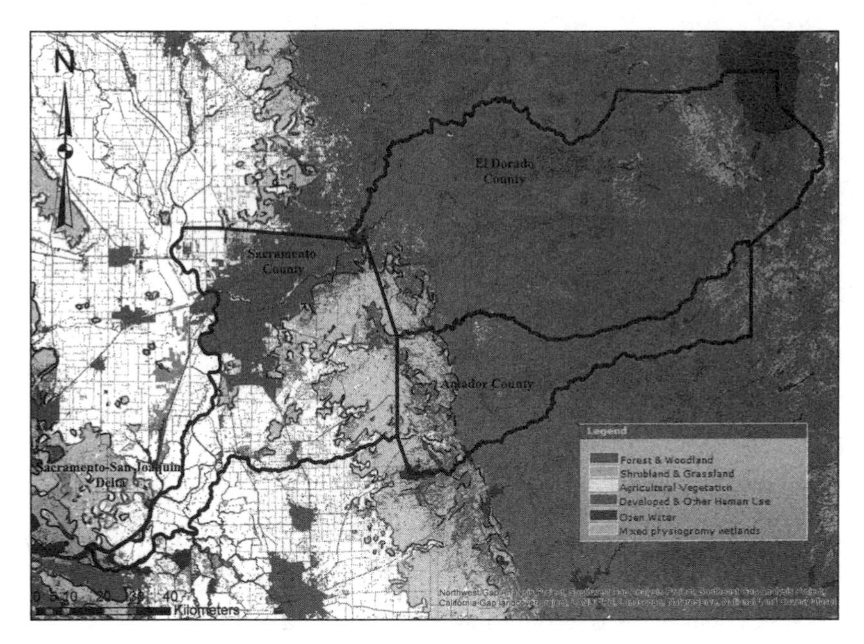

FIGURE 6.3 Overview of the study area.

by indigenous Plains Miwok (Bennyhoff 1977; Bouey and Waechter 1992; Johnson 1976; Kroeber 1925; Levy 1978).

Like many California watersheds, the Cosumnes River has a high amount of variability of flow on both a seasonal and an annual basis. Historically the Cosumnes River was a perennial stream, with flows in later summer being supported by the upwelling of groundwater (Moyle et al. 2003). However, the increased agricultural and rural use of groundwater has lowered groundwater levels as much as 30 meters in some reaches of the river, therefore reducing the amount of water available for late-summer flows (Mount et al. 2001). Due to the low elevation of its headwaters, much of the Cosumnes River watershed is fed by rainfall rather than by snowmelt (USGS 1979). This results in larger and flashier volumes of runoff than occur in snow-fed river systems.

Within the Lower Cosumnes River watershed, the adjacent riparian corridors and grasslands are subject to annual flooding, creating an interspersion of gallery riparian forest, oak woodland, permanent and seasonal wetlands, and aquatic habitats within the floodplain (Vahti and Greco 2007). High winter flows are a critical factor in the creation of the floodplains through the channelization process (Moyle et al. 2003), and several

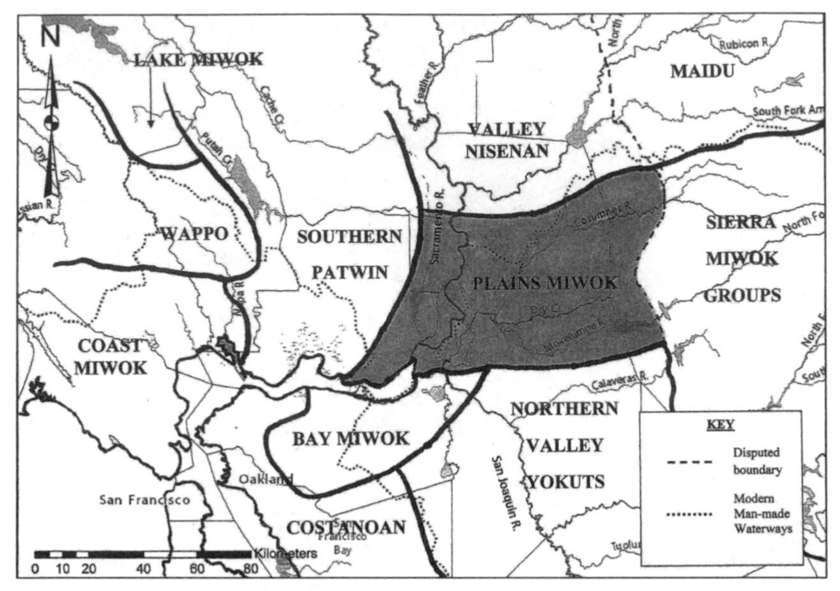

FIGURE 6.4. Plains Miwok territory map.

floodplains are hydrologically connected to the Cosumnes River in its lower region (Swenson et al. 2003). While the mean annual average flow is 529 cubic feet per second , peak winter discharges of as high as 54,000 cubic feet per second have been recorded for the Cosumnes (USGS 1979). During late summer and early fall the river often has no flow in its lower reaches, which can adversely impact fish survival.

The People of the Cosumnes River

The Archaeological Record

In its lower reaches, the Cosumnes River flows through one of the most biologically rich environments in the California Central Valley; this area supports a structurally diverse mosaic of vegetation types interspersed with aquatic habitats before merging with the Mokelumne River to flow into the Sacramento–San Joaquin Delta (Vahti and Greco 2007). This productive interspersion of gallery riparian forests, oak/woodland savannas, grasslands, freshwater marshes, and riverine and floodplain habitats was also home to groups of Native Californians who came to be known collectively as the Plains Miwok or Mewuk. Figure 6.4 illustrates the territories of Native Californians within the study area and the immediate vicinity.

Populations of close to 80,000 people have been estimated for the

Sacramento Valley prior to European arrival (Cook 1956). These estimates are based on the kinds of resources available and the size of each group's respective territories. For the Plains Miwok numbers potentially as high as 57 individuals per square mile along the streams and sloughs have been estimated for prehistoric times (Johnson 1976).

Archaeological sites in the study area are divided into temporal frameworks designated as the Early period (5000–2800 BP), the Middle period (2800–1200 BP), and the Late period (1200–100 BP). For this discussion, we will focus on the Late period, a time that encompasses the calendar dates of AD 750–1848 and which can be successfully linked to Plains Miwok occupation within the study area.

During Plains Miwok occupation, the study area's vegetation was dominated by open grasslands and vast freshwater marshes, with riparian forests along the natural levees of the major rivers (Central Valley Historic Mapping Project 1999; West et al. 2007). Palynological evidence suggests that the study area has supported the same vegetation pattern for the past 6,000 years (West et al. 2007). Further, dated peat deposits suggest that the eastern Sacramento–San Joaquin Delta margin stabilized 5,000 years ago, allowing for a resilient wetland plant community to become established (Pierce 1988).

There are at least 130 archaeological sites located within the northeastern Sacramento–San Joaquin Delta. Geomorphologically, nearly 50 percent of these sites are located on stream banks and natural levees near rivers such as the Cosumnes, Mokelumne, and Sacramento rivers; 17 percent of the sites are in the floodplain; 14 percent are at lakes, abandoned channels, sloughs, and marshes; 8 percent are on alluvial or marine sedimentary terraces; and 7 percent are found on top of Pleistocene aeolian sand dunes (Pierce 1988). As Figure 6.3 illustrates, the majority of Cosumnes River sites are located on either stream banks or natural levees.

Ethnography of the Plains Miwok

The Lower Cosumnes River was home to the Plains Miwok, a people with high cultural regard for the salmon fishery from the beginning of tribal memory to the present day. The river derives its name either from the Cosomne tribelet, which means the "People of the Salmon Place" in the Miwok language, or from the South-Central Miwok words for salmon, *kos'-sum* and *kis'-sum'mi* (Bennyhoff 1977; Latta 1977; Powers 1877). The

Cosomne village of Supu (possibly a variant of *Cosu* and meaning "Salmon Place") was located approximately two miles northeast of Bruceville, approximately nine miles above the mouth of the Cosumnes River (Bennyhoff 1977; Yoshiyama et al. 2001). Throughout its history, the Cosumnes River experienced a fall run of Chinook salmon. This run was extirpated from the Cosumnes River in 1988, and salmon remained absent at least through the 1990s (Yoshiyama et al. 2001). Then, sometime around 2000, the Chinook salmon returned to the Cosumnes River for spawning and rearing (Jeffres et al. 2008; Moyle et al. 2007).

Linguistic and archaeological evidence suggests that the ancestors of the Plains Miwok were resident in the central California delta region for at least 4,500 years (Golla 2007). The people of the Lower Cosumnes watershed who came to be collectively known as the Plains Miwok split off from other Miwok groups approximately 2,000 years ago (Levy 1978); the Plains Miwok are identified as one of the five Eastern Miwok groups who all spoke a subgroup of the Utian language. The traditional territory of the Plains Miwok can be roughly defined by the Deer Creek/Sloughhouse vicinity on the north, the edge of the Sierra Nevada foothills from Bridgehouse southward to present-day Camanche Reservoir on the east, both banks of the Lower Sacramento River to the western edge of the delta tidal plain in the Yolo basin on the west, and both banks of the Mokelumne River on the south (Bennyhoff 1977; Levy 1978). Plains Miwok territory is presented in Figure 6.4.

The Plains Miwok utilized much of what their land had to offer, indicated by archaeological deposits suggestive of a varied diet of many types of grass seeds, acorns, rabbits and hares, pronghorn, tule elk, deer, minnows, salmon, sturgeon, and numerous waterfowl (Barrett and Gifford 1933; Bennyhoff 1977; Kroeber 1925; Levy 1978). Much of the food consumed was cooked in earth ovens. Plains Miwok dwellings included conical semisubterranean houses, assembly or dance houses, sweat lodges, circular or rectangular ceremonial structures, grinding booths (similar to ramadas), acorn granaries, and hunting blinds (Bouey and Waechter 1992; Levy 1978).

Fishing Technologies

The efficiency, variation, and kinds of fishing technologies used by the Plains Miwok and other indigenous Californian groups in the lower hills along the large rivers indicate how important fishing was to their diet. The prominent fish species listed in ethnographies are salmon (*Oncorhynchus* spp.), sturgeon (*Acipenser* spp.), and lamprey eels (*Entosphenus tridentatus*). Fishing was performed from river- and stream banks or from tule rafts. Fishing technology included clay ball– and stone-weighted nets, weirs, seines (especially in the marshes), the toggle harpoon, bipointed fishhooks, spears, and poison from plants such as buckeye (*Aesculus californica*) and soaproot (*Chlorogalum pomeridianum*) (Barrett and Gifford 1933; Kroeber 1925; Levy 1978).

Barrett and Gifford (1933) describe four types of nets used by Miwok peoples, including the Plains Miwok. The first is a dip net with a circular opening and a very long pole that was used in the deep holes of rivers. The second kind, the *yo'ho*, was from six to eight feet wide and as much as 40 feet long and was usually placed across a river or lagoon. The fish would then be driven into the net, where they were caught by their gills or seized as the net was drawn ashore. The *yo'ho* was used in conjuncture with tule rafts to trap all types of fish, including salmon, and particularly in the slow waters of the delta "along rush-bordered rivers and marshes" (Barrett and Gifford 1933:188). The net's lower edges would be weighted with clay balls wrapped in leaves, and many such tule-impressed clay net weights are found in delta archaeological collections. The third type of net was the set net, referred to by the Plains Miwok as the *yû'gû*. This net was weighted with stones and set into a riffle or depressions of a stream. Vertical trigger strings would signal the watcher on the banks when fish were in the net. The net would then be raised; the fish, removed; and the net, reset. Sometimes divers would drive fish into this net from downstream. The last type was the *mōla'nna*, a casting net with a large circular opening that automatically spread wide as the net was cast onto the water. It was attached to a long rope that closed as it was drawn to the shore.

Material cultural remains found in archaeological collections indicate that fish nets required a tremendous amount of plant materials to construct. Many of the plant species used for net construction were maintained through the setting of annual fires. Large quantities of milkweed (*Asclepias speciosa, A. fasicularis, A. eriocarpa*) and Indian hemp (*Apocynum cannabinum*) were used to construct fishnets and fishline. Since no complete examples of Plains Miwok netting are known, correlatives can be based on known examples from neighboring groups. Washoe and Northern Paiute gill nets (with the dimensions of 1⁄16-inch two-ply cordage, 100-feet-×-4.5-feet-×-1.5-inch mesh) required 60,110 stalks; bag nets required 4,425 stalks; and A-frame dip/lift nets required 39,450 stalks (Anderson 1993; Lindstrom 1992).

In general, native plants used for textiles, such as milkweed and Indian hemp, produce the best-quality stems for fiber after being burned (Anderson 2005; Bates and Lee 1990). Stalks were harvested when dry in the fall, and fires would have been set after harvesting to stimulate the growth of new stems in the spring. Both milkweed and Indian hemp are relatively scarce in the contemporary riparian landscape. The widespread loss and degradation of riparian habitats has resulted in most native riparian understory species becoming relatively scarce. These species must have been in greater abundance in prehistoric times in order to support the construction of fishing nets and other textiles needed by large indigenous populations.

Aside from being caught with nets, salmon were speared with the two-pronged harpoon called a *sīla'nna* (Barrett and Gifford 1933). The harpoon head (or tip) was usually made of deer bone or antler and was secured to the shaft by a short, very strong leader of native string. Sturgeon were caught by a bipointed fishhook, *ya'lūtc,* and line; a "large sucker" was used as bait. Barrett and Gifford (1933) state that the hook-and-line method was usually performed from a tule raft. Lamprey eels were taken with ordinary fishnets, and no special eel net or trap has been reported as being used by Plains Miwok (Barrett and Gifford 1933).

Poisons made from plants were also used to procure fish. Mashed buckeye and soaproot were used as fish poisons (Barrett and Gifford 1933). Mashed soaproot was put into calm or standing water, and the stupefied fish would rise to the surface, where the Indians gathered them with baskets or dip nets (Kroeber 1925). Soaproot worked best in late summer when the water was low.

Traditional Resource Management

In order to support a sustainable harvest of their resources, the Plains Miwok actively tended the plants and animals of their land by employing various cultivation and harvesting techniques. Today, such techniques and practices are collectively called traditional resource management (TRM). TRM includes multiple species management, resource rotation, succession management, landscape patchiness management, and other ways to respond to and manage environmental uncertainty in order to optimize sustainable resource extraction (Berkes 1999; Berkes et al. 2000).

TRM practices by Native Californians include:

- annual burning of senescent vegetation to stimulate new growth and create microhabitats;
- multiple species management of plant resources, waterfowl, fish, bird eggs, insects, and small mammals;
- resource rotation;
- selective harvesting on a seasonal and phenological basis;
- spatial and temporal restriction of fish harvest during spawning; and
- landscape patchiness management (Anderson 2005; Hankins 2005; Stevens 1999, 2003, 2004a, 2004b).

These traditional practices have similarities to adaptive management, with its emphasis on feedback learning and its treatment of the uncertainty and unpredictability intrinsic to all ecosystems.

Prayer, thanksgiving, and asking permission to harvest are inherent components of traditional resource management, although the specifics vary among individuals and local traditions. Traditional relationships with plants include asking permission to harvest and gratitude for the opportunity to gather and tend plants in the area. Based on our experiences of gathering plant materials with present-day local Miwok (Mewuk) people, prayer and asking permission always occur before gathering, and thanks are always offered after gathering. TRM practices specific to Native California groups consist of harvesting techniques that utilize only a portion of the plant population, with all age classes left behind to reproduce.

Traditional ecological knowledge implies a reciprocal or kincentric relationship with the ecosystem. In 2000, Enrique Salmón described kincentric ecology as "the manner in which indigenous people view themselves as part of an extended ecological family that shares ancestry" (Anderson 2005:57). In terms of traditional land-management techniques, interactions resulting from kincentric ecology can enhance and preserve the ecosystems within which indigenous people have lived for centuries.

Fire

Fire was the most important TRM land-management tool on the pre-European landscape. Native American groups regularly and widely set fires in the Central Valley (Heady 1988; Lewis 1973; Thompson 1961). Sierra

Miwok Elder Bill Franklin told Dr. Kat Anderson what he had learned about burning from his father and grandfather. He said,

> They said the Indians used to burn in the fall—October and November. They set the fires from the bottom of the slope to decrease the snowpack, get rid of the debris so there's no fire danger and they burned in the hunting areas so there was more food for the deer. They burned every year and in the same areas. (Anderson 2005:148–149)

An 1848 account from the Sacramento Valley states,

> The plains are burned over every year by the Indians; and the consequence is, that the young trees, which would otherwise have grown into forests, are destroyed, and the large trees often killed. Nevertheless, the oak (Valley Oak), the plan tree (Sycamore), the ash (Oregon ash)...fringe the stream everywhere, and divide the country into beautiful glades and savannas.... [W]ithin the verge of the valley, grows a belt of oak trees, about three hundred yards wide.... [B]eyond this belt, on either side of the river, stand clumps of forests over the endless seas of grass that reach away to the distant mountains. (Stewart et al. 2002:306)

As reflected in the above statement, the quick, hot burning would kill oak seedlings in the grassland and inhibit their growth but would have a lesser effect on healthy established trees because of the adult oak's very thick, fire-adapted bark (Thompson 1961). The burning of tules in the freshwater marshes would have produced similar results, keeping them in pure stands and inhibiting the growth of willows and other water-tolerant trees on the swampy floodplains.

Annual burning also stimulated the production of plants used for fishing and basketry technology (Anderson 2005; Bibby 1996; Merrill 1923; Yamane and Aguilar 1997). Thousands of stalks of milkweed and Indian hemp, as well as other basketry and fiber materials, were required to support the material culture. These species are relatively uncommon today and not in the abundance necessary to support this level of technology (Stevens 1999). Therefore, traditional burning and kincentric tending practices helped to produce and sustain the plants needed for the material culture.

Removing senescent vegetation through burning and tending also maintained a more open and parklike physiognomy in the riparian corridor within the study area (Stevens 1999). Riparian corridors within the study area occur on natural levees (Katibah 1984; Thompson 1961; Vahti and Greco 2007). Breaks in the natural levees are used by young fish to enter and leave their floodplain nurseries when mature. Burning would have kept vegetation from blocking the natural levee breaks. The majority of indigenous groups within the study area also lived on the natural levees (Pierce 1988).

Last, burning in organic soils creates or enhances depressional microtopography, prolonging ponding and increasing habitat complexity in the floodplain (Sommer et al. 2001a; Sommer et al. 2001b). Indigenous burning of the floodplain is likely to have created openings in the substrate through the removal of surface organic material and oxidizing peat soils. Reducing decadent and senescent vegetation is also likely to have provided a good substrate for the eggs and larvae of floodplain spawning fish such as Sacramento splittail, Sacramento perch, and the extinct thicktail chub. Additionally, burning mobilizes nutrients, resulting in algal and zooplankton blooms, providing important nutrition for all species of native juvenile fish.

The Fish of the Cosumnes

Today the Cosumnes River is home to 41 species of fish, 14 of which are natives (Cosumnes River Preserve 2007). Table 6.1 lists the fish currently found in the Cosumnes River.

Fourteen native fish occurring in the Cosumnes River are found in the study area; 12 of these species are also found in the archaeological record. For the purposes of the following discussion, green and white sturgeon will be collapsed into the general category of sturgeon. Illustrations of the native fish found in the study area are provided in Figure 6.5.

The Pacific lamprey (*Entosphenus tridentatus*) and the prickly sculpin (*Cottus asper*) are the two native fish species in the contemporary fish assemblage missing from the archaeological record. The Pacific lamprey is an ancient anadromous agnathous fish with a skeleton that is not likely to preserve (McGinnis 2006; Wheeler and Jones 1989). The only semibony parts

TABLE 6.1. Cosumnes River Fish Species.

Common Name	Scientific Name
American shad	*Alosa sapidissima* [a]
Bigscale logperch	*Percina caprodes* [a]
Black bullhead	*Ictalurus melas* [a]
Bluegill	*Lepomis macrochirus* [a]
Brook trout	*Salvelinus fontinalis*
Brown bullhead	*Ameiurus nebulosus* [a]
Brown trout	*Salmo trutta*
California roach	*Lavinia symmetricus* [b]
Carp	*Cyprinus carpio* [a]
Channel catfish	*Ictalurus punctatus* [a]
Chinook salmon	*Oncorhynchus tshawytscha* [a,b]
Crappie (black)	*Pomoxis nigromaculatus* [a]
Crappie (white)	*Pomoxis annularis* [a]
Fathead minnow	*Pimephales promelas* [a]
Golden shiner	*Notemigonus crysoleucas* [a]
Goldfish	*Carassius auratus* [a]
Green sunfish	*Lepomis cyanellus* [a]
Hardhead	*Mylopharadon conocephalus* [b,c]
Hitch	*Lavinia exilicauda* [a,b]
Inland silverside	*Menidia beryllina* [a]
Largemouth bass	*Micropterus salmoides* [a]
Pacific lamprey	*Entosphenus tridentatus* [a,b]
Prickly sculpin	*Cottus asper* [a,b]
Rainbow trout	*Salmo gairdneri* [b]
Redear sunfish	*Lepomis microlophus* [a]
Redeye bass	*Micropterus coosae* [a]
Riffle sculpin	*Cottus gulosus* [b,c]
Sacramento pikeminnow	*Ptychocheilus grandis* [a,b]
Sacramento blackfish	*Orthodon microlepidotus* [a,b]
Sacramento sucker	*Catostomus occidentalis* [a,b]
Smallmouth bass	*Micropterus dolomieu*
Speckled dace	*Rhinichthys osculus* [b,c]
Splittail	*Pogonichthys macrolepidotus* [a,b]
Spotted bass	*Micropterus punctulatus* [a]
Striped bass	*Morone saxatilis* [a]
Threadfin shad	*Dorosoma petenense* [a]
Tule perch	*Hysterocarpus traski* [a,b]
Wagasaki	*Hypomesus nipponensis* [a]
Warmouth	*Lepomis gulosus* [a]
Western mosquitofish	*Gambusia affinis* [a]
White catfish	*Ameiurus catus* [a]

Source: Cosumnes River Preserve 2010b.

[a] Species found on the Cosumnes River Preserve.

[b] Native species.

[c] Likely extirpated.

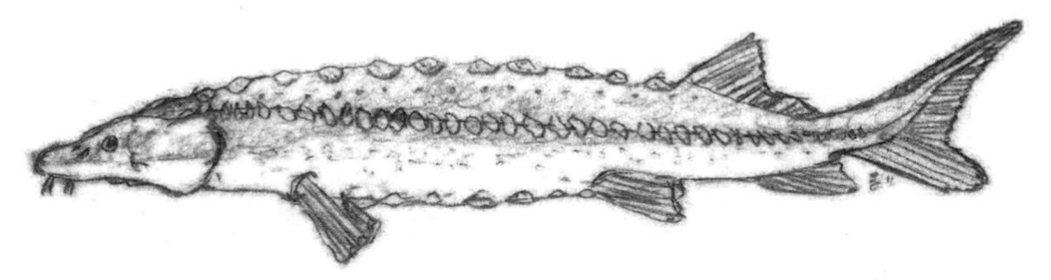

White Sturgeon (*Acipenser tansmontanus*)
Up to 300 cm SL

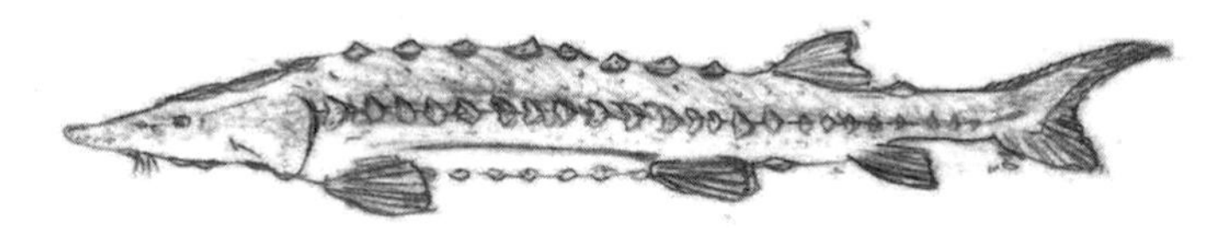

Green Sturgeon (*Acipenser medirostris*)
Up to 160 cm SL

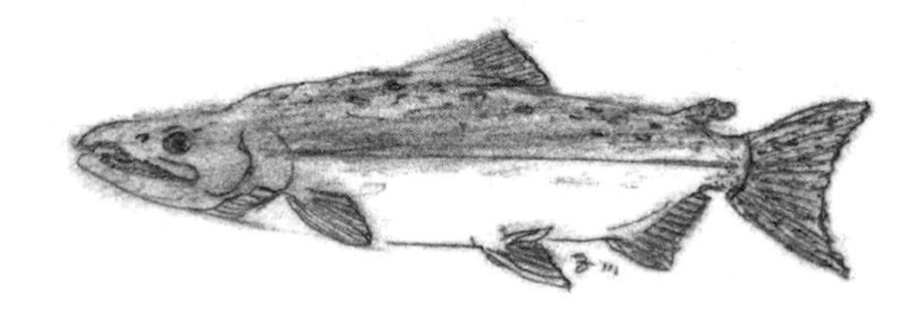

Chinook Salmon (*Oncorhynchus tshawytscha*)
Up to 100 cm SL

Pacific Lamprey (*Entosphenus tridentatus*)
Up to 76 cm SL

FIGURE 6.5A. Illustrations of native fish of the Cosumnes River found in the study area. SL = standard length. Illustrations not to scale (drawn by Emilie Zelazo).

of this fish are its keratinized teeth, which are also susceptible to decay. As such it is unlikely to preserve at all in the archaeological record; agnathans have rarely been recorded in the archaeological record even with the use of very fine-meshed sieves (Wheeler and Jones 1989).

The Central Valley prickly sculpin lives in freshwater and the San Francisco Estuary (Moyle 2002). Central Valley prickly sculpins are tiny fish, ranging in size from three to nine centimeters, with very small bones (McGinnis 2006; Moyle 2002). Even if these tiny fish were taken during aboriginal times, the small size of their bones would preclude recovery under

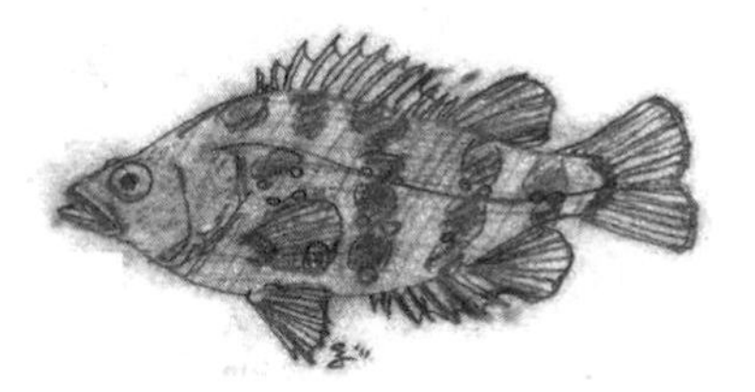

Sacramento Perch (*Archoplites interruptus*)
Up to 61 cm SL

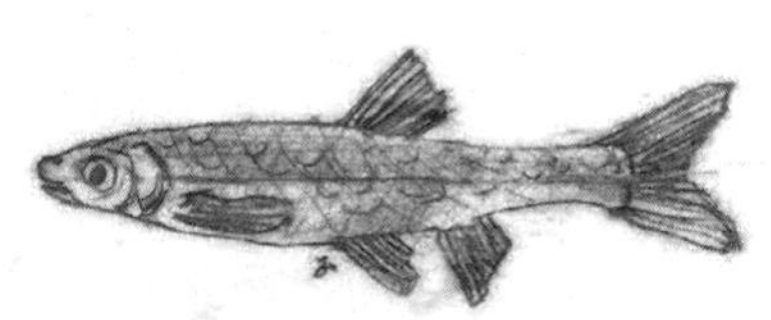

Hardhead (*Mylopharodon concephalus*)
Up to 60 cm SL

Sacramento Blackfish (*Orthodon microlepidotus*)
Up to 50 cm SL

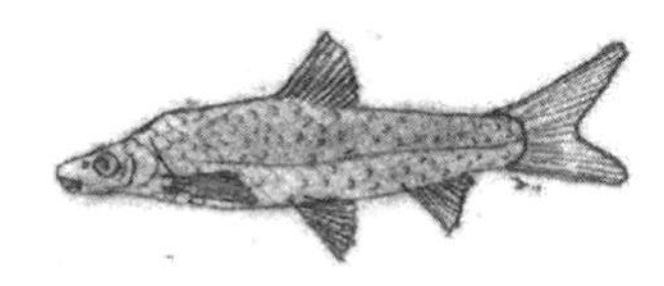

Sacramento Splittail (*Pogonichthys macrolepidotus*)
Up to 45 cm SL

Thicktail Chub (*Gila crassicauda*) extinct
Up to 40 cm SL

Sacramento Sucker (*Catostomus occidentalis*)
Average 30 cm SL

Sacramento Pikeminnow (*Pogonichthys grandis*)
Average at 25 cm SL

Tule Perch (*Hysterocarpus traski*)
Up to 23.5 cm SL

Hitch (*Lavina exilicauda*)
Average at 15 to 20 cm SL

Prickly Sculpin (*Cottus asper*)
up to 20 cm SL

FIGURE 6.5B. Illustrations of native fish of the Cosumnes River found in the study area. SL = standard length. Illustrations not to scale (drawn by Emilie Zelazo).

the normal ⅛-inch screening methods used by archaeologists during excavation. There is ethnographic information citing Pacific lamprey capture and utilization (Barrett and Gifford 1933; Levy 1978), but no information concerning Native American usage of Central Valley prickly sculpin within the study area is available at this time. Therefore, only the Pacific lamprey will be included in the remaining discussion.

Currently, only a fall run of Chinook salmon (*Oncorhynchus tshawytscha*) is observed on the Cosumnes (P. B. Moyle, personal communication, November 29, 2010; Yoshiyama et al. 1996, 1998; Yoshiyama et al. 2001). Salmon require high flows for migration, and due to low-elevation drainage, the Cosumnes River only has suitable flows during late fall rains (Yoshiyama et al. 2001). Further, there is no indication, historically or otherwise, that a spring run of Chinook salmon ever occurred here. Thus, a fall run of Chinook salmon is assumed for Plains Miwok occupation of the Cosumnes River.

Three different types of fish habitats could be found at varying degrees throughout the year within the study area. Habitat settings are based both on the variation of river discharge between seasonal high flows and seasonal low flows and on the interspersion of upland, wetland, and aquatic habitats within the larger floodplain (Moyle et al. 2007). When combined, the three fish habitat settings for the study area are described as slow water, such as sloughs, marshes, lakes, and seasonal floodplains; fast water, such as those associated with the continuous flowing waters of riparian habitats; and varied water flow conditions containing both fast and slow water.

Native slow-water fish found in the archaeological record of the Lower Cosumnes River watershed are tule perch (*Hysterocarpus traski*), Sacramento perch (*Archoplites interruptus*), thicktail chub (*Gila crassicauda*), hitch (*Lavina exillicauda*) and Sacramento blackfish (*Orthodon microlepidotus*). Fast-water fish found include Pacific lamprey (*Entosphenus tridentatus*), hardhead (*Mylopharodon conocephalus*), fall-run Chinook salmon (*Oncorhynchus tshawytscha*), white sturgeon (*Acipenser transmontanus*), and green sturgeon (*Acipenser medirostris*). Fish preferring varied settings include Sacramento sucker (*Catostomus occidentalis*), Sacramento splittail (*Pogonichthys macrolepidotus*), and Sacramento pikeminnow (*Ptychocheilus grandis*); the Sacramento pikeminnow has also been referred to as the Sacramento squawfish.

All of these fish are found today in the Cosumnes River Preserve except Sacramento perch, which are no longer present throughout their native range but have been introduced elsewhere, and the thicktail chub, which is now extinct (Cosumnes River Preserve 2007; McGinnis 2006; Moyle, personal communication, November 29, 2010). Table 6.2 lists each of these native fish, their current status, pertinent characteristics, and the habitats they prefer throughout their life stages.

TABLE 6.2. Cosumnes River Native Fish Habitat Requirements.

Common Name	Scientific Name	Status	Setting	Adults
White sturgeon	*Acipenser transmontanus*	Healthy	Fast water	Bay, estuary, river
Green sturgeon	*Acipenser medirostris*	Threatened	Fast water	Ocean, river
Chinook (king) salmon	*Oncorhynchus tshawytscha*	Special concern	Fast water	Ocean, river
Pacific lamprey	*Entosphenus tridentatus*	Watch	Fast water	Various freshwater, estuary
Sacramento sucker	*Catostomus occidentalis*	Healthy	Varied	Various freshwater
Hardhead	*Mylopharodon conocephalus*	Watch	Fast water	River, stream
Sacramento blackfish	*Orthodon microlepidotus*	Healthy	Slow water	Delta sloughs, various freshwater
Hitch	*Lavinia exilicauda*	Watch	Slow water	Estuary, slow-flow freshwater
Sacramento pikeminnow	*Ptychocheilus grandis*	Healthy	Varied	Various freshwater
Sacramento splittail	*Pogonichthys macrolepidotus*	Special concern	Varied	Various freshwater, estuary, alkaline lakes
Thicktail chub	*Gila crassicauda*	Extinct	Slow water	Delta sloughs, backwaters, floodplain lakes
Sacramento perch	*Archoplites interruptus*	Special concern	Slow water	Various freshwater, saline and alkaline waters
Tule perch	*Hysterocarpus traski*	Healthy	Slow water	Estuary, various freshwater

Standard Length (cm)	Spawning (Eggs Laid)	Type of Spawning	Juveniles	Spawning Season	Present in Study Area Archaeology
Up to 300	River	Broadcast	Estuary	Late winter to summer	Yes, as general sturgeon
3	River	Broadcast	River, estuary	Spring to early summer	Yes, as general sturgeon
Up to 100	Stream, river	Nest	River, flood-plain, estuary	Fall to winter	Yes
Up to 76	Stream, river	Nest	Estuary	Spring to early summer	No
Average at 30	Stream, some lakes	Broadcast	Stream, river margins, floodplain	Spring (use floodplain late in flood cycle in May)	Yes
Up to 60	Stream	Broadcast	Shallow stream margins, backwaters, floodplains	Spring	Yes
Up to 50	Lakes, rivers, backwaters, floodplain	Broadcast	Shallow lake, floodplains, river margins	Spring to early summer	Yes
Average at 15 to 20	Stream	Broadcast	Stream, lake margins, marsh, floodplains	Spring to early summer	Yes
Average at 25	Stream	Broadcast	Stream, river	Spring	Yes
Up to 45	Floodplain	Broadcast	Floodplain, sloughs	Late winter to early summer	Yes
Up to 40	Delta sloughs, floodplain	Broadcast	Unknown; assumed sloughs, shallow river margins, floodplain	Unknown; assumed spring	Yes
Up to 61	Shallow sloughs, river and lake margins, floodplain	Nest	Shallow river and lake margins, floodplain	Spring to summer	Yes
Up to 23	Live birth; various fresh-water, estuary	Live birth	Various freshwater, estuary	Summer	Yes

Habitat Utilization by Fish Life Stages

We hypothesize that traditional resource management enhanced floodplain habitats in a way that optimized conditions for juvenile fish. Table 6.2 lists the habitats used during the three life stages of native fish found in the archaeological and ethnographic record of the study area. The three life stages of native fish are (1) the spawning and egg-laying stage, (2) the fry or juvenile stage, and (3) the adult stage. Floodplains are used by many of these fish for growth and development in the juvenile stage, which is generally the most vulnerable point in native fish's life cycle.

It is important to note that floodplains must retain a passage to and from the fluvial systems that supply them. Within the study area, natural breaks found in the river levees provided fish passage. These breaks allow the exchange of fresh oxygenated water, keeping the floodplain ecosystem productive and healthy for juvenile fish (Moyle et al. 2007). Floodplain passageways also provide egress for older juvenile fish later in the year, preventing stranding and death as floodplains desiccate. The utilization of traditional resource-management practices such as burning enhanced floodplain rearing habitats by removing senescent vegetation, burning organic material in the upper soil layers, enhancing macroinvertebrate populations, and maintaining fish passage. Thus, traditional management practices enhanced fish growth and productivity, as well as reducing fish mortality.

A floodplain habitat is crucial to various stages of native California fish. Several native fish utilize the floodplain for spawning, and one native fish, the Sacramento splittail, is an obligate floodplain spawner. Endemic river spawners in the study area prefer to spawn upstream of floodplains, thereby allowing downstream currents to deliver their young to the floodplain for development in large numbers (Moyle et al. 2007). Twelve of the 14 native fish spawn within the spring months when the rainy season peaks and snowpacks begin to melt (see Table 6.2).

Native fish also have ecologically segregated life stages, which allow eggs, juveniles, and adult fish to exploit separate environments. This segregation reduces competition and predation and provides opportunities for increased growth and development. Floodplains provide an optimal nursery environment for the growth and development of young fish—and therefore a greater survival rate. Young fish of fast-water habitats enter the floodplain as larvae or small juveniles; these juveniles usually enter the floodplain early in the flooding cycle (early spring) in order to take advantage of zooplankton and large insect larvae. For example, Chinook salmon reared on Central Valley floodplains grew faster and achieved larger sizes than fish reared in the main river (Jeffres et al. 2008). Juvenile species of slow-water fish also have substantially faster growth and higher survival rates when they move to the floodplain late in the flood cycle as the water becomes warmer (Moyle et al. 2007).

The characteristics of high fecundity and large body size indicate that the environmental conditions present in California river floodplains are optimal for the growth and development of native fishes (Moyle 2002). Further, native fish have the ability to know when to leave the floodplain and avoid becoming stranded when floodplain pools dry up. Alien species lack this adaptation (Moyle 2002; Moyle et al. 2007).

The Archaeological Ichthyofaunal Record of the Cosumnes

Faunal remains from the study area's archaeological deposits dated from 5000 BP up to the historic era (ca. 1848) confirm that many of the historically observed fauna were also important to the prehistoric indigenous people's diet. In general, the archaeological and ethnographic record reveals that a wide variety of plants and animals were being consumed, including large amounts of grass seeds, roots, greens, insects, small mammals, waterfowl, and fish (Bennyhoff 1977). Salmon may be the most important and common fish cited, but direct archaeological evidence shows that many other different fish species made up the bulk of the indigenous diet in the study area. It has been estimated that fish species may have provided more than a third of the protein intake for most delta populations (Pierce 1988).

Fish remains from several archaeological sites occupied by the Plains Miwok located within the Lower Cosumnes River watershed can be used to help reconstruct the past ecology of the study area and serve as a reference to the mosaic of prehistoric delta ecological habitats. For this study, we have selected four Late period archaeological sites with well-preserved ichthyofaunal records to represent the study area. These sites are CA-SAC-329, CA-SAC-265, CA-SAC-267, and CA-SAC-133. Because the amount of ichthyofaunal remains identifiable to species varied at each site, percentages rounded to the nearest whole number will be used to discuss relative abundance. Figure 6.3 depicts an overview of the archaeological

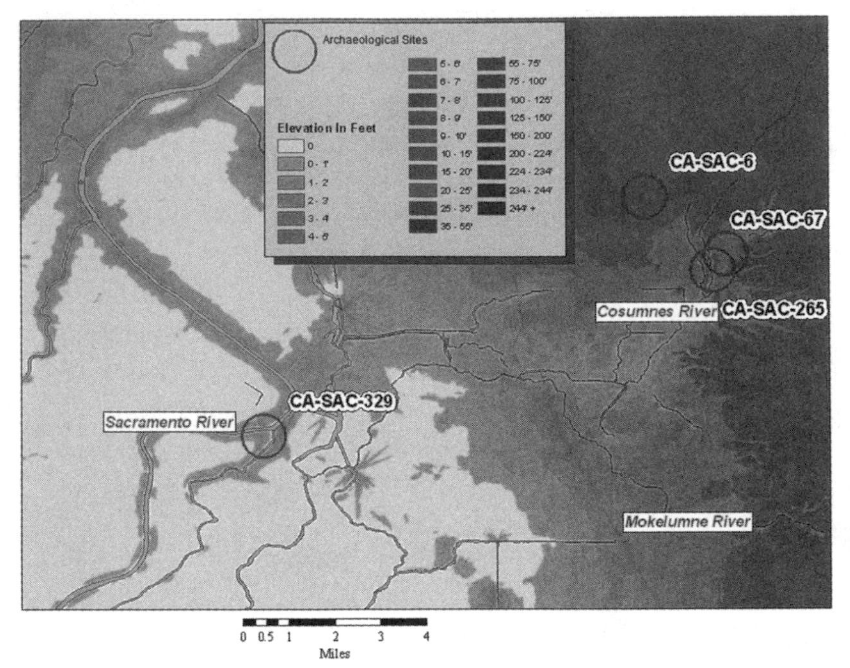

FIGURE 6.6. Site CA-SAC-329.

sites within the study area, and Figures 6.6 through 6.8 depict the general locations of each site discussed in this study.

CA-SAC-329

CA-SAC-329 is located on the southern bank of the Sacramento River at its junction with Georgiana Slough, within the historic confluence of the Cosumnes and Mokelumne rivers (see Figure 6.6). This site is described as a seasonal camp and is associated with a tule marsh habitat (Pierce 1988; Soule 1976). Occupation is dated from approximately AD 780 to 1600.

The faunal remains from this site show a predominance of slow-water fish species (see Figure 6.9). Sacramento perch composes more than half of the assemblage. Thicktail chub is the next most common species in the archaeological record, followed by Sacramento sucker and hitch. No salmon and very few sturgeon are accounted for. The location of CA-SAC-329, near a slough and marsh with a sandy substrate and away from the gravelly substrates of the upstream seasonal spawning grounds, could explain why salmon and sturgeon are underrepresented at this site. CA-SAC-329 is also the only site with tule perch remains, reflecting the lowland habitat preference of this species.

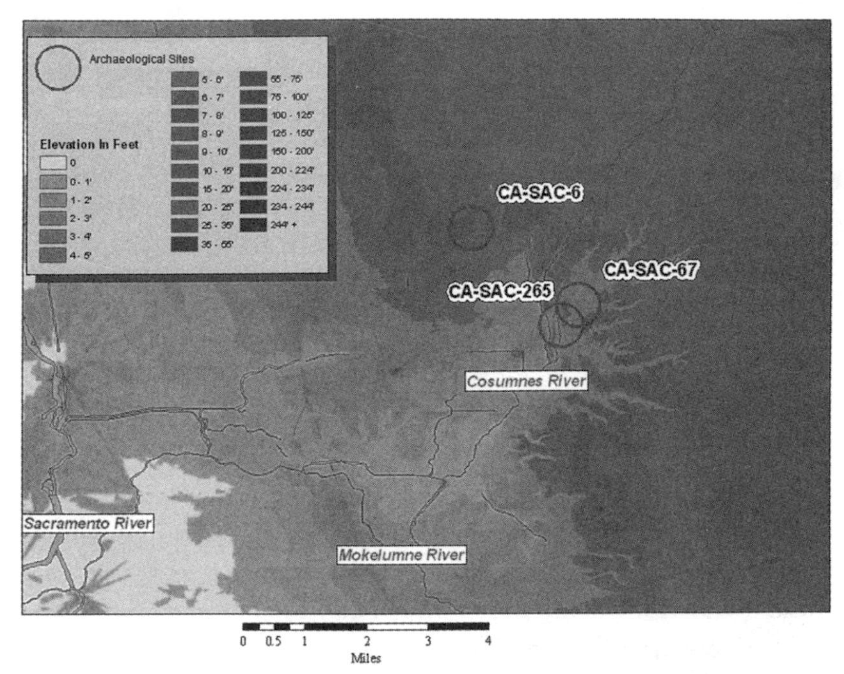

FIGURE 6.7. Site CA-SAC-265.

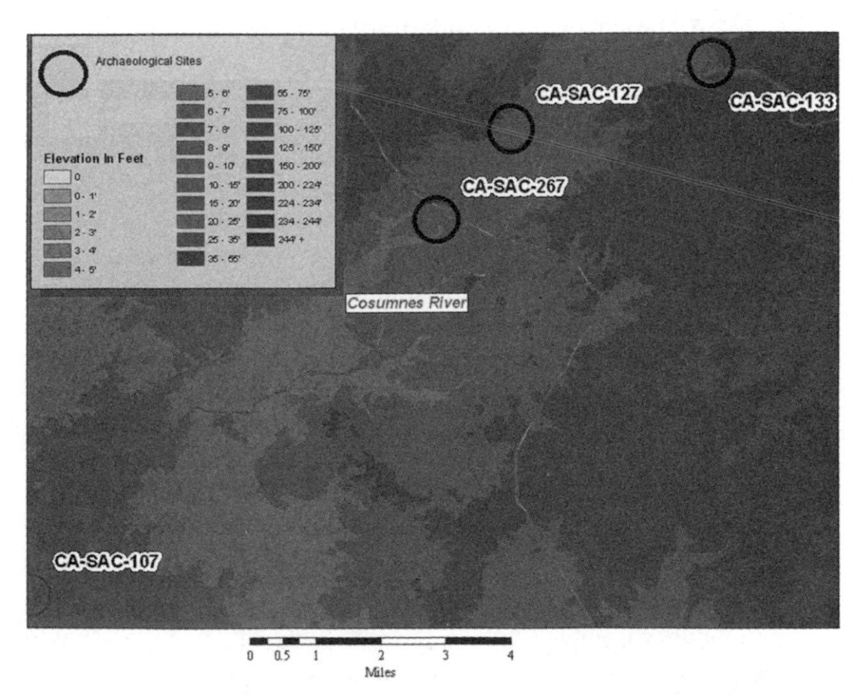

FIGURE 6.8. Sites CA-SAC-267 and CA-SAC-133.

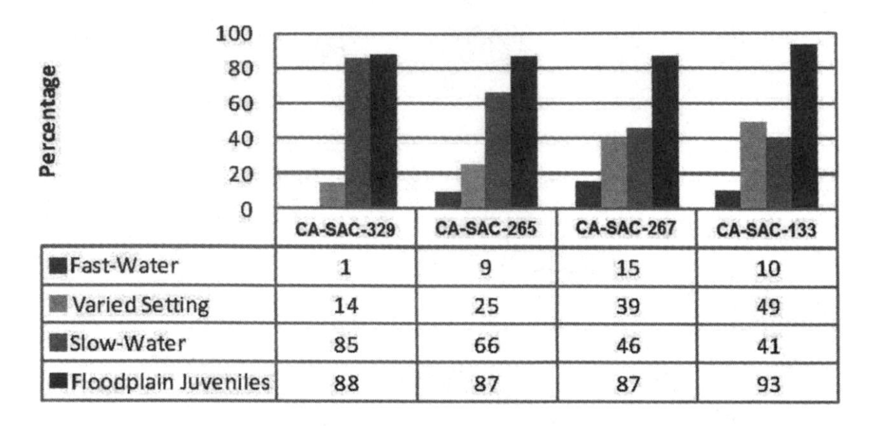

	CA-SAC-329	CA-SAC-265	CA-SAC-267	CA-SAC-133
Fast-Water	1	9	15	10
Varied Setting	14	25	39	49
Slow-Water	85	66	46	41
Floodplain Juveniles	88	87	87	93

FIGURE 6.9. Fish species composition by site.

An assemblage dominated by slow-water fish species is consistent with the location of CA-SAC-329; 85 percent of the fish represented are slow-water fish. As stated above, the growth and development of juvenile native fish are enhanced when they can utilize floodplain resources. An examination of the fish assemblage species composition reveals that 88 percent of the fish assemblage represented at CA-SAC-329 most likely utilized the floodplains in their juvenile stage.

The predominance of Sacramento perch remains in the ichthyofaunal assemblage indicates that the species composition within the vicinity of Georgiana Slough has changed over time. Today Sacramento perch are no longer present here and are a species of special concern for California. The decline of this species is due to a combination of factors, including habitat destruction (particularly the draining of sloughs), reduction of aquatic plant beds, embryo predation by introduced species, and competition for food and space with other introduced species (Moyle 2002).

CA-SAC-265

CA-SAC-265 is described as a specialized fishing camp located on the south bank of Laguna Creek, just north of its confluence with the Cosumnes River (see Figure 6.7; Sheeders 1982). This location is a low-elevation grasslands habitat bordered by a large expanse of seasonal floodplains and sloughs. Before current conditions, this site would have been adjacent to the terminus of the tidal flood basin (Moyle et al. 2003).

The ichthyofaunal assemblage from CA-SAC-265 is slightly more varied than that from CA-SAC-329. Although it is still dominated by slow-water fish (66 percent), fast-water species constitute 9 percent of the assemblage, and varied-setting species compose 25 percent of the assemblage. The fish remains from CA-SAC-265 are dominated by Sacramento perch, followed by equal amounts of thicktail chub and Sacramento sucker. Other minnow species follow. Salmon are also present but only make up less than 5 percent of the assemblage. The habitat preferences of the fish species identified indicate that CA-SAC-265 was located at the interface of slow-water and fast-water environments. Species that would have utilized the floodplains as juveniles compose 87 percent of the CA-SAC-265 assemblage.

CA-SAC-267

CA-SAC-267 most likely represents the remains of a large village or ceremonial center. The site is located on a knoll along the edge of a high terrace just west of the Cosumnes River, 14 miles north of CA-SAC-265 (see Figure 6.8). The site contains the remains of several large cooking features, house pits, and a probable dance house (Johnson 1976). The site was occupied from approximately AD 500 until sometime between 1830 and 1840 (Morgan 2001).

The species composition for CA-SAC-267 indicates that the inhabitants were obtaining fish from a variety of habitats. Fish remains are dominated by Sacramento sucker, followed by Sacramento perch and Chinook salmon. The increase in salmon remains and in fast-water species in general is noteworthy. Together these species compose 15 percent of the assemblage, a figure almost double that found at CA-SAC-265. Despite this variety, 87 percent of the fish species found at CA-SAC-267 likely used floodplains as juveniles, supporting the assumption that healthy floodplains would have benefited multiple species of native fish.

CA-SAC-133

Although the archaeological deposit at CA-SAC-133 is slightly older than the previous sites discussed (AD 670–820), its archaeological assemblage is still relevant to our discussion. CA-SAC-133 is a village site located on a small mound adjacent to the Cosumnes River near the community of Sloughhouse, at the edge of the Sierra Nevada foothills. This location is above the floodplain formed by the Cosumnes River on the east and Deer

Creek on the west (see Figure 6.8). Similar to the case in other sites in the study area, 93 percent of the fish species represented most likely utilized the floodplain as juveniles.

The fish assemblage of CA-SAC-133 is 49 percent varied-setting species, the majority of which are Sacramento sucker. The amount of slow-water species is almost equal to that of varied-setting species, while fast-water species, the majority of which are Chinook salmon, represent only 10 percent of the assemblage. This result is unexpected because historical records document that the Chinook salmon migration went 34 miles up the Cosumnes and the best spawning beds were reported to be between Sloughhouse and Bridgehouse, located upstream to the west (Cosumnes, American, Bear, and Yuba Integrated Regional Water Management Plan 2010; Yoshiyama et al. 2001). Regardless of this finding, the fish species represented at CA-SAC-133 reflect the varied geographic placement of the site at an area where the Cosumnes River becomes more channelized and swifter but is also bordered by a large floodplain.

Conclusions: Reciprocal Relationships and the Water–People–Fish Connection

Based on this synthesis of multiple sources of information, traditional resource management of the riparian floodplain appears to have helped optimize habitat conditions for California native fish species, contributing to their ability to adapt to fluctuating environmental conditions and supply one-third of the study area population's diet for at least 1,100 years. The loss of traditional tending practices, compounded by widespread degradation of habitat, alteration of flows, and introduction of exotic species, has resulted in the catastrophic decline of most California native fish species. Minnows and other native fish that were originally abundant in lowland lakes, freshwater marshes, sloughs, and slow-moving sections of the river have diminished significantly from pre-European settlement numbers or disappeared. Just over 50 percent of the fish species present within the archaeological record for the study area are now either on watch status, threatened, of special concern, or extinct. The Sacramento perch, which composed 49 percent of the entire archaeological ichthyofaunal record presented here, is no longer present within the study area. The thicktail chub, which composed 13 percent of all the assemblages, is now extinct.

Chinook salmon and Pacific lampreys, which are profusely referred to in the ethnographic record, are listed as species of special concern and on watch status, respectively. Recent research has shown that salmon reared in seasonally inundated habitats, such as floodplains, with annual vegetation have higher growth rates (Jeffres et al. 2008; Sommer et al. 2001a; Sommer et al. 2001b). Such floodplains may have been available in areas adjacent to the Cosumnes River during prehistoric times; burning techniques practiced by Native Californians would have likely enhanced optimal habitats. Today, Chinook salmon have only recently returned to the Cosumnes River because restoration efforts have reestablished suitable habitats (Moyle et al. 2007). The return of salmon to the Cosumnes River does not negate the fact that the salmon runs traditionally managed and used as resources by Native Californians were extirpated after 1988.

The extent of burning as a keystone management tool in the indigenous landscape has been well documented (Anderson 2005; Hankins 2005; Lewis 1973; Martinez 2000, 2002; Vahti and Greco 2007). Burning of the floodplains within the study area not only helped rejuvenate vegetation stands important for the production of the indigenous material culture but also rejuvenated and nourished the soils and kept the floodplain clean and clear for the growth and development of juvenile fish. For over 90 percent of the fish considered in this discussion, a deep, open, oxygenated floodplain saturated with spring waters and teaming with insect larvae would have been an optimal environment for the rearing of juvenile fish: "Burning and grazing of tules was probably good for fish; the ranchers used to do this along Suisun Marsh, keeping areas open and more floodable at high tides" (Moyle, personal communication, November 29, 2010). Such a practice reflects a lesson already learned and well practiced by California's indigenous population.

In the timeless past, Miwok ancestors cared for and managed their ecosystem and conducted specific world-renewal ceremonies. We present our information in recognition and in honor of the California Indian cultures in the Cosumnes River watershed—namely, the Ione Band of Miwok Indians, the Sierra Native American Council, and the California Indian Basketweavers Association. We also recommend that this information be used for the conservation of native California fish species, for resource management of the Cosumnes River and the Sacramento–San Joaquin Delta, and as a template for cultural and ecological restoration of this valuable habitat complex.

Acknowledgments

We would like to thank Dr. Peter Moyle and Dr. Ron Yoshiyama, University of California, Davis, for their invaluable assistance and knowledge on fish ecology and historic ecology. We would also like to thank Scott Tidball, California State University, Sacramento, environmental studies student, for geographic information system data and help with Figures 6.1–6.4, 6.6–6.8. And we would like to thank Sandra Varela, California State University, Sacramento, student, for help with Table 6.2.

References Cited

Anderson, M. K.

1993 *Indian Fire-Based Management in the Sequoia–Mixed Conifer Forests of the Central and Southern Sierra Nevada*. Final report for cooperative agreement no. 8027-2-002. On file at the Yosemite Research Center, Yosemite National Park.

2005 *Tending the Wild: Native American Knowledge and the Management of California's Cultural Resources*. Berkeley: University of California Press.

Barrett, S. A., and E. W. Gifford

1933 Miwok Material Culture. *Bulletin of Milwaukee Public Museum* 2(4):117–276.

Bates, C. D., and M. J. Lee

1990 *Tradition and Innovation: A Basket History of the Indians of the Yosemite–Mono Lake Area*. Yosemite National Park: Yosemite Association.

Bennyhoff, J. A.

1977 *The Ethnogeography of the Plains Miwok*. Center for Archaeological Research at Davis Publication no. 5. Davis: University of California.

Berkes, F.

1999 *Sacred Ecology: Traditional Ecological Knowledge and Resource Management*. Philadelphia: Taylor and Francis Publishing.

Berkes, F., J. Colding, and C. Folke

2000 Rediscovery of Traditional Ecological Knowledge as Adaptive Management. *Ecological Applications* 10(5):1251–1262.

Bibby, B.

1996 *The Fine Art of California Indian Basketry*. Sacramento: Crocker Art Museum; and Berkeley: Heyday Books.

Blackburn, T. C., and K. Anderson, eds.

1993 *Before the Wilderness: Environmental Management by Native Californians*. Menlo Park: Ballena Press.

Bouey, P. D., and S. A. Waechter

1992 *Final Report on Phase II Test Excavations at CA-SAC-133 near Sloughhouse, Sacramento County, California*. Report prepared by the Far Western Anthropological Group, Davis, for contract no. 03G196/Task Order 1, December.

On file at the California Department of Transportation, District 3, Sacramento.

Central Valley Historic Mapping Project

1999 Pre-1900 (Base Map). Electronic document, http://www.gic.csuchico.edu/historic/4_1.html, accessed September 26, 2010.

Cook, S. F.

1956 *The Population of the California Indians, 1796–1970*. Berkeley: University of California Press.

Cosumnes, American, Bear, and Yuba Integrated Regional Water Management Plan

2010 Salmon and Steelhead in CABY Region Watersheds. Electronic document, http://cabyregion.org/projects-1/work-groups/fish-passage-and-habitat-improvement-project-development/western-placer-creeks-documents/salmon-and-steelhead-in-the-caby-region-watersheds/, accessed September 26, 2010.

Cosumnes River Preserve

2007 Cosumnes River Fish Species List. Electronic document, http://www.cosumnes.org/flora_fauna/Fish.pdf, accessed September 26, 2010.

2010a About Cosumnes River Preserve. Electronic document, http://www.cosumnes.org/about_crp/index.html, accessed September 19, 2010.

2010b Cosumnes River Fish Species List. Electronic document, http://cosumnes.org/documents/fish.pdf, accessed October 12, 2010.

Egan, D., and E. A. Howell, eds.

2001 *The Historical Ecology Handbook: A Restorationist's Guide to Reference Ecosystems*. Washington, DC: Society for Ecological Restoration, Island Press.

Golla, V.

2007 Linguistic Prehistory. In *California Prehistory: Colonization, Culture, and Complexity*. T. L. Jones and K. A. Klar, eds. Pp. 71–82. Plymouth, UK: AltaMira Press.

Grossinger, R. M.

2001 Documenting Local Landscape Change: The San Francisco Bay Area Historical Ecology Project. In *The Historical Ecology Handbook: A Restorationist's Guide to Reference Ecosystems*. Dave Egan and Evelyn A. Howell, eds. Pp. 425–442. Washington, DC: Island Press.

Grossinger, R. M., R. A. Askevold, and C. J. Striplen

2006 *Coyote Creek Watershed Historical Ecology Study: Historical Condition, Landscape Change, and Restoration Potential in the Eastern Santa Clara Valley, California*. San Francisco Estuary Institute Report no. 426. Report prepared for the Santa Clara Valley Water District, Oakland. Electronic document, http://www.sfei.org/sites/default/files/executive_summary_8.5x11_CoyoteCk_HE_SFEI_2006.pdf.

Hankins, D.
2005 Pyrogeography: Spatial and Temporal Relationships of Fire, Nature, and Culture. Unpublished Ph.D. dissertation, University of California, Davis.
Heady, H. F.
1988 Valley Grassland. In *Terrestrial Vegetation of California: New Expanded Edition*. Michael G. Barbour and Jack Major, eds. Pp. 491–514. California Native Plant Society Special Publication no. 9. Sacramento.
Jeffres, C. A., J. J. Opperman, and P. B. Moyle
2008 Ephemeral Floodplain Habitats Provide Best Growth Conditions for Juvenile Chinook Salmon in a California River. *Environmental Biology of Fishes* 83:449–458.
Johnson, J. J., ed.
1976 *Archaeological Investigations at the Blodgett Site (CA-SAC-267), Sloughhouse Locality, California*. Report on file at the North Central Information Center, Sacramento.
Katibah, E. F.
1984 A Brief History of Riparian Forests in the Central Valley of California. In *California Riparian Systems: Ecology, Conservation and Productive Management*. R. E. Warner and K. M. Hendrix, eds. Pp. 23–29. Berkeley: University of California Press.
Kroeber, A. L.
1925 *Handbook of the Indians of California*. Bureau of American Ethnology Bulletin 78. Washington, DC.
Latta, F. F.
1977 *Handbook of Yokuts Indians*. Santa Cruz, CA: Bear State Publishers.
Levy, R.
1978 Eastern Miwok. In *Handbook of North American Indians, vol. 8: California*. R. F. Heizer, ed. Pp. 398–413. Washington, DC: Smithsonian Institution.
Lewis, H. T.
1973 *Patterns of Indian Burning in California: Ecology and Ethnohistory*. Ramona, CA: Ballena Press.
Lindstrom, S.
1992 Great Basin Fisherfolk: Optimal Diet Breadth Modeling the Truckee River Aboriginal Subsistence Fishery. Unpublished Ph.D. dissertation, University of California, Davis.
Martinez, D.
2000 Traditional Ecological Knowledge, Ecosystem Science, and Environmental Management. *Ecological Applications* 10(5):1249–1250.
2002 *Traditional Indian Burning, Fire Hazard Reduction and Restoration Forestry*. Mendocino, CA: New Settler.
McGinnis, S. M.
2006 *Field Guide to Freshwater Fishes of California*. Berkeley: University of California Press.

Merrill, R.E.

1923 Plants Used in Basketry by the California Indians. *University of California Publications in American Archaeology and Ethnology* 20:215–242.

Morgan, S.M.

2001 Biological Distance Study of Four Late Horizon Central California Populations. Unpublished M.A. thesis, California State University, Sacramento.

Mount, J.F.

1995 *California Rivers and Streams: The Conflict between Fluvial Process and Land Use*. Berkeley: University of California Press.

Mount, J.F., G.E. Fogg, L. Kavvas, J.H. Fleckenstein, M. Anderson, Z. Chen, and E. Suzuki

2001 *Linked Surface Water Groundwater Model for the Cosumnes River Watershed: Hydrologic Evaluation of Management Options to Restore Fall Flows*. Final report, U.S. Fish and Wildlife Service, cooperative agreement no. 11332-8-J264. Sacramento.

Moyle, P.B.

2002 *Inland Fishes of California*. Rev. and expanded edition. Berkeley: University of California Press.

Moyle, P.B., P.K. Crain, and K. Whitener

2007 Patterns in the Use of a Restored California Floodplain by Native and Alien Fishes. *San Francisco Estuary and Watershed Science* 5(3):1–27. Electronic document, http://escholarship.org/uc/item/6fq2f838.

Moyle, P.B., P.K. Crain, K. Whitener, and J. Mount

2003 Alien Fishes in Natural Streams: Fish Distribution, Assemblage Structure, and Conservation in the Cosumnes River, California, USA. *Environmental Biology of Fishes* 68:143–162.

Pierce, P.

1988 A Geoarchaeological Analysis of the Prehistoric Sacramento–San Joaquin Delta, California. Unpublished M.A. research paper, University of California, Davis.

Powers, S.

1877 *Tribes of California*. Contributions to North American Ethnology, vol. 3. Washington, DC: Government Printing Office.

Salmón, E.

2000 Kincentric Ecology: Indigenous Perceptions of the Human–Nature Relationship. *Ecological Applications* 10:1327–1332.

Sheeders, D.J.

1982 An Archaeological Analysis of the Whaley Site, CA-SAC-265. Unpublished M.A. thesis, California State University, Sacramento.

Sommer, T.R., B. Harrell, M. Nobriga, R. Brown, P. Moyle, W. Kimmerer, and L. Schemel

2001a California's Yolo Bypass: Evidence that Flood Control Can Be Compatible with Fisheries, Wetlands, Wildlife, and Agriculture. *Fisheries* 26:6–16.

Sommer, T. R., M. L. Nobriga, W. C. Harrell, W. Batham, and W. J. Kimmerer
2001b Floodplain Rearing of Juvenile Chinook Salmon: Evidence of Enhanced Growth and Survival. *Canadian Journal of Fisheries and Aquatic Science* 58:325–333.

Soule, W. E.
1976 Archaeological Excavations at SAC-329 near Walnut Grove, Sacramento County, California. Unpublished MS on file at the Archaeological Research Center, California State University, Sacramento.

Stevens, M. L.
1999 The Ethnoecology and Autecology of White Root (*Carex barbarae*): Implications for Restoration. Unpublished Ph.D. dissertation, University of California, Davis.
2003 The Contribution of Traditional Resource Management (TRM) of White Root (*Carex barbarae Dewey, Cyperaceae*) by California Indians to Riparian Ecosystem Structure and Function. In *California Riparian Systems: Processes and Floodplain Management, Ecology, and Restoration*. 2001 Riparian Habitat and Floodplains Conference Proceedings. P. M. Faber, ed. Pp. 502–511. Sacramento: Riparian Habitat Joint Venture.
2004a Ethnoecology of Selected California Wetland Plants. *Fremontia* 32(4):7–13.
2004b White Root (*Carex barbarae*). *Fremontia* 32(4):3–6.

Stewart, O. C., H. T. Lewis, and K. Anderson
2002 *Forgotten Fires: Native Americans and the Transient Wilderness*. Norman: University of Oklahoma Press.

Swenson, R., K. Whitener, and M. Eaton
2003 Restoring Flood to Floodplains: Riparian and Floodplain Restoration at the Cosumnes River Preserve. In *California Riparian Systems: Processes and Floodplain Management, Ecology, and Restoration*. 2001 Riparian Habitat and Floodplains Conference Proceedings. P. M. Faber, ed. Pp. 224–229. Sacramento: Riparian Habitat Joint Venture.

Thompson, K.
1961 Riparian Forests of the Sacramento Valley, California. *Annals of the Association of American Geographers* 51(3):294–315.

U.S. Geological Survey
1979 *Water Resources Data for California, Water Year 1978, vol. 4: Northern Central Valley Basins and the Great Basin from Honey Lake to Oregon State Line*. U.S. Geological Survey Water Data Report CA-78-4. Sacramento.

Vahti, M. G., and S. E. Greco
2007 Riparian Vegetation of the Great Valley. In *Terrestrial Vegetation of California*. M. G. Barbour, T. Keeler-Wolf, and A. A. Schoenher, eds. Pp. 425–455. Berkeley: University of California Press.

West, G. J., W. Woolfenden, J. A. Wanket, and R. S. Anderson
2007 Late Pleistocene and Holocene Environments. In *California Prehistory: Col-*

onization, Culture, and Complexity. T. L. Jones and K. A. Klar, eds. Pp. 11–34. Plymouth, UK: AltaMira Press.

Wheeler, A., and A. K. G. Jones

1989 *Fishes*. Cambridge: Cambridge University Press.

Yamane, L., and D. Aguilar

1997 *Weaving a California Tradition: A Native American Basketmaker*. Minneapolis: Lerner Publications.

Yoshiyama, R. M., F. W. Fisher, and P. B. Moyle

1996 Historical and Present Distribution of Chinook Salmon in the Central Valley Drainage of California. In *Sierra Nevada Ecosystem Project: Final Report to Congress*, vol. III. Don C. Erman, ed., and the SNEP Team. Pp. 309–362. Davis: University of California Centers for Water and Wildland Resources.

1998 Historical Abundance and Decline of Chinook Salmon in the Central Valley Region of California. *North American Journal of Fisheries Management* 18:487–521.

Yoshiyama, R. M., E. R. Gerstung, F. W. Fisher, and P. B. Moyle

2001 Historical and Present Distribution of Chinook Salmon in the Central Valley Drainage of California. In *Contributions to the Biology of Central Valley Salmonoids*, vol. 1. Randall L. Brown, ed. Pp. 71–176. State of California Department of Fish and Game Fish Bulletin 179. California Fish and Game, Sacramento.

At the Intersection of Ecology, History, and Evolution

Archaeological and Ethnographic Perspectives on Fishing in North America's Interior Northwest

ANNA MARIE PRENTISS

Fishing was a critical subsistence pursuit for traditional interior peoples of the greater Pacific Northwest. Anthropologists have learned a great deal about variability in traditional fishing practices in recent decades (e.g., Hunn 1990; Kew 1992; Prentiss and Kuijt 2012; Romanoff 1992). There have also been important contributions from archaeologists regarding the antiquity of fishing traditions within the region (e.g., Butler and Campbell 2004; Chatters 1989, 1995; Chatters et al. 1995; Speller et al. 2005). There is a widespread assumption among Plateau archaeologists that fish were of fundamental importance, yet few have engaged in direct consideration of variability in fish procurement and processing or considered reasons behind that variation. As the chapters in this volume make clear, the problem of variability in fishing and its impacts on the archaeological record are complex. Explanation of variability in fishing asks us to consider both ecology and human cultural history. Were socioeconomic decisions made by ancient actors contingent on local ecological conditions? To what degree were those decisions programmed by historical precedence—as in "we have always done it this way"? The latter implies impacts of long-term cultural traditions. It also implies the evolution of strategies that can persist and spread into new areas.

Chapters in this volume explore the intersection of ecology, history, and evolution. We discover that hunter-gatherers of the interior Northwest engaged in a variety of fishing tactics and integrated fish in sometimes quite different ways into their economies. Some of this was triggered by variability in local ecologies affecting fisheries production. Some groups actively manipulated their environments to enhance productivity. Fishing among all groups was also affected by inherited cultural traditions. There can be little doubt, for example, that some, if not many, of the cultural differences in subsistence practices between ethnographic Numic speakers in southern Idaho and Salish or Chinookan occupants of the main stems of the Fraser and Columbia can be attributed to cultural heritage. The former transported a more mobile strategy for living in arid Great Basin environments, relying upon harvesting and processing of a diverse array of foods. Salmon was merely one small contributor to a wide diet. In contrast, to many of the latter groups, salmon was the keystone resource, mass harvested and stored for reliance throughout the cold-season months by semisedentary groups, the critical element of a socioeconomic strategy that we can trace back to at least the middle Holocene on the Northwest Coast (Chatters 1995; Chatters and Prentiss 2005; Matson and Coupland 1995; Prentiss and Chatters 2003).

These case studies illustrate the complexity of cultural decision making and the challenge for archaeologists attempting to make sense of the archaeological record associated with fishing peoples. In this chapter I explore the relationships among ecology, human organization, and evolutionary history. I argue that we will not fully understand variability without attention to the interaction of complex factors affecting human behavior and consequently the archaeological record. Authors of this book are not charged with explication of the epistemology behind their arguments. Yet each implicates significant theoretical and methodological issues behind the explanation of variability in foraging behavior and its reflection in the archaeological record. In the present chapter I review some of the critical contributions of this book and close with a consideration of their implications for our current understanding of variability in Middle Fraser Canyon (British Columbia) fishing and socioeconomic systems during the past 2,000 years.

Salmon Ecology

Life histories of salmon are affected by variability in a range of environments. Chapters in this volume aptly illustrate many of these conditions and offer important implications for understanding human predation tactics and their role in larger socioeconomic systems. Grabowski provides a valuable summary of variability in salmon life histories, pointing out significant variation between and even within species of salmonids. He recognizes that while most species of salmon spawn in the late summer and fall, some populations come in the spring. Even today, Native people of the Fraser–Thompson system often refer to Chinook salmon as "spring salmon." Another important factor for Native fishing people concerned variability in access to particular species and their potential utility. Grabowski notes that while several species were known to run substantial distances up interior river systems (e.g., sockeye and Chinook), others (chum and pink) never made it past lower reaches of the region's rivers. Next, different fish offered different packages of nutrients to indigenous consumers. Chum or "dog" salmon as well as pink salmon have little fat. Consequently, while they offered significant protein and stored well, they were less well regarded than the fatter sockeye and Chinook species (e.g., Kew 1992; Romanoff 1992). This distinction could be critical for groups seeking to survive long winters on dried fish (among other stored foods).

Grabowski points out that while salmonids are highly resilient, there was still significant potential for variability in numbers during any given year. Fundamentally, anadromous salmon spend their lives in freshwater stream and marine ecosystems. Variability in the conditions of each can affect numbers available to human predators. The spawning and outmigration of smolts is affected by stream conditions, particularly water temperature, sediment loads, and thermal cover. Plew and Guinn, in their contribution, add examples of how local conditions in specific stream systems could have significant impacts on numbers of fish. They point to hydrologic effects of tectonic events, fire-induced erosion, and even landslides as critical factors leading to the potential degradation of salmon streams. Some of these factors have been considered by previous scholars. For example, Hayden and Ryder (1991), famously, explained the collapse of Middle Fraser Canyon villages as the consequence of landslides blocking salmon in the Fraser River. When questioned by Kuijt (2001) on the issue, they (Hayden and Ryder 2003) added the possibility that coordinated slides around the region could have been the result of tectonic activity. Regardless of outcomes from debates concerning dramatic slides in the Middle Fraser River area, it is clear that such factors could have played important roles affecting local variability in salmon resources.

Grabowski makes it clear that since salmon spend a significant portion of their life cycles in marine contexts, oceanic conditions and global weather phenomena (e.g., El Niño and La Niña) can also play important roles in the salmon populations available to fishing peoples. Sea surface temperatures, upwelling, and predator–prey distributions affect the ability of young fish to mature and survive to spawning age (Beamish and Bouillon 1993; Benson and Trites 2002; Downton and Miller 1998; Mueter et al. 2002). It is also well known that some river systems such as the Fraser could be harsh to spawning fish (Gilhousen 1990; Heard 1991; MacDonald 2000; Quinn 2005). There has been an assumption among some scholars (e.g., Hayden and Mathewes 2009) that salmon numbers were simply so high that despite these factors, there could never have been fluctuations large enough to significantly impact human fishing groups. In contrast, recent research suggests that interannual fluctuations in numbers of spawning salmon have been extreme in the Fraser system, for example, from as little as three million to more than 34 million fish in a 30-year period (Bernton 2010; English et al. 2006). Paleoecological research suggests that extreme fluctuations such as these undoubtedly occurred in the past (Chatters et al. 1995; Finney et al. 2002).

Some groups on the eastern Columbia Plateau lived in contexts lacking (or nearly so) anadromous salmon and instead harvested different species of trout and mountain whitefish along with shellfish. Lyons makes the argument that the predictable life cycles of these fish made them equally amenable to intensive harvest in the absence of anadromous salmonids in the Pend Oreille watershed. Bull trout in particular may have been attractive given their larger size and highly predictable spawning patterns. Jones points to shellfish as an equally attractive option in the Spokane River area. An important point to also consider is that even in areas where access to anadromous salmonids was possible, trout and shellfish could still provide a critical link in the annual subsistence cycle. For example, Canadian Plateau peoples often harvested trout in the spring and fall when stored salmon, roots, and dried deer meat were not available (Alexander 1992).

All things considered, it is clear that indigenous fishing groups often coped with significant variability in access to fish. However, indigenous groups were not always passive consumers but were quite capable of manipulating environments to enhance and maintain productivity. Stevens and Zelazo outline tactics undertaken by the Plains Mewuk people of northern California to improve habitats for the production of a wide range of resources. These people employed a range of strategies that included species management, landscape rotation, and landscape patchiness management. Most critically, they used fire to maintain open habitats for harvesting and habitation, to prevent vegetation from blocking natural levee breaks (and preventing fish from spawning on floodplains), and for creating depression topographies to enhance fish spawning in floodplains. Enhanced floodplains permitted exceptional spawning and rearing habitats for many fish, including Chinook salmon. Archaeologists and paleoecologists have only recently begun research to assess evidence for Native landscape management in the greater Pacific Northwest (e.g., Lepofsky et al. 2005), but this will be a critical area of research in the future, and it will offer important implications for resource managers and policy makers.

Cultural Traditions and Locally Contingent Tactics

While variability in the predictable access to fish was undoubtedly critical to indigenous fishing groups of the interior Northwest, having the cultural apparatus to organize the harvest and process the return was equally critical. Contributors to this book make it clear that a range of culturally distinct socioeconomic strategies may have operated in the region during the ethnographic period. If we cast the net wider, so to speak, the range of variability only grows (e.g., fire-enhanced collectors of California). Plew and Guinn recognize four possible strategies used by Shoshonean groups in the Snake River system. Some were classic collectors (sensu Binford 1980), intensively harvesting and storing fish and living in small winter villages. Others were more mobile, making use of horses to transport loads of dried fish to more distant residential bases. These latter groups were not tethered to caches of fish along the rivers and could afford to move with their stores. A third pattern reflects classic forager (again sensu Binford 1980) strategy whereby groups of "White Knife" Shoshone used the Snake River fishery as one node in a highly mobile residential system. These groups did not harvest a surplus for storage purposes but merely made use of the salmon resource while available before moving on to the next resource. The final strategy may have emphasized the storage of camas in upland prairie winter base camps, supplemented by harvested, dried, and transported salmon from the Snake River.

Other contributors identify evidence for the operation of the Plateau winter village pattern (e.g., Chatters 1989; Chatters and Pokotylo 1998). Yu and Cook see intensive late prehistoric salmon fishing in the Upper Columbia area associated with often large winter villages, specialized fish-harvest and -processing sites, and accumulations of specialized processing tools. Lyons describes a wide range of techniques for intensively harvesting trout in service of retaining a winter village strategy in the absence of anadromous fish. Jones posits that shellfish occurred in sufficient abundances to favor intensive harvest and storage and offer another alternative to salmon. Stevens and Zelazo step beyond procurement techniques to also consider a wider range of resource-management tactics incorporated into annual subsistence and mobility cycles. This adds a new and interesting dimension to our knowledge of fishing peoples, requiring us to imagine not just the enhanced technologies and advance planning incorporated into Mewuk subsistence systems but also the unintended constraints that such a system may have imposed on the people's mobility options. If locked into a cycle of burning and vegetation maturation coupled with fisheries schedules, the people may have had few options for making contingent adjustments (e.g., Lightfoot et al. 2011). On the other hand, their effective maintenance of maximally productive wetland and upland communities may have made the issue of mobility options somewhat irrelevant. Contrast this with the Shoshone groups of the northern Great Basin, periodically stopping off in the Middle Snake for short-term salmon harvests. Mobility options for these people were likely paramount in their annual cycles.

The origin of collector-like strategies is a significant issue for Plateau archaeologists (Chatters 1989, 1995; Lohse and Sammons-Lohse 1986; Nelson 1973; Prentiss and Chatters 2003; Prentiss and Kuijt 2004; Schalk 1981). Drawing from Davis (2007), Plew and Guinn point out that while Prentiss and Chatters (2003) argue for a post-3500 BP emergence of collectors on the Plateau, some evidence from the Salmon River in Idaho suggests a post-2000 BP development. Implicit in their argument is the assumption that collector-like organization is one of many choices that could be instituted at any time given the right ecological conditions (e.g., predictably abundant salmon). Binford (1980) did argue that logistical and residential mobility options might be employed in different mixes in different ecological contexts. However, Binford was surely not excluding the possibility that unique combinations of mobility, technological organization, and food procurement and processing could evolve as integrated strategies and compete with other such packages held by different groups (e.g., Bettinger and Baumhoff 1982). His argument merely implies that certain patterns of organization will more likely be favored over time under certain ecological conditions (e.g., collectors commonly appear in high effective temperature contexts [Binford 1980]). As argued by Chatters and Prentiss (2005; see also Prentiss 2009), the shift from a full-time forager-like to a winter village collector-like socioeconomic organization may have implied a highly risky process of radically altering long-held tactics of mobility and land-use scheduling, technological organization, and labor allocation, making such a change unlikely to have been a socioecologically or politically simple undertaking.

The Holocene record of Plateau hunter-gatherers is extensive and complex. It is very clear that different groups have employed a range of mobility options. There is little doubt that Western Stemmed Tradition groups predating 8000 BP engaged in logistical mobility, but there is virtually no evidence for reliance upon intensive food storage or occupation of winter villages (Chatters et al. 2012). Early Holocene groups postdating the Western Stemmed Tradition (e.g., Cascade phase and Nesikep traditions) demonstrate mobility, food procurement/consumption, and technological organization closely aligned with Binford's (1980) conception of residentially mobile foragers (Chatters et al. 2012; Prentiss and Kuijt 2004). Early house pit groups (e.g., Pithouse I [Chatters 1995]) on the Plateau clearly employed some degree of logistical mobility along with semisedentism. However, not only is there little evidence for food storage in the form of cache pits, but the zooarchaeological record (Butler and Campbell 2004; Chatters 1995; Prentiss et al. 2005) provides virtually no indication of specialized diet and resource processing associated with winter village collectors (compare with Middle Fraser Canyon villagers at ca. 1200–1600 BP [Prentiss et al. 2007]). It is not until the post-3500 BP period that we recognize the region-wide appearance of such organizational behavior on the Plateau (Chatters 1989, 1995, 2004; Goodale et al. 2004; Prentiss and Kuijt 2004). Collector-like organization also does not become obvious until after 3500–4000 BP on the central Northwest Coast (Matson and Coupland 1995). However, new research on the northern coast of British Columbia suggests that collector-like organization may have developed earlier in that context (e.g., Christensen and Stafford 2005; McLaren et al. 2011).

These data suggest either that local groups independently made the switch to collector organization or that one or a few made the jump, had some success, and either spread to new areas or transmitted the core concepts between groups. The former idea seems unlikely given the high degree of intergroup contact that likely existed between Pacific Northwest groups during the premodern period. In contrast, cultural transmission probably played a significant role in the spread of collector organization in parts of both the coast and the Interior (Chatters and Prentiss 2005). But the near abandonment of the Plateau region at circa 4000–3600 BP (Chatters 1995; Goodale et al. 2004; Prentiss and Kuijt 2004) may have also provided a significant opportunity for outside groups. Prentiss and Kuijt (2004) document evidence for the expansion of coastal collectors onto the Canadian Plateau post-3500 BP. Further research is necessary to document origins of early Columbia Plateau collectors (e.g., Pithouse II [Chatters 1995]), but strong stylistic similarities between early Columbia Basin collectors and northern Plateau and coastal groups suggest a likely coastal origin (Prentiss et al. 2005). This kind of population expansion is also implied by studies in historical linguistics (Elmendorf 1965; Foster 1997).

If Davis (2007) and Plew and Guinn are correct that winter village collector organization did not make entry into portions of the Salmon River drainage until after circa 2000 BP, there are some interesting implications for eastern Plateau prehistory. If the salmon habitat was truly poor until this time, it of course makes perfect sense that groups operating a collector-like strategy would have simply avoided this area, permitting it to be used by other groups organized differently. Plew and Guinn's review of variability in ethnographic organization on the Middle Snake River makes this kind of scenario highly likely. Another possibility is that groups normally employing a winter village collector strategy may have had the flexibility to reorganize mobility tactics and to reduce their emphasis on food storage during poor fishing years, and as documented above, there were undoubtedly seasons when salmon fishing was indeed very poor (see also Yu and Cook, this volume). Such groups might have periodically moved through valleys (e.g., the Salmon) not normally occupied for winter sedentary purposes, leaving a record of more forager-like behavior during these resource-poor periods. Amsden (1977) documented just this kind of behavior when Nunamiut collectors lost significant access to their keystone food resource (caribou) a little more than 100 years ago. Ultimately, these kinds of scenarios cause us to recognize that one of the advantages held by many hunter-gatherers over agricultural societies was the ability to move and/or to alter some elements of their socioeconomic organization in the face of socioecological contingencies. But simultaneously we cannot also rule out the possibility of poor decision making, economic disaster, and demographic collapse as has been recognized among hunter-gatherers in other areas (e.g., Holly 2011).

Subsistence Intensification on the Plateau

An important hallmark of Columbia Plateau archaeology has been its focus on understanding processes of subsistence intensification among hunting and gathering groups. Subsistence intensification remains a fundamentally important yet often misused concept in hunter-gatherer archaeology. The first problem comes with how the term is actually used. Morrison (1994) points out that intensification is not an event but, rather, a process. An important implication of this is that intensification may follow different pathways and result from the application of different organizational and technological strategies. Next, as originally defined by Boserup (1965), intensification involves a process of increased production, but this is not the same thing as simple increase. Intensification must be measured against a constant, as in more production per unit of land or labor (Morrison 1994). Thus, increased production paralleling increased productivity is not necessarily intensification. But with different constants, intensification can still mean very different things, and it is critical for researchers to be clear on their definitions.

Probably the most common view of intensification among hunter-gatherer archaeologists derives from Boserup's original configuration of intensification as an essentially maladaptive process whereby despite greater production per unit of land, there is a parallel loss of efficiency as people worked harder to generate more (thus less per unit of labor). For agriculturalists this can mean increasing cropping frequency or employing multicropping (Morrison 1994). For hunter-gatherers it can mean adding lower-ranking food resources requiring greater handling time prior to consumption (Basgall 1987; Bouey 1989; Broughton 1994; Janetski 1997). One potential outcome of this process is local resource depression as preferred resources are overexploited, leading to hardship among foragers (Broughton 1994; Holly 2011; Janetski 1997). This process tends to be marked archaeologically by indicators of rising diet breadth and reduction in prey size.

Less frequently discussed are processes of intensification whereby increased production per unit of land parallels increased production per unit of labor (Brookfield 1984; Morrison 1994). This concept should also be of critical importance to hunter-gatherer archaeologists, particularly those who work with more sedentary "complex" groups relying upon intensive harvest of select resources. Within this scenario, technological and organizational innovations permit lower-cost harvest and processing of critical foods that can then be made even more efficient by storage for long-term use. One interesting implication of this process is that a formerly low-ranking food (e.g., salmon) could quickly shift to high rank if efficiently mass harvested and processed. Collector organization may have been the fundamental innovation that favored late prehistoric intensification focusing on salmon, given the fact that fishing technologies and fish-processing techniques had already been around in the Pacific Northwest for some time prior to the late middle Holocene (Ames and Maschner 1999; Matson and Coupland 1995). Similarly it was collector organization that probably also made root food processing worthy of an intensification process in the interior Northwest, as roots had been roasted intermittently for thousands of years prior to their intensification after circa 4,000 years ago (Chatters 2009).

Subsistence intensification has been discussed and debated on the Plateau and in the wider Pacific Northwest for decades. Some models link enhanced production with productivity and thus seem to be talking more about simple increase (per Morrison 1994) than about formal intensification (e.g., Ames and Marshall 1980; Schalk 1981). Others implicate population growth and imbalances between consumers and the resource base as critical factors in Plateau intensification processes, thus implicating intensification as a potentially maladaptive process (Galm 1985; Thoms 1989). Chatters (1995) recognizes examples of both population- and technology-driven intensification in his contrast of Pithouse I and Pithouse II subsistence strategies. Chatters sees wider diet breadth, thus subsistence diversification, as associated with the former and specialization on salmon as a characteristic of the latter. In this volume Lyons and Jones suggest that trout and shellfish, respectively, might have been candidates for intensification. However, their use of the term *intensification* seems to imply intensification as "event" not "process." Regardless, their thoughts are provocative and ask us to explore the possibility that some groups employing collector-like socioeconomic organization might have specialized in foods other than salmonids and roots. Our challenge is to derive the means for measuring such behavior in the archaeological record.

Frames of Reference

An important contribution of this book is in its emphasis on integrating multiple sciences (biology, ecology, geology) with archaeological and ethnographic research to facilitate the creation of frames of reference (e.g., Binford 2001) for archaeological interpretation. The Pacific Northwest region (inclusive of northern California) offers abundant opportunities for this kind of research and has significantly benefited from traditionally close relationships among tribes, First Nations, and anthropologists and archaeologists. This tradition continues with the productive work currently carried out by Jones and Lyons with the Spokane and Kalispel tribes. It is also reflected in the innovative research of Yu and Cook in the Upper Columbia fishery and Stevens and Zelazo in the Cosumnes River watershed. It is a tradition well known to Canadian Plateau researchers (e.g., Hayden 1992; Prentiss and Kuijt 2012).

Contributors to this volume offer important new information regarding not only fishing techniques but also resource-management and organizational tactics associated with mobility, technology, labor, demographics, and food processing and consumption. Yu and Cook introduce new research into lithic tools associated with fish processing, describing a variety of forms ranging from costly (in labor and raw materials) hafted ground-slate knives of the Northwest Coast to more "expedient" tabular chert knives of the Kettle Falls area of the Columbia Plateau. Moving beyond simple item descriptions, they offer a number of propositions regarding the organizational characteristics of these items. They suggest that tabular chert knives were low-cost solutions to the need to process large numbers of fish during short periods. Such tools thus could be expected to accumulate in locations of intensive fish-processing activity and to exhibit signs of resharpening and reuse potentially for a variety of functions. Indeed many tools may have acted in the roles of "site furniture" (e.g., Binford 1979) for logistically mobile hunter-gatherers of the region. This research offers great promise for developing measures of variability in the importance of fish processing in other contexts where it is less well known.

Jones implicates the role of shellfish in traditional Spokane subsistence. He offers the critical point that despite reliance on some other keystone resource (e.g., salmon), hunter-gatherers depended upon a wide range of other food resources to make it through entire annual cycles. Shellfish may have been such a crucial food resource, providing one link in a chain of resources stretching across the seasons. Lyons describes a range of fishing techniques, including a unique series of traps used by the Kalispel people implicating the importance of trout and whitefish to these eastern Plateau people. He links the disparate tactics and technologies to a subsistence system organizationally similar to those favoring salmon elsewhere on the Plateau. In so doing he provides archaeologists with indicators of residential and logistical organization typical of collectors where winter villages and storage features are less obvious in the archaeological record. Stevens and Zelazo offer similarly detailed descriptions of fishing and landscape management by the Mewuk people of California, providing archaeologists with tools for thinking about variability in fishing but also the manipulation of local ecosystems to enhance productivity.

These chapters are unified in their consideration of alternative food resources to salmon for Pacific Northwest peoples. They make the critical argument that even if the caloric value was small compared with the greater contribution of salmon (or root foods), the loss of these resources could still be catastrophic, particularly if it came at a time when other resources were in short supply or had failed for any reason. This offers the additional implication that any interruption to annual subsistence schedules could have big impacts on human demographics and organizational viability. As we imagine processes of culture change in the ancient past we must remember that not all change came as a consequence of conscious innovation (as in "necessity is the mother of invention"). Organizational change in subsistence and mobility could derive from simple interruptions to annual schedules (say, missing a key food resource such as shellfish), leading to further adjustments.

Fishing and Complex Hunter-Gatherers of the Middle Fraser Canyon

This volume offers a number of important implications for understanding variability in fisher-hunter-gatherer socioeconomic organization in North America's Interior and Pacific Northwest region. Most fundamentally, contributors demonstrate that while salmon were a critical and often dependable resource, access to that resource could be highly variable depending upon a wide range of factors ranging from global climate change to local factors such as forest fires and landslides. Native peoples coped via a variety of strategies for integrating fish into annual subsistence rounds, which included everything from immediate consumption to intensive harvesting and processing for long-term storage. They employed a complex array of tactics for accessing their prey, ranging from the simple hook and line to a creative array of traps and facilities. Some groups actively enhanced fishery habitats to improve access not just to salmon but to a wide array of other fish species. Our archaeological challenge is to recognize such variability in the ancient past, and contributors to this volume offer some useful insights to help achieve that goal.

I close my discussion with a consideration of some implications of these works for our understanding of fishing, demographics, and socioeconomic and political change in the Middle Fraser Canyon of British Columbia. The canyon, located around Lillooet, British Columbia, was traditionally home to the St'át'imc, Salish speakers who lived in moderate to large house pit villages along the terraces of the Fraser Canyon and adjacent drainages such as the Bridge River. The Mid-Fraser area could support high population densities given its fishery centered at the 6-Mile Rapids, recognized as the most productive fishing site on the entire Canadian Plateau (Kew 1992). Ethnographers (e.g., Teit 1906) have documented a pattern of social relations similar to that of the nearby Northwest Coast, featuring hereditary and achieved status ranking, lineage and clan groups, ownership and control of access to critical subsistence resources, and use of public ceremonies such as the potlatch in the status-negotiation process. This complex society was founded economically on a classic winter village collector strategy whereby groups were based in permanent winter villages and used extensive logistical mobility to acquire and transport resources for storage and later consumption (Alexander 1992; Prentiss and Kuijt 2012).

The annual cycle began in the spring following snowmelt (around late February to March), when people began to hunt and fish. By mid- to later spring (April–June) many left the winter villages for mid-elevation trout-fishing, deer-hunting, and root-processing camps. Activities in mid- to late summer and early fall (July–September) were focused on harvesting and processing salmon and berries for winter consumption. By mid-fall (late September–November) many families moved back into the higher elevations for fall deer hunts, more root and berry collecting, and lithic quarrying. Families reassembled in the winter villages by late fall (mid- to late November) for winter (November–February). During winter, families engaged in many activities, including preparation of and attendance at feasts, potlatches, and other ceremonies. This was also a time of rest and preparation for the next warm season. Clothing was prepared, tools were manufactured or refurbished, and plans were made for spring and summer activities. By late winter (about February) many stored foods were in short supply, as were cached supplies of lithic tool stone. The people were poised to begin the cycle again.

The St'át'imc annual cycle very effectively illustrates the importance of keystone and lesser food resources to survival throughout the year. It also very effectively illustrates the role of advance planning in the operation of this delayed-return subsistence system. Summer fishing and berry collecting provided food for immediate consumption, but since most of this was intended for winter use, people also relied heavily on smoked deer and roasted and dried roots from spring foraging trips. Foragers in springtime camps at mid-elevations ate deer and roots, but they also relied upon trout, birds, and other plants and animals. Much the same could be said for fall hunting, gathering, and fishing camps at high elevations. Thus, while salmon, roots, and deer are recognized as keystone foods, such secondary items as berries, trout, tree bark, pine nuts, and small mammals and birds also provided critical links in the annual chain of subsistence. One additional implication of this is that if one of the keystone resources failed or even declined, then heavy pressure could be placed on some of the secondary sources, leading to additional problems.

Archaeological research at two large Mid-Fraser villages, Bridge River and Keatley Creek, suggests that mobility, population size, and social arrangements were heavily affected by subsistence issues (Prentiss and Kuijt 2012; Prentiss et al. 2007; Prentiss et al. 2008). Current data indicate that the villages grew significantly between 1,800 and 1,200 years ago under conditions of steadily improving annual salmon runs. Bridge River expanded from as few as three–seven to potentially more than 30 co-occupied large residential pithouses (Prentiss et al. 2008). At approximately 1300–1200 cal. BP, Bridge River achieved peak size but also began to be impacted by declines in critical food sources. Zooarchaeological data suggest that salmon declined by as much as 50 percent in most house pits. Deer bone assemblages in most houses shift from a pattern of complete carcasses to one of partial carcasses emphasizing lower limb bones. A similar pattern has been recognized at Keatley Creek at this time (Prentiss et al. 2007). Shifts in the use of plant resources are not fully understood, though data from Keatley Creek suggest the harvest of higher numbers of high-elevation berries, an expanding role for pine nuts, and a reduction in local root-roasting post-1200 cal. BP (Prentiss et al. 2007). All told, it would appear that there was a trend toward subsistence diversification and an expanding role for lower-ranking food sources such as seeds/nuts and some mammals. It is also at about this time that we recognize indicators of emergent interhousehold social ranking, as marked by significant variability in some subsistence items and prestige-related artifacts such as stone beads, copper pendants, and nephrite jade tools (Prentiss and Kuijt 2012; Prentiss et al. 2012). Villages were abandoned beginning circa 1100 cal. BP.

I have argued that declining access to salmon during the early Medieval Warm Period may have played a critical role in expanding diet breadth, increasing interhousehold competition for resources, emergent inequality, and the eventual abandonment of the villages (Kuijt and Prentiss 2004; Prentiss and Kuijt 2012; Prentiss et al. 2005; Prentiss et al. 2007; Prentiss et al. 2008; Prentiss et al. 2012). This argument is disputed by Hayden (2005; Hayden and Mathewes 2009), who asserts that salmon spawned in such numbers that most fluctuations would not have been significant to groups with premodern fishing technology. Hayden believes that the Mid-Fraser villages are much older and were characterized by inequality throughout their history and that the abandonment was triggered only by a catastrophic landslide (Hayden and Ryder 1991), though the latter is disputed by Kuijt (2001). Most fundamentally, Hayden rejects the notion that human groups could have been impacted by anything other than a major calamity or that human decision makers could have had any impact upon their local environment.

Chapters in the book demonstrate that Native peoples of the Pacific Northwest could be affected by change in their environment but that they could also play a significant role in enhancing or degrading their local ecosystems. Work by Grabowski and by Plew and Guinn makes it very clear that salmon populations could be significantly affected by marine and freshwater environments and that this could in turn have major impacts on human groups. Stevens and Zelazo argue that Native land-management practices could significantly enhance harvests. There is some evidence for this in the Mid-Fraser as well, particularly in reference to root resources (Turner 1992). The flip side of resource enhancement is adverse impacts. In the Mid-Fraser reductions in salmon circa 1300–1200 cal. BP may have forced people to more intensely harvest local terrestrial plants and animals, leading to local shortages in some critical secondary resources. If this was the case, then increased interhousehold competition and eventual abandonment may have been triggered not just by declining salmon but by the actions of densely packed human predators.

There remains much that we do not know. Probably the biggest question remaining in late-period Mid-Fraser archaeology concerns the abandonment of the packed villages and subsequent dispersal. Far more extensive research is needed to identify changes in the uses of canyon-bottom fishing sites and highland hunting and root-processing camps. After the abandonment did Mid-Fraser groups' use of these places shift from logistical to residential? This would make sense if they dispersed into more mobile and less storage-dependent foraging groups for several hundred years, perhaps similar to the Middle Snake River foragers described by Plew and Guinn. Then, did harvest of salmon cease or become less intensive, particularly if people were using them primarily for immediate consumption? One measure of variability in the use of fishing sites could come from assessments of fish-processing knives at such sites, as is suggested by Yu and Cook. Finally, were there changes in cooking and storage practices? Research by Lyons and Jones allows us to develop new hypotheses about the use of alternative foods and changes in procurement and processing traditions.

Final Thoughts

All told, the chapters in this volume point us in new directions. They aptly illustrate the potential complexity of the archaeological record that accumulates at the intersection of local and regional ecology and historical cultural tradition. Future researchers will need to build upon these themes as we seek more nuanced understanding of past cultural systems. Resource managers and planners will be wise to take heed of the message in these essays that humans have played an essential role in Pacific Northwest ecosystems for millennia.

Acknowledgments

I thank Pei-Lin Yu for inviting me to write this chapter and for her comments on the manuscript. I also thank Ron Yoshiyama and several anonymous reviewers for their valuable comments. Archaeological research at the Bridge River and Keatley Creek sites was funded by grants from the National Science Foundation (grants 0108795, 0313920, and 0713013), the Wenner-Gren Foundation for Anthropological Research Inc., and the University of Montana. I thank the Bridge River (Xwisten) and Pavilion (Ts'kway'laxw) bands (both St'át'imc Nation) for being wonderful collaborators in our research at the Bridge River and Keatley Creek sites.

References Cited

Alexander, Diana

1992 Prehistoric Land Use in the Mid-Fraser Area Based on Ethnographic Data. In *A Complex Culture of the British Columbia Plateau.* B. Hayden, ed. Pp. 99–176. Vancouver: University of British Columbia Press.

Ames, Kenneth M., and A. G. Marshall

1980 Villages, Demography, and Subsistence Intensification on the Southern Columbia Plateau. *North American Archaeologist* 2:25–52.

Ames, Kenneth M., and Herbert D. G. Maschner

1999 *Peoples of the Northwest Coast: Their Archaeology and Prehistory.* London: Thames and Hudson.

Amsden, Charles

1977 A Quantitative Analysis of Nunamiut Settlement Dynamics: 1898 to 1969. Unpublished Ph.D. dissertation, Department of Anthropology, University of New Mexico.

Basgall, Mark E.

1987 Resource Intensification among Hunter-Gatherers: Acorn Economies in Prehistoric California. *Research in Economic Anthropology* 9:21–52.

Beamish, Richard J., and Daniel R. Bouillon

1993 Pacific Salmon Production Trends in Relation to Climate. *Canadian Journal of Fisheries and Aquatic Science* 50:1002–1016.

Benson, Ashlen J., and Andrew W. Trites

2002 Ecological Effects of Regime Shifts in the Bering Sea and Eastern North Pacific Ocean. *Fish and Fisheries* 3:95–113.

Bernton, H.

2010 Fraser Whopper Sockeye Salmon Run Even Bigger. *Seattle Times,* September 1.

Bettinger, Robert L., and M. A. Baumhoff

1982 The Numic Spread: Great Basin Cultures in Competition. *American Antiquity* 47:485–503.

Binford, Lewis R.

1979 Organization and Formation Processes: Looking at Curated Technologies. *Journal of Anthropological Research* 35:255–273.

1980 Willow Smoke and Dogs' Tails: Hunter-Gatherer Settlement Systems and Archaeological Site Formation. *American Antiquity* 45:4–20.

2001 *Constructing Frames of Reference*. Berkeley: University of California Press.

Boserup, Esther

1965 *The Conditions of Agricultural Growth: The Economics of Agrarian Change under Population Pressure*. Chicago: Aldine.

Bouey, Paul D.

1989 The Intensification of Hunter-Gatherer Economies: Archaeological Indicators of Change and Complexity in the North Coast Ranges of California. Unpublished Ph.D. dissertation, Department of Anthropology, University of California, Davis.

Brookfield, H. C.

1984 Intensification Revisited. *Pacific Viewpoint* 25:15–44.

Broughton, Jack M.

1994 Late Holocene Resource Intensification in the Sacramento River Valley: The Vertebrate Evidence. *Journal of Archaeological Science* 21:501–514.

Butler, Virginia L., and Sarah K. Campbell

2004 Resource Intensification and Resource Depression in the Pacific Northwest of North America: A Zooarchaeological Review. *Journal of World Prehistory* 18(4):327–404.

Chatters, James C.

1989 Resource Intensification and Sedentism on the Southern Plateau. *Archaeology in Washington* 1:1–20.

1995 Population Growth, Climatic Cooling, and the Development of Collector Strategies on the Southern Plateau, Western North America. *Journal of World Prehistory* 9:341–400.

2009 A Macroevolutionary Perspective on the Archaeological Record of North America. In *Macroevolution in Human Prehistory: Evolutionary Theory and Processual Archaeology*. A. M. Prentiss, I. Kuijt, and J. C. Chatters, eds. Pp. 213–234. New York: Springer.

Chatters, James C., Virginia L. Butler, M. J. Scott, D. M. Anderson, and D. A. Neitzel

1995 A Paleoscience Approach to Estimating the Effects of Climatic Warming on Salmonid Fisheries of the Columbia Basin. *Canadian Special Publication in Fisheries and Aquatic Sciences* 21:489–496.

Chatters, James C., Steven Hackenberger, Anna M. Prentiss, and Jayne-Leigh Thomas

2012 The Paleoindian to Archaic Transition in the Pacific Northwest: In Situ Development or Ethnic Replacement? In *From the Pleistocene to the Holocene: Human Organization and Cultural Transformations in Prehistoric North America*. C. Britt Bousman and Bradley J. Vierra, eds. Pp. 37–66. College Station: Texas A&M University Press.

Chatters, James C., and David L. Pokotylo
1998 Prehistory: Introduction. In *Handbook of North American Indians, vol. 12: Plateau*. D. E. Walker Jr., ed. Pp. 73–80. Washington, DC: Smithsonian Institution Press.

Chatters, James C., and William C. Prentiss
2005 A Darwinian Macro-Evolutionary Perspective on the Development of Hunter-Gatherer Systems in Northwestern North America. *World Archaeology* 37:46–65.

Christensen, Tina, and Jim Stafford
2005 Raised Beach Archaeology in Northern Haida Gwaii: Preliminary Results from the Cohoe Creek Site. In *Haida Gwaii: Human History and Environment from the Time of Loon to the Time of the Iron People*. Daryl W. Fedje and Rolf Mathewes, eds. Pp. 245–273. Vancouver: University of British Columbia Press.

Davis, Loren G.
2007 Paleoseismicity, Ecological Change, and Prehistoric Exploitation of Anadromous Fishes in the Salmon River Basin, Western Idaho, USA. *North American Archaeologist* 28:233–263.

Downton, Mary W., and Kathleen A. Miller
1998 Relationships between Alaskan Salmon Catch and North Pacific Climate on Interannual and Interdecadal Time Scales. *Canadian Journal of Fisheries and Aquatic Science* 55:2255–2265.

Elmendorf, W. W.
1965 Linguistic and Geographic Relations in the Northern Plateau Area. *Southwestern Journal of Anthropology* 21:63–78.

English, K. K., R. E. Bailey, and D. Bobichaud
2006 *Assessment of Chinook Returns to the Fraser River Watershed Using Run Reconstruction Techniques, 1982–2004*. Report prepared by LGL, Ltd. On file at the Department of Fisheries and Oceans, Nanaimo.

Finney, Bruce P., Irene Gregory-Eaves, Marianne S. V. Douglas, and John P. Smol
2002 Fisheries Productivity in the Northeastern Pacific Ocean over the Past 2,200 Years. *Nature* 416:729–733.

Foster, M. K.
1997 Language and the Culture History of North America. In *Handbook of North American Indians, vol. 17: Language*. I. Goddard, ed. Pp. 64–111. Washington, DC: Smithsonian Institution.

Galm, Jerry R.
1985 The Avey's Orchard Site in Regional Perspective. In *Avey's Orchard: Archaeological Investigation of a Late Prehistoric Columbia River Community*. J. R. Galm and R. A. Masten, eds. Pp. 321–334. Eastern Washington University, Reports in Archaeology and History 100-61. Cheney.

Gilhousen, P.
1990 *Pre-Spawning Mortalities of Sockeye Salmon in the Fraser River System and*

Possible Causes. International Pacific Salmon Fisheries Commission Bulletin 26. New Westminster.

Goodale, Nathan B., W. C. Prentiss, and Ian Kuijt

2004 Cultural Complexity: A New Chronology of the Upper Columbia Drainage Area. In *Complex Hunter-Gatherers: Evolution and Organization of Prehistoric Communities on the Plateau of Northwestern North America.* W. C. Prentiss and I. Kuijt, eds. Pp. 36–48. Salt Lake City: University of Utah Press.

Hayden, Brian

2005 Emergence of Large Villages and Large Residential Corporate Group Structures among Complex Hunter-Gatherers at Keatley Creek. *American Antiquity* 70:169–174.

Hayden, Brian, ed.

1992 *A Complex Culture of the British Columbia Plateau.* Vancouver: University of British Columbia Press.

Hayden, Brian, and Rolf Mathewes

2009 The Rise and Fall of Complex Large Villages on the British Columbian Plateau: A Geoarchaeological Controversy. *Canadian Journal of Archaeology* 33:281–296.

Hayden, Brian, and June Ryder

1991 Prehistoric Cultural Collapse in the Lillooet Area. *American Antiquity* 56:50–65.

2003 Cultural Collapses in the Northwest: A Reply to Ian Kuijt. *American Antiquity* 68:157–160.

Heard, William R.

1991 Life History of Pink Salmon (*Oncorynchus gorbuscha*). In *Pacific Salmon Life Histories.* Cornelis Groot and Leo Margolis, eds. Pp. 119–230. Vancouver: University of British Columbia Press.

Holly, Don

2011 When Foragers Fail, in the Eastern Subarctic, for Example. In *Hunter-Gatherer Archaeology as Historical Process.* Kenneth Sassaman and Donald Holly, eds. Pp. 79–92. Amerind Foundation SAA Seminar Series. Tucson: University of Arizona Press.

Hunn, Eugene S.

1990 *Nch'i-Wána, "the Big River": Mid-Columbia Indians and Their Land.* Seattle: University of Washington Press.

Janetski, Joel C.

1997 Fremont Hunting and Resource Intensification in the Eastern Great Basin. *Journal of Archaeological Science* 24:1075–1088.

Kew, Michael

1992 Salmon Availability, Technology, and Cultural Adaptation in the Fraser River Watershed. In *A Complex Culture of the British Columbia Plateau.* Brian Hayden, ed. Pp. 177–221. Vancouver: University of British Columbia Press.

Kuijt, Ian
2001 Reconsidering the Cause of Cultural Collapse in the Lillooet Area of British Columbia: A Geoarchaeological Perspective. *American Antiquity* 66: 692–703.

Kuijt, Ian, and William C. Prentiss
2004 Villages on the Edge: Pithouses, Cultural Change, and the Abandonment of Aggregate Pithouse Villages. In *Complex Hunter-Gatherers: Evolution and Organization of Prehistoric Communities on the Plateau of Northwestern North America*. William C. Prentiss and Ian Kuijt, eds. Pp. 155–170. Salt Lake City: University of Utah Press.

Lepofsky, Dana, Ken Lertzman, Douglas Hallett, and Rolf Mathewes
2005 Climate Change and Culture Change on the Southern Coast of British Columbia 2400–1200 Cal. BP. *American Antiquity* 70:267–293.

Lightfoot, Kent G., Edward M. Luby, and Lisa Pesnichak
2011 Evolutionary Typologies and Hunter-Gatherer Research: Rethinking the Mounded Landscapes of Central California. In *Hunter-Gatherer Archaeology as Historical Process*. Kenneth Sassaman and Donald Holly, eds. Pp. 55–78. Tucson: University of Arizona Press.

Lohse, E. S., and D. Sammons-Lohse
1986 Sedentism on the Columbia Plateau: A Matter of Degree Related to Easy and Efficient Procurement of Resources. *Northwest Anthropological Research Notes* 20:115–136.

MacDonald, J. S.
2000 *Mortality during the Migration of Fraser River Sockeye Salmon (*Oncorynchus nerka*): A Study of Ocean and River Environmental Conditions in 1997*. Canadian Technical Report of Fisheries and Aquatic Science 2326. Burnaby.

Matson, R. G., and Gary Coupland
1995 *The Prehistory of the Northwest Coast*. San Diego: Academic Press.

McLaren, Duncan, Andrew Martindale, Daryl Fedje, and Quentin Mackie
2011 Relict Shorelines and Shell Middens of the Dundas Island Archipelago. *Canadian Journal of Archaeology* 35:86–116.

Morrison, Kathleen D.
1994 The Intensification of Production: Archaeological Approaches. *Journal of Archaeological Method and Theory* 1:111–157.

Mueter, Franz J., Randall M. Peterman, and Brian J. Pyper
2002 Opposite Effects of Ocean Temperature on Survival Rates of 120 Stocks of Pacific Salmon (*Oncorhynchus* spp.) in Northern and Southern Areas. *Canadian Journal of Fisheries and Aquatic Science* 59:456–463.

Nelson, C. M.
1973 Prehistoric Culture Change in the Intermontane Plateau of Western North America. In *The Explanation of Culture Change: Models in Prehistory*. Colin Renfrew, ed. Pp. 371–390. London: Duckworth.

Prentiss, Anna Marie

2009 The Emergence of New Socioeconomic Strategies in the Middle and Late Holocene Pacific Northwest Region of North America. In *Macroevolution in Human Prehistory: Evolutionary Theory and Processual Archaeology*. Anna Marie Prentiss, Ian Kuijt, and James C. Chatters, eds. Pp. 111–132. New York: Springer.

Prentiss, Anna Marie, Guy Cross, Thomas A. Foor, Mathew Hogan, Dirk Markle, and David S. Clarke

2008 Evolution of a Late Prehistoric Winter Village on the Interior Plateau of British Columbia: Geophysical Investigations, Radiocarbon Dating, and Spatial Analysis of the Bridge River Site. *American Antiquity* 73:59–81.

Prentiss, Anna Marie, Thomas A. Foor, Guy Cross, Lucille E. Harris, and Michael Wanzenried

2012 The Cultural Evolution of Material Wealth-Based Inequality at Bridge River, British Columbia. *American Antiquity* 77:542–564.

Prentiss, Anna Marie, and Ian Kuijt

2012 *People of the Middle Fraser Canyon: An Archaeological History*. Vancouver: University of British Columbia Press.

Prentiss, Anna Marie, Natasha Lyons, Lucille E. Harris, Melisse R. P. Burns, and Terrence M. Godin

2007 The Emergence of Status Inequality in Intermediate Scale Societies: A Demographic and Socio-Economic History of the Keatley Creek Site, British Columbia. *Journal of Anthropological Archaeology* 26:299–327.

Prentiss, William C., and James C. Chatters

2003 Cultural Diversification and Decimation in the Prehistoric Record. *Current Anthropology* 44:33–58.

Prentiss, William C., James C. Chatters, Michael Lenert, David S. Clarke, and Robert C. O'Boyle

2005 The Archaeology of the Plateau of Northwestern North America during the Late Prehistoric Period (3500–200 BP): Evolution of Hunting and Gathering Societies. *Journal of World Prehistory* 19:47–118.

Prentiss, William C., and Ian Kuijt

2004 The Evolution of Collector Systems on the Canadian Plateau. In *Complex Hunter-Gatherers: Evolution and Organization of Prehistoric Communities on the Plateau of Northwestern North America*. William C. Prentiss and Ian Kuijt, eds. Pp. 49–66. Salt Lake City: University of Utah Press.

Quinn, Thomas P.

2005 *The Behavior and Ecology of Salmon and Trout*. Bethesda: American Fisheries Society.

Romanoff, Steven

1992 Fraser Lillooet Salmon Fishing. In *A Complex Culture of the British Columbia Plateau*. B. Hayden, ed. Pp. 222–265. Vancouver: University of British Columbia Press.

Schalk, Randall F.
1981 Land Use and Organizational Complexity among Foragers of Northwestern North America. *Senri Ethnological Studies* 9:53–75.
Speller, Camilla F., Dongya Y. Yang, and Brian Hayden
2005 Ancient DNA Investigation of Prehistoric Salmon Utilization at Keatley Creek, British Columbia, Canada. *Journal of Archaeological Science* 32:1378–1389.
Teit, James
1906 The Lillooet Indians. *Memoirs of the American Museum of Natural History, Jesup North Pacific Expedition* 2:193–300.
Thoms, A. V.
1989 The Northern Roots of Hunter-Gatherer Intensification: Camas and the Pacific Northwest. Unpublished Ph.D. dissertation, Washington State University, Pullman.
Turner, Nancy J.
1992 Plant Resources of the *Stl'átl'imx* (Fraser River Lillooet) People: A Window into the Past. In *A Complex Culture of the British Columbia Plateau*. Brian Hayden, ed. Pp. 405–469. Vancouver: University of British Columbia Press.

Contributors

Jackie M. Cook
Department of History and Archaeology, Confederated Tribes of the Colville Reservation

Stephen J. Grabowski
U.S. Bureau of Reclamation, ret.

Stacey Guinn
Department of Anthropology, Boise State University

Jason M. Jones
Stell Environmental Enterprises

Kevin J. Lyons
Cultural Resources, Kalispel Tribe of Indians

Mark G. Plew
Department of Anthropology, Boise State University

Anna Marie Prentiss
Department of Anthropology, University of Montana

Michelle L. Stevens
Department of Environmental Studies, California State University, Sacramento

Pei-Lin Yu
Department of Anthropology, Boise State University

Emilie M. Zelazo
California Department of Transportation

Index